the Fruit Tree
handbook

T0322386

the Fruit Tree
handbook

Ben Pike

GREEN BOOKS

LONDON • OXFORD • NEW YORK • NEW DELHI • SYDNEY

GREEN BOOKS
Bloomsbury Publishing Plc
50 Bedford Square, London, WC1B 3DP, UK
29 Earlsfort Terrace, Dublin 2, Ireland

BLOOMSBURY, GREEN BOOKS and the Green Books logo are trademarks of
Bloomsbury Publishing Plc

First published in 2011 in the United Kingdom by Green Books Ltd
This edition published 2023

Bloomsbury Publishing Plc does not have any control over, or responsibility for, any third-party
websites referred to or in this book. All internet addresses given in this book were correct at the time of
going to press. The author and publisher regret any inconvenience caused if addresses have changed
or sites have ceased to exist, but can accept no responsibility for any such changes

Please use pesticides responsibly. This publication is intended as a guide only. Whilst every care
has been taken in this publication's compilation pesticide regulations and safety guidance may have
changed, so please check for any updates on each occasion you use pesticides. If you are unsure on the
use or effects of a pesticide please consult a professional before using and never disregard their advice
because of something you have read in this publication. The decision to use and rely on the information
contained in this publication is entirely at your discretion and responsibility.

A catalogue record for this book is available from the British Library
Library of Congress Cataloguing-in-Publication data has been applied for

ISBN: PB: 978-1-9003-2274-4; ePub: 978-0-8578-4100-1 ;ePDF: 978-0-8578-4041-7

Design by Jayne Jones
Printed and bound in India by Replika Press

To find out more about our authors and books visit www.bloomsbury.com and sign up for our
newsletters

AUTHOR'S CAUTIONARY NOTE REGARDING PESTICIDES

Since this book was published, EU pesticide regulations have changed and look set to change
further. Some of the pesticides recommended in the book may be withdrawn from sale. As this is
a fluid situation, it is sensible to check the current status before using pesticides, organic or
otherwise.

In the UK the best resource for this is www.pesticides.gov.uk/garden In other EU countries,
http://ec.europa.eu/food/plant/protection/evaluation gives further information.

Contents

Acknowledgements

So many people have given their time and encouragement to help me write this book. They are too numerous for me to be able to thank them all individually, but suffice to say that many a kind word or friendly email has smoothed the way for a novice navigating the obstacles encountered in writing a first book.

Particular thanks go to those who have helped in providing photographs for this book. Jerry Cross, Ursula Twomey and Penny Greeves of East Malling Research were most generous with their time and advice. Matt Ordidge of Reading University and Mary Pennell of FAST Ltd at The National Fruit Collection have both offered their help freely. Hamid Habibi of Keepers Nursery was most hospitable in allowing his many trees to be photographed. Nick Dunn of Frank P. Matthews Ltd has been generous in providing photos from his collection. Jacquie Sarsby, Tim Selman of the Tamar Valley AONB, Liz Copas and Sherry Orchard have also gone beyond the call of duty in allowing access to their lovely photos. Michael Gee, of Orchards Live, has helped in finding sites to photograph. Thanks to the Royal Horticultural Society at Wisley and Rosemoor, Hatton Fruit Garden and the Lost Gardens of Heligan for allowing me to take photos in their lovely gardens.

Thanks to John Guest (the English Apple Man) and Andrew Bakere of the Devon Wildlife Trust for their help. My employer, the Sharpham Trust in Devon, kindly allowed me time off work to write this book.

Thanks to Steph and Ember for their patience and encouragement at just the right times, and to my mother, Sheila Sermon, for her unwavering support.

Lastly, thanks to all at Green Books, who have shown the support and encouragement that a first-time author needs. My editors Amanda and Alethea have guided me unfailingly; their attention to detail has been outstanding. Jenny Johnson, who painted the lovely illustrations, was wonderfully talented in interpreting my muddled instructions.

Introduction

Go forward [and] graffe, set, plant and nourish up trees in every corner of your ground, the labour is small, the cost is nothing. The commodity is great, your selves shall have plenty . . .

John Gerard, *Great Herball* (1597)

A day out in August, in my childhood haunt of East Anglia, reminded me of why I am so passionate about growing fruit. We had travelled only a few miles when we came across one of those old-fashioned fruit farms that are now rarely seen in England. From all the delicious fruits on display, we managed to choose Stella cherries and Opal plums. Sometime later, we parked the car to stop for lunch, only to be greeted by a feast of large blackberries in front of us. Lunch was eaten half an hour later, with purple hands staining our sandwiches. Plums, cherries and blackberries, warmed by the hot sun, combined to make a wonderful dessert.

After lunch we found a stall selling greengages. I find greengages irresistible: that taste of toffee apples combined with a slightly sharp juiciness sends me into raptures of delight, all the more so when they are so perfectly ripe that the juice drips down your chin. While out walking later on, we came across wild cherry plums at the side of the road. Having used up all our containers by now, we tied the sleeves of jumpers to collect these delectable fruits, thoughts of plum crumbles never far from our minds.

Yet the pièce de résistance was still to come. At the end of a deserted lane we came across a stall laden with all kinds of wonderful fruit and vegetables from a garden tantalisingly hidden behind a large brick wall. Limited by what we could carry or eat, we chose some fascinating squashes, Devonshire Quarrenden apples and flat Chinese peaches. Needless to say, the peaches did not last long.

Now all these fruits were wonderful, but they were grown by someone else. There are so many advantages to growing your own fruit – so much fun – though of course there's also the odd heartache when nature has different plans from you. So, why grow your own fruit trees?

Left: Nouveau Poiteau pears trained against a wall.

Choice

Shopping in the supermarket, you might have a choice of half a dozen varieties of apple: most of them will have been transported halfway around the world, sprayed many times, picked before they are fully ripe and then sprayed again. If you are buying cherries, plums or peaches, you will be lucky to find any choice of varieties; you take what you are given.

In your own orchard, you can grow Bardsey Island apples (a lovely lemony tasting apple discovered on a remote island off the Welsh coast), Court Pendu Plat (an ancient variety that might have been grown by the Romans), or Grand Sultan (a wonderful cooking apple from North Devon that is perfect for baked apples). The choice goes on and on; you can grow the kind of apple that is perfect for you.

Of course the same is true for peaches, plums, pears and cherries: you can grow just the sort of fruit that you like to eat. When did you last find Morello cherries or a medlar in your supermarket?

Personal enjoyment

Not only do you have the enjoyment of eating your favourite fruit fresh from the tree, but you also have the satisfaction of nurturing something that might look rather like a stick when you plant it, seeing it grow into a mature tree covered in tasty fruit. You might find yourself becoming rather attached to your trees, rather like an anxious parent, looking out for their joys and sorrows.

Aside from the delight of tending to your trees, you will also have the pleasure of their beauty. Sitting amongst your trees on a warm spring day, you can enjoy the beautiful pink-and-white blossom, looking forward to the luscious fruit that will arrive in a few short months.

Environmental benefits

By growing an orchard, even of just a few trees, you will be creating a habitat for all kinds of wildlife. Birds, such as redwings, will be attracted to the fruit and to the insects that live in the trees. You can manage the orchard floor to grow wildflowers. Even in a small garden, growing fruit trees will have a positive effect on the ecosystem. On a larger scale, you will be creating a habitat that has now been recognised as being so valuable that it has been granted BAP (Biodiversity Action Plan) status. This is a book that encourages you to grow fruit in harmony with the natural world.

The scope of this book

The above are just some of the reasons for growing fruit trees. You will doubtless have more of your own. Whatever they are, you are likely to find fruit growing a rewarding and occasionally frustrating hobby. In these pages I aim to provide you with the knowledge that you need, so that you can move forward with confidence. You will know that your trees will pollinate each other, that your pruning cuts will help and that you can overcome problems of pests and diseases.

This book, as the title implies, encompasses the cultivation of tree fruits. Apples, pears, plums and cherries are all covered in depth, but after those favourites it becomes harder to judge what can be included as tree fruits suitable for growing in Britain. Some fruits are becoming more suitable for growing here because new varieties more suited to our climate are becoming available. Other fruits could become easier to grow here as the effects of global warming unfold. Peaches and nectarines are good examples. Peaches have usually been grown in greenhouses; outside they have struggled to cope with peach leaf curl, particularly in the wetter regions of Britain. Now a new cultivar, Avalon Pride, is showing good resistance against this disease, which would allow peaches to be grown outdoors more readily. Nectarines are a little more delicate and still appreciate the extra warmth of a greenhouse, but in a slowly warming climate they might grow well outdoors.

Other fruits, such as figs, mulberries, medlars, quinces, peaches and apricots are included, whereas more obscure or difficult-to-grow fruits such as loquats and citrus are not. The aim is to help you to grow fruits that can easily be cultivated outdoors in the British climate; the section on a changing climate (see Chapter 4, page 52) covers those fruits that might become viable in the future.

ORGANIC GROWING

You will have gathered by now that I care deeply for our natural environment, and may guess that I don't advocate spraying fruit trees with chemicals. The main reason for this is that it's not necessary. If you choose varieties that are suited to the climate and soil conditions where you live, you will be able to grow perfectly good fruit without resorting to chemical warfare. There will be times when nature, in the form of insects or diseases, threatens the well-being of your fruit. Rather than rushing for the latest chemical spray, this can be a time to consider whether you are more concerned with blasting away any problem as soon as it is seen, or could adopt a gentler approach, of keeping problems under control as part of a rich and varied ecosystem.

For example, if your trees are threatened by aphids, there are various alternatives to using chemical pesticides. Firstly, you could encourage insect-eating birds to your orchard or garden, thus enriching your ecosystem as well as helping to protect your trees. Ladybirds and lacewings are other natural predators of aphids. Secondly, don't panic! Aphids rarely cause significant harm, except occasionally to young trees. Thirdly, if you do decide that further action is needed, you have a range of alternatives, including the use of soft soap as a contact insecticide. You might even decide that sharing some of your harvest with nature is a price worth paying for having a garden teeming with wildlife.

If you do choose to spray your trees, there is plenty of information in these pages to tell you how to do it, but I describe only those methods that are more in harmony with nature. They might not all be strictly organic, but they will stop your garden shed looking like a chemical factory. Sometimes you will have to use your ingenuity to outwit pests, sometimes you will experiment to see what works, but the likelihood is that you will have fun and will learn to recognise your friends in the natural world, such as bees and lacewings, as well as your foes.

Part 1

. . . .

Preparation, planning and planting

Chapter 1

The site of your orchard

There is such a thing as a perfect site for growing fruit trees. It would be a south-facing spot sheltered from strong winds and away from frost pockets. The soil would be a fertile, well-drained loam with a pH of around 6.5. Although such sites are to be found, it is unlikely that you will live in such a place.

There are many variables affecting the cultivation of fruit trees. Some, such as soil fertility, drainage and shelter, can be adjusted, while others, such as altitude or aspect, must be worked with as they are. Although the site of your orchard might seem far from ideal, there is much that you should be able to do to improve it. Most places in the British Isles are suitable for growing fruit trees, although you will need to choose the type of fruit trees you intend to grow according to the locality. If you live on a sheltered site in the south of England, you can take your pick from the different fruits featured in this book. It is only if you live in a cold mountainous area with little topsoil that you will not be able to grow fruit trees. If, like most of us, you live somewhere in between, you will have to tailor your fruit growing to the conditions, but you will be able to harvest crops of delicious home-grown fruit.

Observation over the seasons will show whether a site is suited to growing fruit trees. On a wet site like this, it would be best to improve the drainage before planting.

It may be that you have room for only one or two trees, but, unless you have a really small garden, you will have some choice about where you plant them. Choosing between different parts of your site involves understanding variables such as sun and shade, soil and exposure, and the effect that they have on your fruit trees. Making the right decisions about the position of your trees can be a key factor in the success of your orchard: it is not just a question of growing the right trees, but also of planting them in the right place.

Finding a suitable site for your trees is largely a matter of avoiding extremes of drainage, pH, exposure, soil type and microclimate. This chapter explains about the ideal conditions for growing fruit trees and ways to overcome any difficulties that may be present on your site.

The best way to assess the conditions is simply to observe the site over a period of time. Look to see where the frost lies heaviest in the winter, where the sunlight falls at different times of the year and how the water drains away after heavy rainfall. Such observation will build a picture of the conditions in your garden that you can then use to determine the best place to plant fruit trees. You can supplement your own knowledge with a soil test, which will give a scientific analysis of the soil, pinpointing any deficiencies that need remedying.

Soil

Soil is a miraculous substance that forms a thin skin over the surface of the earth. When you look at a landscape, what you see is the soil and the plants that grow in it, but this is almost a mirage, because what lies just underneath the surface is rock. It is this rock that the soil is formed from originally, but it also contains a host of other organisms that give life to the soil, such as fungi, earthworms, bacteria and humus.

Soil types

Soil types are divided into different classifications according to the biggest constituent, although, in practice, most soils contain a mixture of the different types.

Clay soils

The most common method of classifying soil types is by particle size. Clay soils contain the finest particles. They bind together into a tight mass, which can be heavy and sticky when wet, or hard and unforgiving when dry. Clay soils often crack as they dry out during the summer. They are easily damaged by treading on them while wet, which compacts the soil. They are potentially fertile soils, but this fertility can be locked away in the tightly bound structure.

Clay soils tend to warm up slowly in the spring and also drain more slowly than other soils.

Sandy soils

Sandy soils contain the largest particles. The resultant larger spaces between the particles mean that sandy soils drain well – often too well for the gardener's liking. They warm up quickly in the spring, but also dry out quickly. They are often low in nutrients, which can be easily leached away by heavy rainfall. They tend to be more acidic and low in organic matter.

Silty soils

Silty soils contain intermediate-sized particles, somewhere between those of clay and sandy soils. They tend to have some of the characteristics of clay soils, such as high fertility and easy compaction, and some characteristics of sandy soils, such as good drainage, while avoiding the extremes of either.

Loamy soils

There are also a number of combination soil types, of which loamy soils are the most important. They are a mix of different types of soil types that may include clay, silt and sand. They often have a relatively high organic content, particularly where the soil has been improved over the years. Loamy soils tend to be ideal for growing fruit trees because they are fertile and avoid the extremes of drainage found in clay and sandy soils.

Peaty soils

Peaty soils are largely composed of decaying organic matter. As such, they hold moisture well and are generally very fertile. Peaty soils

are mostly found in the area around The Wash, in East Anglia, as well as in other localised pockets.

Chalky soils

Chalk soils are found in large swathes of southern England. They are alkaline and often lacking in fertility. They are often described as 'thin' soils, being light and crumbly to the touch. They may contain pieces of chalk.

Identifying your soil type

Simply looking at your soil will give you clues to its composition. You might notice elements of the bedrock in the soil, such as shale or chalk, or you might see a dark peaty look or a light sandy texture. Digging the soil will give you further clues. A heavy cloddy texture will point you in the direction of a clay soil, for example. Digging deeper will provide more evidence; the greater the depth

At first glance a site might seem unsuitable, but digging could reveal a sufficient depth of soil.

of soil you find, the better. Exposing the sub-soil or bedrock will give you more idea of what the soil is composed of.

The easiest way of identifying the presence of clay in the soil is to attempt to roll the soil into a ball in your hand. Take a small lump of moist soil, then roll and squeeze in one hand until it forms a ball or otherwise. If the soil refuses to form a ball and feels gritty, then you have sandy soil. If the soil readily forms a tight ball, then you have soil with a high clay content. If the result is somewhere between the two, you are likely to have a loamy soil.

Soil pH

Soil pH is a way of measuring the acidity or alkalinity of the soil. In the UK, this might vary from 4, which is extremely acid, to 9, which is extremely alkaline. A measurement of 7 shows a neutral soil, which is close to ideal for most fruit trees. The pH require-ments of particular fruits can be found in Chapters 12 to 16.

Soil tests

A soil test, or soil analysis as it also called, is a scientific method of determining the com-position of your soil. The most important factors to test for are the pH of the soil and the amounts of the major nutrients present. Nitrogen, potassium, phosphorus and mag-nesium are the important nutrients and will show up with a simple testing kit. These are available from garden centres and are simple enough to use at home.

Alternatively, there are various professional bodies that will test your soil for you. Care-fully chosen soil samples are tested in a lab-oratory. Although more expensive, having your soil tested professionally will produce a much more accurate result.

PROFESSIONAL SOIL TESTING

The Royal Horticultural Society (see Resources) is one organisation that will test your soil for potassium, phosphorus and magnesium, as well as testing the pH, structure of the soil and organic matter content. It will provide recommen-dations for improving any deficiencies found. There are also many companies that will provide a similar service.

Drainage

Achieving good drainage is, again, a matter of avoiding extremes. Sandy soil can be very free-draining, to the extent that trees will often be short of water, whereas clay soil can give rise to waterlogged conditions that can be detrimental to fruit trees. Poor drainage leads to a lack of oxygen for the tree roots and can also contribute to the development of fungal diseases such as phytophthora, which can kill fruit trees.

Where possible it is always best to avoid badly drained areas of your land when plant-ing fruit trees. Where this is not possible, planting on ridges or mounds will help, but in serious cases you will need to consider installing land drains.

Quince trees will tolerate damp conditions better than most fruits, as will some varie-ties of apple – Lord Derby being the best-known example.

Improving the soil

You have a choice of improving the soil over the whole area, or improving conditions in the planting hole when the tree is planted.

All that remains here is the stake where an apple tree was planted in an unsuitable location.

Adding manure to the soil will improve the structure as well as increasing nutrient levels.

Improving the soil over a large area is a good investment for the future but it can require a lot of time and effort. Improving conditions at planting time will help the tree to establish, but won't help once the tree roots have grown beyond the planting hole.

This section explains how to improve the soil before your trees are planted; improving the soil at planting time and ongoing feeding requirements are covered in Chapter 7. While specific deficiencies that show up in a soil test can be remedied as needed, there are more general ways of improving different types of soils, as described below.

Improving clay soils

Clay soils benefit from digging over in the autumn to break up the hard pan that tends to form. Leaving them exposed to winter frosts will also help to break them up. The addition of lime will assist this process, but it should be used only if the soil is not alkaline. If the soil is very heavy, adding course grit will help, although considerable quantities will be needed to make a real improvement. Adding organic matter, such as manure or compost, will provide extra nutrients at the same time as improving the soil structure, and therefore drainage. Manure should not be added at the same time as lime as they react badly with each other, releasing ammonia.

If the only area you have to plant fruit trees in is prone to waterlogging, you may need to consider installing land drains as well as improving the soil. This is a task best undertaken by a professional such as a landscape gardener.

Improving silty soils

Silty soils, having small particles, tend to have similar problems to clay soils. Digging in autumn is helpful, as is the addition of organic matter. Soils with poor drainage should not be walked on, as this will compact the soil and damage the soil structure. Use a board to walk on while digging.

Improving sandy soils

Sandy soils also benefit from the addition of organic matter. Manure or compost will increase the nutrient levels in the soil as well as helping it to hold more moisture. Growing green manures (see right) is another way of adding nutrients and organic matter to sandy soils. Crimson clover and bitter blue lupins are excellent green manures for improving sandy soils.

Improving loamy soils

Loamy soils, being a mixture of the other soil types, tend to avoid their extremes of drainage or nutrient deficiencies. Although loamy soils might not need specific improvements, they will still benefit from the addition of organic matter or the cultivation of green manures.

Improving peaty soils

Peat soil is one of the easiest types of soil to cultivate, with an easily workable soil structure. These soils have a high organic matter content but can be somewhat acid and will therefore benefit from the application of lime or mushroom compost. Peat soils are often found in areas where there is a high water table, in which case the drainage might need to be improved with land drains.

Improving chalky soils

Chalk soils will benefit greatly from the addition of organic matter such as manure or compost. Being slightly acidic, these materials will counteract the alkalinity of the chalk, while also improving the water retention and increasing the amount of organic matter in the soil. Winter tares and alfalfa are green manures particularly suitable for alkaline soils.

Correcting soil pH

The ideal soil pH for most fruit trees is between 6.5 and 7, i.e. slightly to the alkaline side of neutral. However, they tend to be tolerant of all but the most extreme conditions, so it is fine to aim for a slow improvement rather than to expect sudden change.

It is easier to make soil more alkaline than it is to make it more acidic. Adding garden lime to an acid soil will increase the soil pH easily and predictably, so long as the directions are followed. Mushroom compost, which is composed of chalk, manure, peat and gypsum, is alkaline, and will feed the soil at the same time as increasing the pH. Manure, and to a lesser extent compost, are acid in nature, so adding these to soil will increase the acidity over time. You can increase the acidity of compost by adding pine needles or bracken to it.

Green manures

Sowing a green manure crop in the season before planting is a valuable means of improving the soil. Green manures do this either by drawing up nutrients from the lower levels of the soil or by fixing nitrogen from the air, making it available in the soil. They also provide large amounts of material for composting.

Tares, also known as vetch, is a leguminous (nitrogen-fixing) green manure that can be overwintered.

Heavy rainfall leaches nutrients from the topsoil, depositing them lower down in the soil structure. Green manures with extensive roots, such as buckwheat or rye, help to draw nutrients up to where they are needed, as well as reducing further leaching. Leguminous plants, such as field beans, tares or bitter blue lupins, will fix nitrogen. Different green manures are suited to different soils and different times of the year, so it is worth finding out which is the best for your needs and soil conditions.

Correcting nutrient deficiencies

Specific deficiencies can show up in a soil test. These can all be remedied using organic methods. In addition, green manures can be used to draw up nutrients from lower in the soil and to fix nitrogen from the air.

Nitrogen is the nutrient that is responsible for the vegetative growth of a tree. Too little nitrogen will result in a starved-looking tree that puts on little growth. A deficiency of nitrogen in the soil can be corrected by using a high-nitrogen fertiliser such as dried blood, or a more balanced fertiliser such as pelleted chicken manure or blood, fish and bone.

Phosphorus is largely responsible for root growth, so is particularly important in the establishment of a tree after planting. Applying bonemeal is the most common organic method of redressing phosphorus deficiency.

Potassium, or potash, is the nutrient that is largely responsible for the formation of flowers and fruit. Potassium deficiency can be corrected by applying rock potash or comfrey-based preparations.

Other important minerals are magnesium, iron, zinc and copper. Levels of all these minerals can be improved by the application of seaweed or preparations made from it, such as seaweed meal. Seaweed-based feeds will also provide the other trace elements that are needed. The use of seaweed, manure or compost will ensure the development of a healthy soil with adequate nutrients and a good soil structure.

Remedying compacted soil

If you are planting a large orchard, access to agricultural machinery can be helpful. Land that has been used for intensive agriculture in the past may have become compacted by heavy machinery. If you find that the soil is dense and difficult to chop through with a spade, you may be suffering from this problem (although clay soils can present a similar picture). If you suspect your soil is compacted, contact a local farmer who can loosen the soil with a tractor-mounted sub-soiler.

Shelter and exposure

Fruit trees appreciate shelter from harsh conditions. Warm, sheltered conditions will lead to strong, healthy growth and favourable conditions for pollination. Plenty of sunlight is needed for the formation of fruit buds and the ripening of fruit. While all gardeners might wish for a warm sunny site, we have to make the best of what we do have. There are favoured spots in any garden and, even where conditions appear adverse, there is much that can be done to improve matters.

The exposed site

Exposure to strong winds can hinder the growth of fruit trees as well as making successful pollination less likely. Gales can blow trees over and knock ripening fruit to the ground. When looking at conditions in your garden or orchard site, it is important to know the direction of the prevailing wind. Over most of Britain, this will be between the south-west and north-west, but it can vary with local topography. Wind will follow the path of least resistance, so is likely to funnel down a valley or blow between hills, giving rise to local variations.

There is no substitute for patient observation of your own site, identifying the direction of the prevailing wind, as well as its strength in different areas of your land. You might find that local features such as a hedge or trees will provide the kind of shelter that you are looking for, but make sure that they are not blocking out sunlight at the same time. Trees and hedges will usefully filter strong winds, whereas solid objects such as walls and fences can create a harmful whirlwind effect.

Shelter from cold easterly winds in the spring will also be helpful. Young growth is particularly susceptible to scorching by cold winds, and pollination can be badly affected. Although strong winds can be damaging anywhere, the problems of exposure can be compounded by altitude and aspect.

Altitude

Higher ground tends to be colder and to suffer from stronger winds. Fruit crops begin to decline over an altitude of 125m (410'). The temperature decreases by about 0.5°C (0.9°F) for every 100m (328') of height. This doesn't mean that you can't grow fruit trees at higher altitudes, just that you will need to provide a suitable environment for them, by planting windbreaks, for example, or using sheltered sites.

Aspect

Aspect is another variable over which you have little control. North-facing slopes receive less sun than areas with other aspects and are slow to warm up when the spring arrives. This is a minor problem on a gentle slope in the south of England, but a serious one in a cold place in Scotland. If the aspect of your

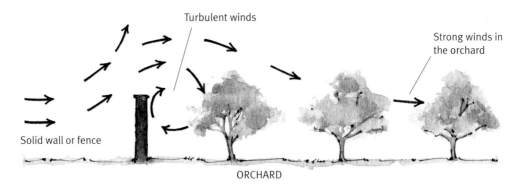

Turbulent winds

Strong winds in the orchard

Solid wall or fence

ORCHARD

Diagram 1 A damaging whirlwind effect created by a solid barrier.

site is unfavourable, you will need to work harder at improving those things over which you do have control.

Windbreaks

A windbreak, or shelterbelt, is a planting of trees designed to filter the wind and to lift it up and over an area of orchard that needs protection. A well-planted windbreak can give protection for a distance of up to 20 times the height of the tallest trees in the windbreak. This is in marked contrast to a solid barrier, such as a wall or fence, which can create a damaging whirlwind effect in the orchard.

Suitable trees for planting in a shelterbelt include silver birch, alder, poplar and some types of willow. These are fast-growing species that will give an ever-increasing level of protection. Traditionally tough species of fruit trees, such as damsons and cherry plums, were sometimes added to shelterbelts. These trees will give you the added bonus of a crop of fruit.

As time goes by, the trees in a shelterbelt will tend to become bare around the base of the trunk, allowing wind to blow underneath the effective area of the windbreak. Planting a

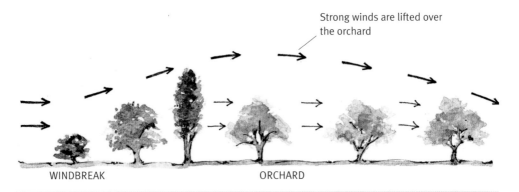

Strong winds are lifted over the orchard

WINDBREAK   ORCHARD

Diagram 2 A windbreak protecting an orchard.

American red alder
used as a windbreak.

row of dense shrubs to the windward side of the trees will prevent this problem. Holly, sea buckthorn and blackthorn are all suitable shrubs to give an extra layer of protection.

Existing hedges can also give a useful amount of protection, especially if allowed to grow a little higher. If the hedge is becoming thin and bedraggled, hedge laying could be a suitable option. Laying is a traditional method of hedgerow management, which will reduce a hedge in the first year, but rejuvenate and thicken it after that.

Proprietary windbreak netting can be useful, either as temporary feature while a living windbreak becomes established, or as a permanent feature, if there is not space to plant a shelterbelt. It is worth doing all you can to protect an orchard site from the effect of strong winds; it really does make a difference.

The sheltered site

A sheltered site is a blessing when looking for somewhere to plant fruit trees. The shelter might come from the local topography, or from buildings, hedges or trees. If one area of your site is more sheltered than others, you can use it to grow the more tender species of fruit, such as apricots, peaches or figs.

The most favourable conditions in a garden are to be found against a south- or west-facing wall, particularly a house wall that will radiate the heat from the house. Here you can grow the most tender fruit trees, such as peaches and nectarines, that will benefit from the extra warmth and shelter of the wall. All types of fruit tree will thrive in these benign conditions, and growing them in restricted forms such as cordons, fans or espaliers will keep them close to the shelter of the wall. See Chapter 6, page 81, for information on growing restricted forms of tree.

Frost pockets

The types of fruit tree normally grown in the British Isles are generally hardy. This means that the tree will not be harmed by the temperatures that are normally found here. It is late frosts that are much more likely to cause a problem, by damaging a fruit tree's flowers and so preventing successful pollination. Severe damage is usually found only when temperatures fall below -2°C (28.5°F). Peach trees, for example, are hardy to around -25°C (-13°F), but the blossom can be damaged by temperatures just below freezing.

The likelihood of your area experiencing late frosts is affected by both regional and local factors. The map on the right shows the frequency of air frosts found in Britain during April (you can see that most of the country can experience heavy frosts during April, when many fruit trees are flowering). It is local conditions that will determine whether damaging frosts are found on a particular site, and often the most sheltered sites are prone to the heaviest frosts. Sites in valley bottoms might seem ideal for growing fruit, until late frosts are taken into consideration.

This can seem strange until the formation of frost pockets is understood. Frost pockets are areas of low-lying ground that suffer from more frost than the valley slopes just above them. This happens because cold air is dense and flows downhill, replacing warm air, which tends to rise. Now that thermometers are becoming commonplace in cars, we can drive along in cold weather and observe the difference in temperature between the valley floor and the surrounding hillsides in cold weather. It is not uncommon to find a variation of 4°C (7°F) between the two. Gently sloping ground 30-80m (approx. 100-260') above a valley floor will often be an ideal site

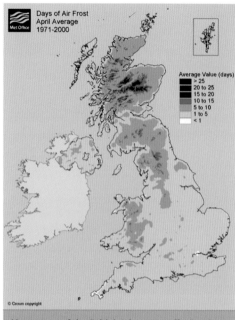

Days of Air Frost
April Average
1971-2000

Average Value (days)
> 25
20 to 25
15 to 20
10 to 15
5 to 10
1 to 5
< 1

© Crown copyright

Most parts of the British Isles can suffer hard frosts in April, when many fruit trees are flowering. © Crown Copyright 2011, the Met Office

as far as avoiding frost damage is concerned. It might seem that there is little that you can do to influence frost, but features such as banks, hedges, walls and fences will all influence the movement of cold air on a very local scale. Barriers such as these at the top of a garden can divert cold air away, whereas at the bottom of a site they can trap cold air. If you have such a barrier, which is trapping frost within your garden, it can be beneficial to create a gap in the barrier, allowing cold air to flow away. It may seem strange to think of air behaving in this way, but cold air will behave much like water, following the path of least resistance.

Sun and shade

Sunlight is needed as a vital link in the process of photosynthesis, whereby a tree creates

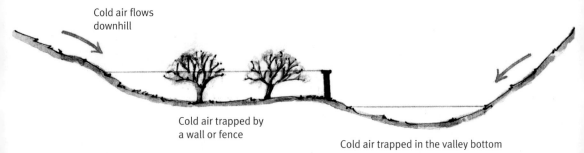

Cold air flows
downhill

Cold air trapped by
a wall or fence

Cold air trapped in the valley bottom

Diagram 3 How a wall or fence can create a frost pocket.

the carbohydrates needed for growth, from carbon dioxide and water. Adequate levels of sunlight are also important in the formation of fruit buds and the ripening of fruit. A minimum of six hours of potential sunlight per day is necessary for most types of fruit trees to produce good levels of fruit. Acid cherries are an exception to this, even growing satisfactorily on a north-facing wall. Cooking plums and some apples will also tolerate some shade.

Once again, it is patient observation over the seasons that will show you which areas of your site are most suitable for growing fruit trees. A tree or a building that casts no shade in the summer may cause considerable shade during the spring and autumn.

Some aspects of sun and shade will be under your control, while others will not. You can do nothing about surrounding buildings, whereas trees and tall hedges that are casting shade can be managed appropriately. Even the shade cast by a large tree can be reduced by crown lifting or thinning, although this is likely to be a job for the professional.

QUICK GUIDE TO THE SITE OF YOUR ORCHARD

- Observe your site carefully over the seasons to become aware of the conditions that exist.
- The soil, wind, climate, sun and shade all need to be taken into account.
- The soil type, drainage and pH need to be assessed and then corrected as necessary.
- Growing green manures and adding manure or compost will improve all soil types.
- Fruit trees flourish in sheltered conditions. Plant shelterbelts or hedges to shelter trees from strong winds.
- Avoid frost pockets where possible, or modify their effect with walls or hedges.
- Wherever possible, choose a sunny site for planting your fruit trees.

Chapter 2

Rootstocks

More than 99 per cent of fruit trees are grown on a rootstock. In order to choose a fruit tree for your orchard, you will need to know a little about rootstocks, particularly because the rootstock has a large influence on the eventual size of your tree. For example, a Cox's Orange Pippin grown on a vigorous M25 rootstock will grow into a large tree up to 10m (33') tall, whereas the same variety grown on a dwarfing M27 rootstock might only grow to about 1.5m (5') tall.

For nearly every fruit tree you plant, there will be a choice of rootstocks. While some rootstocks are suitable for certain soils and some confer resistance to certain diseases, by far the most important characteristic of a rootstock is the effect it has on the eventual size of the tree.

This allows you a lot of flexibility when planning your orchard. Choosing the correct rootstock will save you a lot of heartache later on. It is no use trying to prune a fruit tree hard because it is getting too big for your garden; you will only succeed in creating a tree with lots of upright vegetative growth that will gradually lose its fruiting potential.

Why use a rootstock?

If you grow an apple tree from a pip, you will not end up with the same variety of tree you started with, because apple trees are cross-pollinated. This means that the flower of an apple needs pollen from another apple variety to successfully produce a fruit. The pips of that apple will share the characteristics of both varieties. So if you plant the pips from a Cox's Orange Pippin, you will end up with a fruit that shares the characteristics of a Cox and the variety that pollinated it.

Some apple varieties that are well known today originated from seedlings. The Bramley's Seedling cooking apple originated from a chance seedling planted in 1809 (see box overleaf). Very few apples will grow successfully from cuttings, so to reproduce a known variety of apple, grafting is necessary.

The process of grafting

Grafting is the process of fixing a cutting, known as graftwood or scion wood, to a rootstock in such a way that the living tissue in both will fuse together to make a strong bond. This is achieved by cutting a shape in the top of the rootstock that is mirrored by a

Left: A large apple tree in a traditional orchard. The size of a tree is largely determined by the rootstock.

THE STORY OF BRAMLEY'S SEEDLING

The story of our quintessential English cooking apple started in around 1809 when a young woman called Mary Ann Brailsford planted some apple pips. One of the resulting trees turned out to be fine green cooking apple that cooked to a sharp purée.

In around 1857, or so the story goes, a local nurseryman by the name of Henry Merryweather came across the local vicar carrying a basket of these apples. Recognising a good apple, he asked the vicar where they came from. The vicar took him to Mary's tree and the rest is history.

Merryweather took graftwood from the tree and started selling the young trees, naming them after Matthew Bramley, who was now living in the house where Mary had lived. In the late nineteenth century the Bramley apple achieved fame and recognition at the Royal Horticultural Society shows. By the 1920s, large acreages of Bramley trees were being planted as commercial orchards.

Amazingly, the Bramley has now eclipsed all other British cooking apples. It keeps well, has a good flavour and cooks to a pulp, which English cooks prefer.

Bramley's Seedling.

The bulge in the trunk is the union between the rootstock and the scion. This should be well above ground level after planting.

corresponding but inverted shape in the graftwood, so that they can come together without any gaps. The two parts are held firmly together and then wrapped tightly with a biodegradable tape that will perish once the union is strong enough. Once the bond is formed and the tree is growing, the graft or union will be recognisable as a distinct knobbly shape on the lower trunk.

It is important to recognise this shape, to ensure that it is above the soil when the tree is planted (see Chapter 6).

Some orchard groups run courses that teach you to graft your own fruit trees. (You can find your local group via the website www.orchardnetwork.org.uk.) This is an excellent

and satisfying way to reproduce an old favourite tree, if you don't know its variety. Grafting is usually carried out in late winter. There is also another method of producing fruit trees, known as 'budding', often used by commercial nurseries: this where just one bud is inserted into the rootstock, usually in the late summer. Amazingly, a whole apple tree will develop from just that one bud.

Characteristics of different rootstocks

In the early days of grafting, tree nurseries did not exist, so grafting would have been largely the preserve of farmers and smallholders wishing to propagate successful trees. They did not have access to specially prepared rootstocks as we do today, so they would use whichever trees were close to hand. The rootstock also had to be compatible with the graftwood. For example, pear graftwood can be grafted on to a quince or a wild pear rootstock, but not on to a cherry or plum. Apples were usually grafted on to crab apples or apple seedlings.

More recently, with the commercialisation of the fruit industry, much research has been carried out into rootstocks, particularly with apples. This has resulted in a range of rootstocks, named with codes such as M25 or MM106 – which can be confusing to the novice fruit grower.

By far the most important characteristic of these rootstocks is their effect on the eventual size of the fruit tree, but their imprint will also affect the tree in other, more subtle, ways – for example, in resistance to specific pests and diseases and suitability for different soils.

Dwarfing rootstocks

In the past, most fruit trees were of a large size, but modern developments in rootstocks have enabled the cultivation of dwarfing or semi-dwarfing trees. These smaller trees are more suited to both the commercial grower and the amateur because they can be sprayed, pruned and harvested from the ground rather than using the long ladders of days gone by.

As gardens have become smaller, dwarfing trees have become increasingly convenient. Growing trees on dwarfing rootstocks allows you to grow many more varieties in the same area of garden. For example, instead of growing two varieties of a large apple tree, you could plant a number of small trees that would give you both cookers and dessert varieties, early and late, as well as more room for other fruits. Trees grown on more dwarfing rootstocks tend to bear fruit sooner in their lives than trees grown on more vigorous rootstocks.

There are, however, disadvantages of dwarfing rootstocks. Generally, the smaller the tree, the more nurturing it requires. Some of the most dwarfing apple rootstocks, such as M27 or M9, will struggle on poor or chalky soils. More attention will need to be paid to feeding the tree as well as to keeping the area around the trunk free from grass and weeds. Obviously these trees produce much smaller crops than large trees, which might seem like a disadvantage, but then do you need half a tonne of an early apple that will keep for just three weeks or so?

Vigorous rootstocks

A vigorous rootstock will produce a large tree, sometimes over 10m (33') tall and wide.

While there are obvious difficulties with managing trees of this size, if you do have the space for an orchard of such trees, you will be rewarded with not only large quantities of fruit but also the beautiful sight of a traditional orchard in the landscape. These orchards, particularly at blossom time and at harvest time, are a sight to behold; by planting such an orchard you are doing much to enhance the landscape in a way that has been done for centuries.

Such orchards offer the potential for very large crops, much larger than you will be able to eat, even if you have a large family. This is where juicing and cider-making come into play. Because much of a large tree is out of reach, most of your harvest will be windfalls or shaken apples. These are likely to be bruised, so they will not keep long; however, juicing them, either for cider or juice, is a way of using and potentially preserving them in large quantities. Fresh juice can be preserved by pasteurising or freezing.

Another advantage of trees grown on vigorous rootstocks is that they can be trained so that grazing animals can keep the grass under control – which can otherwise be a demanding task on an orchard scale. Although formative pruning is needed, such trees need little looking after once established. They can live for over 100 years, compared with around 20 years for some of the more dwarfing rootstocks.

The main disadvantages of vigorous rootstocks are the difficulties in reaching the trees and the long time before cropping begins. It is not uncommon to wait eight years before a standard tree bears substantial crops.

A traditional apple orchard reclining gently in the landscape.

Semi-dwarfing rootstocks

For many people, semi-dwarfing rootstocks are a suitable compromise between dwarfing and vigorous rootstocks. They are reasonably quick to start fruiting, don't take up too much space and are manageable from the ground – albeit with long-handled tools as they grow taller. Examples of such rootstocks are MM106 for apples, Quince A or C for pears, and St Julien A for plums.

Rootstocks for different fruits

Choosing the correct rootstock is as important as choosing the right variety. The information on the following pages will help you to make this choice with confidence.

Apple rootstocks

The first half of the twentieth century saw much research into apple rootstocks, particu-

PLANTING DISTANCES

The rootstock largely determines the spread of the tree, although this can vary slightly – up to a metre – depending on the vigour of the cultivar. The spread indicates how far apart trees should be planted. So, a tree with a spread of 2m (6'6") could be planted 2.5m (8') from other trees, allowing for room to walk around the tree when harvesting or pruning. Planting trees far enough apart, so that they have gaps between them when mature, decreases their suscepti-bility to fungal disease.

larly in England. Many of the rootstocks now commonly in use were developed at this time, mostly at government research stations, such as those at Merton and East Malling. The names of these research stations gave rise to the prefixes M (East Malling) and MM (Malling-Merton) that are found preceding some of the most common apple rootstocks.

The most useful apple rootstocks are listed here, starting with the most dwarfing (see Chapter 8, pages 109-112, for descriptions of tree forms).

M27 An extremely dwarfing rootstock. Needs permanent staking. Requires fertile soil and lack of competition from weeds or grass. Fruits early in its life. Will not tolerate wet soils. Suitable for dwarf-trained trees. Mature height 1.2-1.7m (4'-5'6"); spread approximately 1.5m (5').

M9 A very dwarfing rootstock. Needs per-manent staking. Requires fertile soil and lack of competition from weeds or grass. Fruits early in its life. Will tolerate wet soils but not drought. Can be prone to canker in wet soils. Suitable for training as a bush or spindlebush; also small trained trees such as stepovers and cordons, and pot-grown trees. Height 1.7-2.5m (5'6"-8'); spread 2.5m (8').

M26 A dwarfing rootstock. Needs perma-nent staking. Will not tolerate wet and heavy soils. Fruits early in its life. Liable to produce

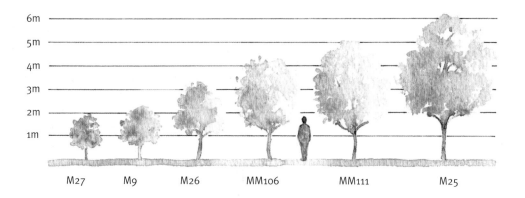

Diagram 4 The size of tree produced by different apple rootstocks.

burr knots, which can be colonised by pests such as woolly aphids. Susceptible to crown rot and fireblight. Suitable for most forms of training, including cordon and espalier, as well as pot-grown trees. Height 2.5-3m (8-10'); spread 3.5m (11'6").

MM106 A semi-dwarfing rootstock. Needs staking early in its life. Suitable for most soil conditions. Susceptible to crown rot. Resistant to woolly aphids and fireblight. Suitable for training as a bush, spindlebush or large wall-trained tree. Height 4-5m (13-16'); spread 4m (13').

MM111 A semi-vigorous rootstock, not often found. Needs staking only early in its life on windy sites. Prone to burr knots but resistant to woolly aphids. Suitable for training as a half standard or standard. Suitable only for orchards and large gardens. Height 5-8m (16-26'); spread 7m (23').

M25 A vigorous rootstock. Needs staking early in its life on windy sites. Susceptible to woolly aphids. Suitable for training as a half standard or standard. Suitable only for orchards and large gardens. Height 6-10m (20-33'); spread 7-10m+ (2-33'+).

Pear rootstocks

Traditionally grown on wild pear rootstocks, most pears these days are grafted on to quince rootstocks. The most common pear rootstocks are as follows.

Quince C A moderately vigorous rootstock producing a tree 3.5- 4 metres (11'6"-13') tall that will start bearing fruit when 4-5 years old. Spread 3-3.5m (10'-11'6"). Prefers fertile soil conditions. Intolerant of dry and chalky soils. Suitable for all forms of tree except standards.

Quince A A medium-vigour rootstock producing a tree of 4-4.5m (13'-14'6") tall that will start bearing fruit when 4 to 6 years old. Spread 3.5-4m (11'6"-13'). Prefers fertile soil conditions. Intolerant of dry and chalky soils. Suitable for all forms of tree except standards.

Pyrodwarf A new medium-vigour rootstock originating from Germany. Similar in size to Quince A rootstock, but more tolerant of less favourable soil conditions. Fruits earlier in its life than quince rootstocks.

Wild pear (*Pyrus communis*) A very vigorous rootstock, producing trees 10-15m (33-49') tall. Some resistance to honey fungus. The spread of trees on pear rootstock can vary considerably, depending on the variety: if you are unsure, allow at least 10m (33') between trees.

Plum rootstocks

In the past, plums have often been grown on their own roots (i.e. without a rootstock) and propagated by the lifting of suckers. The use of rootstocks has now become the norm, with a choice of several rootstocks giving a range of tree size.

Pixy The most dwarfing rootstock, resulting in a tree 2.5-3.5m (8'-11'6") tall and 3m (10') across. It is suitable for bush and pyramid forms and for fan-training. Because of its size and disease resistance, Pixy is increasing in popularity. It has some resistance to silverleaf and bacterial canker, two of the most common diseases on plum trees. It prefers a fertile soil and doesn't tolerate drought well.

St Julien A A semi-vigorous rootstock producing trees with a mature height of around 3.5-4.5m (11'6"-14'6"); spread 4m (13'). It has been the most common plum rootstock for a long time and is tolerant of a range of conditions. Suitable for bush and half standard forms or training as a large fan. Its main drawback is its susceptibility to bacterial canker. It has some resistance to honey fungus.

Brompton A vigorous rootstock that is now declining in popularity because of its large size. It is really suitable only for training as a standard or half standard, giving trees of a height and spread of 5-6m (16-20'). It is suitable for most soil conditions.

Cherry rootstocks

Although related to plums, cherries use completely different rootstocks. In the past, cherries were grafted on to wild cherry seedlings, giving rise to huge trees up to 15m (49') tall, harvested from very long ladders. The introduction of dwarfing rootstocks was particularly important for cherries, because netting is often needed to prevent birds from stripping the fruit from the tree.

Most cherry trees for growing in garden situations are now grown on Gisela 5 rootstocks, although Gisela 6 might also be available from some nurseries. This is a slightly more vigorous rootstock than Gisela 5, more suited to weaker-growing cultivars, such as Lapins. Trees grown on Colt and F12/1 rootstocks are much larger, making them harder to net, spray or harvest.

Gisela 5 A comparatively new rootstock that is replacing Colt (see above right) due to its smaller size (40 per cent smaller) and precociousness. Mature trees are only 2.5-3m (8-10') tall and 3m (10') across, so fairly easy to net.

Colt A semi-dwarfing rootstock, with mature trees 3.5-4.5m (11'6"-14'6") tall and 4.5m (14'6") across. Trees on a Colt rootstock will tolerate a wide range of soil conditions.

F12/1 A vigorous rootstock that can still sometimes be found, giving rise to trees over 6m (20') tall.

Peach, nectarine and apricot rootstocks

Peaches, nectarines and apricots are grafted on to the same rootstocks as plums, to which they are closely related, with one or two important additions.

Montclaire A new, highly productive rootstock for peaches and nectarines that results in a slightly smaller tree than when St Julien A is used. It makes trees less susceptible to frost damage, which could make peaches an easier crop to grow in Britain. Montclaire rootstock produces trees around 3.5-4m (11'6"-13') tall.

Torinel A recently introduced rootstock for apricots, which is becoming more popular. It is slightly smaller than St Julien A, suitable for a wide range of soil conditions and highly productive.

Figs

Figs are grown on their own roots. It is good practice to plant figs where their roots can be restricted, by walls or paving for example, in order to control their growth and promote fruiting.

Mulberries

Mulberries can be propagated by taking cuttings and they can also be grafted. You will not find any choice of rootstock. Growing trees on a rootstock brings them into fruiting earlier in their life. When mulberries are grafted on to a rootstock, it is usually *Morus alba*, the white mulberry.

Quince rootstocks

Quince trees are grown on quince or wild pear rootstocks. Quince rootstocks will produce a small tree, around 3.5-5.5m (11'6"-18') tall and around 5m (16') wide. Hawthorn rootstocks produce slightly bigger trees, but with less stable roots. Although rarely found nowadays, medlars can also be grafted on to wild pear rootstocks, leading to very large trees about 10m (33') in height and spread. All three will tolerate relatively poor soil conditions. See 'Pear rootstocks', page 33, for details of these.

Medlar rootstocks

Medlar trees can be grown on hawthorn (*Crataegus monogyna*), quince or wild pear rootstocks. Hawthorn and quince will produce semi-dwarfing trees, whereas wild pear will produce a large tree. All three will tolerate relatively poor soil conditions. See 'Pear rootstocks', page 33, for details of quince and wild pear rootstocks.

Medlars can be grown on hawthorn, quince or wild pear rootstocks.

QUICK GUIDE TO ROOTSTOCKS

The variety of fruit tree that you want to grow will be grafted on to a rootstock. The following points will help you choose the correct rootstock.

- The rootstock will determine the eventual size of the tree.
- Different rootstocks prefer different soil conditions.
- The more vigorous rootstocks will produce large trees with heavy crops. On the downside, they are harder to harvest and prune. They also start to crop later in life than smaller trees. They are well suited to orchards that will be grazed by livestock.
- While it is tempting in many situations to plant dwarfing rootstocks, it is worth remembering that they do have several disadvantages. They generally do not like wet or heavy soils, and need to be kept weed-free and fed well to really perform well.
- In many situations, a semi-dwarfing rootstock will be a happy compromise.

Chapter 3

Pollination, flowering and fruit development

This chapter considers the various factors that come into play when choosing varieties and deciding where to place them within a particular site. It is not just a question of choosing your favourite varieties: you must also find out whether they will be pollinated successfully by other trees and whether they will grow well in your area. For example, if you garden in a wet climate, you will need to select varieties that are resistant to the diseases that thrive in those conditions. Then you must find the best place to site these varieties in your plot. Sometimes it can seem time-consuming and frustrating to meet these criteria, but time spent at this stage will avoid greater frustration later on.

Pollination of fruit trees

In order to produce fruit, the flowers on your fruit tree must be pollinated. Most fruit trees are what is called self-incompatible, or self-

sterile. This means that the flowers cannot be pollinated using pollen from the same tree, or from another tree of the same variety. They need to be cross-pollinated with pollen from another variety of the same fruit that is flowering at the same time. Some fruit trees, particularly members of the *Prunus* family, such as plums and cherries, have some degree of self-fertility, although crops will be larger if the flowers are cross-pollinated.

If you are keenly watching to see if your flowers are being pollinated, there will not be much to see until the petals fall off and you see the small embryonic fruit emerging. This is a sign of successful pollination. Not all flowers will be pollinated; if they were, your tree would have too much fruit for its own good.

The role of bees in pollination

Bees are the main agent of pollination of fruit trees, with the honey bee being the most effective. Bumblebees and solitary bees, such as the mason bee, also play their part. The honey bee has a symbiotic relationship with fruit trees. The fruit tree provides nectar, an important food for the bee; in return, the bee pollinates the tree by travelling from one flower to another.

Much has been spoken in recent years about the decline of the honey bee. It is recognised that this decline could pose a serious threat to crops that require cross-pollination, including most fruit trees. A parasitic mite called varroa has been responsible for much of the problem, but 'Colony Collapse Disorder' is another factor.

Intensive farming, especially where certain pesticides are used, has also been implicated. A group of pesticides known as neonicotinoids, for example, thiacloprid, has come under suspicion. If you do spray your trees with pesticides, look out for warnings printed on the label such as 'may be dangerous to bees'. These warnings can also apply

A bee pollinating pear blossom.

THE MECHANICS OF POLLINATION

- The **colourful petals** serve to attract pollinating insects to the flower.

- The **sepals** and **petals** are a protection for the delicate reproductive parts of the flower.

- The **stamen** is the male reproductive organ. It consists of the **filament** topped by the **anther**, which contains the **pollen**.

- The female organ consists of a long tube called the **style**, on top of which sits **the stigma**, a sticky receptacle where the pollen is collected.

- The pollen moves down the style into the **ovule** within the **ovary**, where the female genetic material is contained. When male and female genetic materials are fused together, fertilisation occurs.

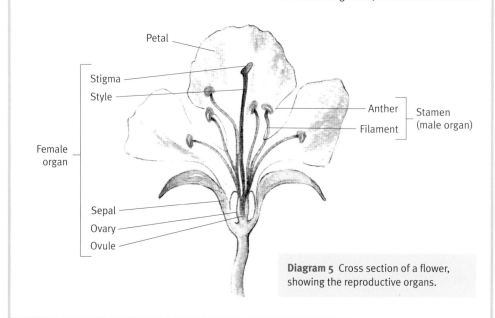

Petal
Stigma
Style
Anther
Filament
Stamen (male organ)
Female organ
Sepal
Ovary
Ovule

Diagram 5 Cross section of a flower, showing the reproductive organs.

to plant-based pesticides that you might assume to be more friendly to wildlife, such as pyrethrum. The best way around such a problem is to spray as late as possible in the day, when bees are less likely to be working.

It is worth taking positive steps to attract bees to your garden or orchard. One way to do this is to ensure that bees have good food sources throughout the year. There are usu-

ally plenty of suitable plants during the summer, but good sources of nectar early and late in the season are particularly important to bees. Fruit trees are one of the best early sources of nectar. Another source late in the year is the flowers of ivy. Growing single-flowered forms of plants, rather than double, will also help. You can make or buy nests that will attract solitary bees to your garden, which consist of sections of bamboo

A home-made mason bee nest.

in a wooden frame. You can even provide nest sites by drilling holes into wood, such as fence posts, in sunny positions.

One factor over which you have no control is the weather. Bees tend to be fair-weather creatures. They will not be working much when it is raining, cold or windy. Poor pollination due to adverse weather conditions can be a significant problem, particularly with early-flowering fruit such as plums or peaches. Where possible, plant your trees in a sheltered position that will provide a more welcoming environment for pollinating insects. There often seem to be cold easterly winds at blossom time, so any shelter that you can provide from this direction will be helpful. If you have no choice but to plant on a windswept site, it can be worth planting a windbreak first (see Chapter 1, page 22).

Where it is known that poor pollination is likely, hand pollination can be worthwhile. This could be necessary when the weather is poor in spring at blossom time, or if you are

growing particularly early fruit. It usually pays to pollinate peaches by hand, because they flower at a time when few bees are working; peach trees are also likely to be covered up at this time of year in order to prevent peach leaf curl. The best tool for the job is a very soft paintbrush, such as one made from camel hair. Hand-pollinating a tree is one of those relaxing jobs that make fruit-growing fun. Simply dab the brush lightly on one flower after another, pretending that you are a bee (see photo overleaf).

Pollination in the orchard

So most fruit trees will need another tree growing nearby to act as a pollinator. But how do you know which trees are suitable for this?

The main criterion is flowering time: both trees need to be in flower at the same time for a bee to spread pollen from one tree to the flowers of another. When you order or buy a tree, you are likely to find a number or letter that will give you a guide to its flowering time.

Pollinating a nectarine flower with a paintbrush.

The most common system is a set of numbers, usually from 1 to 7, but letters from A to G are also used, with 1 or A being the earliest flowering. The principle of these two systems is that you need to have a variety in the same flowering group (also known as pollination group), or one either side of it, in order for your tree to be pollinated. In other words, if you have a tree in flowering group 3, it will be pollinated by trees in groups 2, 3 or 4.

There are exceptions to this rule in the form of self-fertile varieties, triploids and varieties that are not compatible with each other (see right). The charts in the chapters on individual fruits in Part 3 are designed to make the choosing of suitable varieties a simple task.

There are some apple trees that are particularly valuable for pollination, because they flower over a longer period than most apples. Many crab apples, such as John Downie, Golden Hornet and Red Sentinel, are helpful in this way. Other apples that are good pollinators, and also useful varieties in their

own right, are Greensleeves, Grenadier and Lane's Prince Albert.

Self-fertile varieties

These are varieties that are able to produce fruit without another pollinator. Some apples and pears (such as Conference) are able to set a small crop without the help of a pollinator, while a number of plums and cherries are properly self-fertile, being able to set a good crop on their own – although they will nearly always bear a larger crop if pollinated by another tree. Quinces, peaches, nectarines, apricots, medlars, figs and mulberries are all self-fertile.

Triploids

Trees that have healthy pollen and need another tree for pollination are known as diploids. These include the vast majority of apples and pears. However, there are other trees, known as triploids, which carry largely sterile pollen, meaning that they are unable to pollinate other trees; they still need a diploid to pollinate them, but they are unable to pollinate the diploid in return. So, whereas two apple trees can usually pollinate each other, if a triploid is grown, you need two other diploids to ensure that all three trees are successfully pollinated. The diploids will pollinate each other as well as the triploid. So, in practice, if you want to plant a Bramley's Seedling (triploid), you will need two diploid apples, such as James Grieve and Falstaff, all flowering at the same time, to ensure that all three are pollinated.

Incompatible varieties

With some fruits, there are, unfortunately, some varieties that are not able to pollinate each other. The charts in the chapters on individual fruits in Part 3 give details of these incompatible varieties.

Pollination from trees in neighbouring gardens

Fruit trees in neighbouring gardens may be a valuable source of pollen, but it is best not to rely on them. One reason for not doing so is that to achieve the highest level of pollination, the donor tree should be within 20m (66') of the recipient. Also, you have little control over the fate of the donor tree – if your neighbour decides to remove it, you could be left without a pollinator!

Solutions to pollination problems

If you find yourself in a situation where you have a tree of an unknown variety that you would like to get pollinated, you have two choices. One is to get the variety identified, perhaps by using a dedicated fruit-naming service such as those run by the Royal Horticultural Society (RHS) or Brogdale (see Resources; also Chapter 17, page 310). The other is to wait until the tree is in flower and then look for other named fruit trees that are flowering at the same time so that you can buy one for your own garden. If you do this, be aware that problems may arise if yours is a triploid or if the varieties are incompatible.

In extreme circumstances, you could cut a branch of another tree that is flowering at the same time and place it in water close to your tree. This is likely to be only a temporary solution, however, unless you wish to decimate the donor tree.

Flowering and fruit development

Once pollination is successfully completed, the next stage you will notice is the petals turning brown, followed not long after by the embryonic fruit appearing. If all goes well, the fruit will slowly become larger until it reaches full size, ripens and is then ready for harvest.

The June Drop

During June, or July, something is likely to occur which may alarm the newcomer to fruit-tree growing. This is called the June Drop. Young fruits will start dropping from the tree. This is not actually a problem, but rather nature's way of ensuring that the tree does not bear too heavy a crop, which could place a strain on it, cause broken branches or help to induce biennial cropping.

Biennial cropping

Biennial cropping is the tendency of a tree, or sometimes a whole orchard, to crop heavily one year and very lightly the next. It is seen most commonly in apples – cider apples such as Major, Sweet Coppin and Stoke Red being particularly susceptible. There are

Young pears developing. The remains of the blossom can still be seen at the end of the fruit.

ways to counteract biennial cropping, the main one being to not allow a tree to set too heavy a crop in the 'on' year, either by pruning off some off the excessive fruit buds, or by thinning the fruit once it starts to develop.

Fruit thinning

Although it can be time-consuming, thinning the developing fruit can have many other advantages in addition to remedying biennial cropping, such as producing good-quality fruit, reducing the strain on a tree from too heavy a crop and removing damaged or malformed fruit. Successful pollination can result in a large number of fruits developing from one cluster of flowers. If left alone, these fruits are likely to be small and of poor quality. Thinning just after the June Drop will allow the fruits to develop to their potential size and quality (see Chapter 7, page 95).

The chapters on individual fruits in Part 3 give details of the thinning requirements of each fruit. Young trees that are fruiting should have their fruit thinned heavily. While it is tempting to allow a new tree to fruit heavily, it is important to allow the tree to concentrate its energy on vegetative growth rather than fruiting. If trees are allowed to fruit heavily while they are young, subsequent growth can be weak, resulting in a stunted tree.

QUICK GUIDE TO POLLINATION, FLOWERING AND FRUIT DEVELOPMENT

You need to ensure that pollination occurs successfully to produce an abundant harvest of fruit. You can help this process in the following ways.

- Plant varieties that flower at the same time and will pollinate each other. When choosing varieties, look for the number or letter that indicates the time of flowering.

- Ensure that you choose a pollinator with the same number as the variety you want pollinated, or with a number either side of it, or choose self-fertile varieties. Quinces, peaches, nectarines, apricots, medlars, figs and mulberries are all self-fertile.

- Encourage good conditions for pollination. Avoid windswept sites and frost pockets. Encourage bees and other beneficial insects to your orchard by, for example, planting flowers that provide nectar for bees.

If there is a lack of fruit developing from pollinated flowers, look out for the following problems.

- Over-hard pruning, i.e. cutting out much of the wood where fruiting would occur.

- Unproductive trees as a result of poor soil conditions and grass encroachment.

- Diseases such as canker or blossom wilt.

- Bullfinches eating fruit buds.

- Insects such as apple sawfly or pear midge causing damage to the developing fruitlets.

- Frost damage. Planting late-flowering cultivars or protecting with horticultural fleece can help prevent damage.

Appropriate action early on will solve problems quickly. With fruit trees, 'nipping problems in the bud' is certainly true. See Chapter 9 for details of fruit tree problems and remedies.

Chapter 4

Choosing fruit trees

Choosing the right fruit trees for your site and requirements can seem a bewildering task, but it is worth taking time over – making the right choices will result in years of bountiful harvests, while choosing trees just because they are available at the local garden centre could be an expensive mistake that puts you off growing fruit trees for life. This chapter will provide you with the confidence to help you make rewarding choices.

Choosing the right variety

There are a number of factors involved in determining the right variety of fruit tree for you. Personal choice is a large part of this, including the elusive factor of taste. To someone who adores the taste of the Cox's Orange Pippin, nothing else will do. This person might choose to grow a Cox despite the fact that it is one of the most disease-prone varieties in existence. Garden centres are guilty of encouraging such choices, providing few varieties for sale, with correspondingly little information to go with them. Often the varieties sold will be completely unsuitable for

A Cox's Orange Pippin tree. Although they taste wonderful, Cox's are very susceptible to diseases such as scab, canker and mildew.

growing in that particular part of the country, which only leads to disease-ridden trees that give fruit growing a bad name.

It is worth looking more objectively at whether a certain variety will grow and fruit well in the place you live. What do you want to use the fruit for? Do you want apples for cider making, cooking, dessert use or juice making? Some varieties can be useful for several different uses. There is an apple called Tom Putt, for example, that is known as a triple-use apple because it can be used for cooking, eating fresh and cider.

Local varieties

Going back 200 years or more, most fruit growing took place on a very local scale. There would be local cultivars of most fruits, especially apples. Grafting at this time was not a specialist enterprise carried out by nurseries who sell nationwide, as it is today, but something practised by farmers who made their own fruit trees. Graftwood would be passed around on a local scale, sometimes being used in just one or two villages. It is thought that at one time around 6,000 varieties of apple were grown in Britain.

Catshead, an ancient English cooking apple.

Sadly, many have been lost, but there are still over 2,000 known today. Apple-growing counties such as Devon still have many local varieties: there are over 100 varieties of Devon apple still grown, despite the fact that Devon has lost 90 per cent of its orchards since the Second World War.

Old varieties

All over Britain, there are local varieties that have stood the test of time, so are still being grown today. Modern breeding has also introduced many fine new cultivars that are delivering various benefits to fruit growers. Yet it is remarkable how many old varieties are being grown, not for sentimental reasons, but because they produce fruit as good as any from modern cultivars. If we look at the two most popularly grown apples in Britain, Cox's Orange Pippin and Bramley's Seedling, we see two varieties that are both around 200 years old. Modern breeding has failed to surpass them, at least in the public's imagination. Some varieties that are still grown today have origins in the mists of time. Good varieties such as Ashmead's Kernel, Devonshire Quarrenden and Catshead are known to date back to the seventeenth century, while Court Pendu Plat is an apple thought to hail from Roman times. Many well-known and popular apples, such as Bramley's Seedling or Blenheim Orange, were found as chance seedlings.

Climatic and regional factors

Most of the local varieties that have remained in cultivation have done so because they were suited to the local climatic and soil conditions. So, in the West of England, for example, most of the indigenous varieties are suited to a damp climate and are resistant to scab and canker – fungal diseases that can decimate apple trees.

Climatic regions of Britain

If we divide the British Isles into four quadrants as in the illustration here, we find four distinct climatic areas. In the west of Britain, the climate is generally wetter than in the east. A wet climate, while suitable for apples, quinces and damsons, is not enjoyed by many other fruits. Furthermore, some serious diseases – pear and apple canker, scab and bacterial canker – are more common in damp climates. On the other hand, powdery mildew is a fungal disease that is more prevalent in drier areas of Britain. It is very important to consider disease resistance when choosing suitable varieties for your area. See the Appendices at the back of this book for information on specific varieties suited to different climatic conditions.

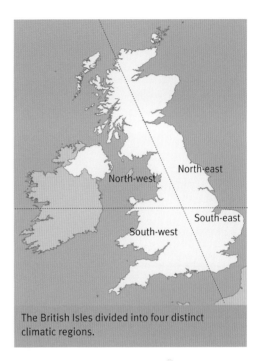

The British Isles divided into four distinct climatic regions.

The horizontal line marks an imaginary dividing line between the comparative warmth of southern England and the colder northern half of Britain.

North-west This area is comparatively cold and wet, although coastal areas such as the west coast of Scotland are warmer than might otherwise be expected because of the influence of the Gulf Stream. You will need to choose varieties that are disease-resistant, suited to cool summers and, in many places, able to resist the effects of late frosts. In the more hostile parts of Scotland, apples, pears, quinces and damsons are all that you will be able to grow successfully. The shelter of a warm wall can be a blessing in such conditions, enabling you to grow fruit that you wouldn't otherwise consider.

North-east This area is cold and dry compared with other parts of Britain. If you live north of Lancashire and Yorkshire, you will find it difficult to succeed with the more tender fruits included in this book, unless your garden is in a sheltered position. Peaches, nectarines, mulberries, apricots and figs are all more at home in the warmer parts of southern England. You can grow them further north, but they may not thrive. Fruiting will be more intermittent and trees will be smaller.

One advantage of the north-east over the north-west is that it is drier and therefore fruit trees are less prone to most fungal diseases. In Scotland, for example, Bramley's Seedling grows well in the east of Scotland, but suffers from canker and scab in the wetter parts of western Scotland. Bacterial canker is more prevalent in wet climates, so Victoria plums can be grown in the east, whereas Opal might be a better choice in the west.

South-east A warm, dry region, this area is

Victoria plum. Because of its susceptibility to bacterial canker, this variety is best suited to drier areas.

ideal for fruit growing in many respects. It is home to the majority of commercial orchards in Britain. Kent, or the 'garden of England', as it is often called, is home to large orchards of apples, pears and cherries. Being geographically close to the continent, its climate is somewhat similar.

The comparative lack of rain in the summer months can be a disadvantage, however, when combined with sandy soils that dry out quickly. In such areas careful watering might be necessary. Large parts of Norfolk, Suffolk and Kent are prone to these conditions.

South-west This area is warm and damp. These are ideal conditions for lush growth, but also ideal conditions for fungal diseases. When reading most nursery catalogues, you will find that canker rarely receives a mention, but in south-west England it is a serious

disease of apples and pears. Varieties such as Cox's Orange Pippin, which are very susceptible to canker, are hardly worth growing unless you envisage constant spraying. Scab can also be a debilitating disease in this area.

In many parts of southern England, fireblight is becoming a serious problem, particularly on pears, yet north of our imaginary line from east to west it is rarely found.

These divisions into quadrants are only approximate, but they are meaningful to the fruit grower looking at the effect that climate plays when choosing varieties. Although regional climatic factors are significant, more local factors, such as frost pockets, must also be taken into account (see Chapter 1, pages 21-5).

Characteristics of different varieties

When choosing varieties of a particular fruit, there are a number of questions you need to ask to ensure that your choice will match your requirements (see box on page 49). This is particularly so with apples, of which there is a seemingly bewildering choice.

Use of the fruit

Fruit can be used for eating fresh, making alcohol or juice, cooking in various ways, or drying. Different varieties will be most suitable for different uses. So, while any apple can be stewed, there are particular varieties that are bred specifically for cooking. Even within the range of cooking apples, there are further choices to be made: there are different tastes, differing degrees of sweetness, and varieties that either keep their shape or cook to a puree. Likewise, there is a choice of pears for dessert use or cooking, as well

Winnal's Longdon is a variety of pear used only for making perry.

as some varieties that are considered suitable for both.

There are specific apples for making cider and pears for making perry. There are further subdivisions within cider apples – into sharps, sweets, bittersweets and bittersharps, as well as vintage varieties suitable for making single-variety ciders. Plums are also divided into culinary and dessert varieties, with many suitable for both. Some varieties are considered especially good for more specialist uses, such as jam making or alcohol production.

So, for each tree you wish to plant, it is worth thinking carefully about what you will use the fruit for. This will make your orchard all the more enjoyable later on.

Seasons of use

With care, you can vastly extend the season in which you are using fruit from your garden. It is common for many people to have a tremendous glut of apples in the autumn, just at the same time that everyone else is giving away apples. However, a judicious choice of varieties can supply you with apples from late July through to April, if they are kept well. Early and mid-season apples can be supplemented by late-keeping apples, which will sweeten in storage for use after Christmas. With cider and juice apples, it is generally an advantage for all the fruit to be ready at the same time, in order to make harvesting and blending easier.

Likewise, pears can also be grown to produce fruit from August until March, with

Striped Beefing is an apple variety that can be kept until April in the right conditions.

Even some pear varieties can be kept until after Christmas. Olivier de Serres will keep till April.

some cooking pears keeping even longer. Plums, being a soft fruit, will not keep for long, but even so a well-chosen collection of varieties will produce fruit from July until October. Cherries, peaches and apricots all offer a shorter season, but a succession of fruits from different varieties is still possible.

There are, of course, many ways of preserving fruits to give a continual supply. The traditional methods of bottling and drying and the modern method of freezing can all help to supply fruit all year round, but this is a matter of the method of preservation rather than the choice of variety. Further information on methods of storing fruit can be found in the chapters on individual fruits in Part 3.

Varieties suitable for keeping can also be found in the chapters on individual fruits in Part 3.

Finding the information

It is all very well knowing that you want a self-fertile juicy dessert plum ready for har-vesting in September that will be suitable for an area that has late frosts, but how do you find out which varieties meet these requirements?

Traditionally, there have been two sources of the information you need: books on fruit growing and specialist nurseries selling fruit trees. There are many books on growing fruit, which give varying amounts of such information. The chapters on individual fruits in Part 3 and the appendices at the back of this book also provide much useful information, but there is insufficient space here to give a comprehensive guide. The most useful books in this respect are Martin Crawford's series of cultivar directories (see Resources), which provide a comprehensive list of varieties suitable for growing in the British Isles, together with all the factors relevant to choosing suitable varieties, such as flowering dates, disease resistance and ripening dates. However, useful as these books are, they are likely to be too expensive and specialist for most interested amateurs.

Nurseries vary widely in their willingness to share their expertise. Some are only too willing to help, while others, seemingly oblivious to the benefits to their business, fail to help the confused gardener. Similarly, the catalogues produced by nurseries vary enormously in the information they provide.

As in many walks of life, the internet is increasingly the place to turn to for detailed and helpful information that is hard to come by elsewhere. At the time of writing, Keepers Nursery (see Resources) maintains a very informative website which includes a search engine that enables browsers to select suitable varieties. Factors such as suitability for difficult conditions, pollination requirements and fruit use can all be included in your search. Of course, the hope is that you will then order trees from this nursery, but this is not a prerequisite.

The National Fruit Collection at Brogdale Farm, near Faversham in Kent (see Resources), also includes much useful information on its website. The collection is open to the public, so a visit at harvest time can be a way of seeing the varieties that you are considering planting in fruit. It is even possible to taste different varieties at certain open days and fruit festivals. At the time of writing, there is also an advice line, with advice on growing fruit trees available free of charge. Many specialist nurseries also hold open days in the autumn, when you can see fruit trees growing, taste the fruit and, of course, order trees.

Local orchard groups can also be mines of information, particularly on the question of local fruit varieties and local nurseries. Some groups offer free advice over the telephone or by email. Some run courses in planning and

QUESTIONS TO ASK WHEN CHOOSING VARIETIES

- What kind of fruit tree am I looking for? (Medlars, apples, plums, peaches, etc?)
- How many of each type of fruit do I want to grow?
- What will I use the fruit for? (Cider, cooking, juicing?)
- What do I want the fruit to taste like? (Sweet, aromatic, melting, buttery, tart, etc?)
- When do I want the fruit to be ready for harvesting?
- Do I want fruit ready for eating from the tree, or for putting into storage for later use?
- Are the type of fruit and the varieties I favour suitable for the climate where I live? Are the varieties resistant to diseases found in my area?
- Do I need late-flowering varieties because late frosts are commonly found in the area where I live?
- Is there a suitable location within my garden/orchard for this tree? (Consider microclimate, shelter, soil conditions, etc.)
- What size of tree at maturity do I require? Which rootstock will provide the right size?
- Are the varieties that I am choosing self-fertile, or do they need pollinating? If pollinators are required, do I have a suitable mix of varieties to give the best chances of successful pollination?

planting young orchards, or even run graft-ing workshops where local varieties can be sourced and fruit trees grafted. If you have a favourite tree that you would like to repro-duce, a grafting workshop is the perfect place to learn how to do it. If you take along a 'cutting' (or, more correctly, graftwood or scionwood), from your tree, you will be able to create a tree by grafting this wood on to a rootstock.

You can find your local orchard group via the website www.orchardnetwork.org.uk, an excellent website run by The National Trust and Natural England.

Growing fruit trees in a warming climate

Because fruit trees are so sensitive to cli-matic conditions, it follows that any long-term changes to the climate will have a knock-on effect on fruit tree growing. It is possible that we will be able to confidently grow fruits in Britain that have been very borderline until now, such as peaches and nectarines, but first we need to know what is happening with our climate.

We all know now that our climate is warm-ing. What might surprise many people is that there have already been significant cli-matic changes in the UK in the last 45 years. Current reports show that our climate is 1°C (1.8°F) warmer than it was in 1961, with increases of around 1.7°C (3°F) in the south and east of England. The UK Climate Projec-tions (UKCP09) report,[*] produced by the Met Office, tells us that "the annual number of days with air frost has reduced in all regions of the UK between 1961 and 2006. There are now typically between 20 and 30 fewer days

of air frost per year". Precipitation patterns are less clear, but there has been a small decline in summer rainfall and a correspond-ing increase in winter precipitation over the same period. These are not huge changes, but they do represent increasingly favour-able conditions for fruit-tree growing.

Prediction of the UK climate in the twenty-first century

What is much more difficult is to accurately predict the future course of events. For the purposes of this discussion, I am using the models provided by UKCP09. The projected figures quoted here are from the 50-per-cent probability level, which is the most likely outcome. The projections are also divided into figures for low-emission, medium-emission and high-emission scenarios. The figures I have used are for the medium-emissions scenario. This is perhaps the most likely course of events, but here we are into the realm of educated guesswork. Personally, I am not convinced that humankind has the capacity to make fundamental remedial changes until it is faced with imminent dis-aster, but I do think that technological and market-led change will bring about eventual reductions in emissions. So, I am content to use this scenario for the purposes of dis-cussing how climate change will affect fruit-tree growing within the next century.

The 50-per-cent probability level projects an increase in UK temperatures of around 1.3°C (2.3°F) between 2010 and 2039, 2.2°C (4°F) from 2010 to 2069 and 3.2°C (5.8°F) between 2010 and 2099. These are average figures, with the increase being higher in the summer than in the winter. Obviously, these are pro-jections rather than accurate figures, but they do show the potential for significant

* UK Climate Projections, available at http://ukclimateprojections.defra.gov.uk.

temperature increases during the lifetime of fruit trees that are being planted now.

Precipitation projections show a mixed picture, with increased winter precipitation and decreases in summer rainfall. In 2069, summer rainfall could be 13 per cent lower and winter precipitation 10 per cent higher than in 2010.

One of the most important projections for fruit growing is that the frequency of heavy rain days (over 25mm [1"]) will increase substantially. This is a potential indicator of increased flooding and storm damage, particularly when these events happen just before harvest, when the both the tree and fruit are most vulnerable to severe weather.

The effects of climate change on growing fruit trees

There are two strands to looking at the effects of climate change on the growing of fruit trees. Firstly, there are the effects on orchards that have already been planted and the need for an adaptive approach to harness the benefits of climate change and to mitigate the challenges. Secondly, there are decisions to be made when considering the planting of new orchards.

Adapting existing orchards to cope with climate change

Depending upon the rootstock used, fruit trees that have recently been planted could easily be around in 50 years' time to experience a considerable increase in temperature and changes in precipitation patterns.

While longer, warmer growing seasons might seem full of promise to the fruit grower, there are also potential problems, as follows.

- Unpredictable conditions can disturb the annual cycle of the fruit tree, causing problems such as poor fruit set and biennial cropping.
- The projected increase in heavy rain days and severe storms can blow trees over, break branches, damage ripe fruit and lead to windrock (where the roots become loose in the soil).
- Some pests and diseases will thrive in the changing conditions, and there is a likelihood that new problems will arrive from abroad, in a similar way to the spread of bluetongue in animal farming. Fireblight is a disease that is particularly damaging to pear trees. At present it is mostly found in southern England, but as climatic belts effectively move northwards, fireblight is likely to follow. Mildew is also

An increase in extreme weather conditions could make scenes like this more familiar.

likely to become more of a problem in hotter, drier summers. Increased winter rainfall could lead to an increased risk of problems with phytophthora, a root-rot disease.

- Water supply in dry summers will become much more of an issue, especially in the south of England. Drought stress, leading to defoliation and fruit drop, could become a serious problem.
- Most fruit trees need a certain period of winter chill in order to develop their fruiting potential for the coming season, which may not be achieved as temperatures rise.

Both preventative and remedial action can be employed to combat these effects of climate change. Most of the methods to combat these potential problems are already part of good orchard practice. For example, providing shelter from strong winds and ensuring that trees are well anchored by good-quality staking are likely to become more important as the severity of storms increases. Mulching in the spring to help preserve soil moisture will need to become common practice as drier summers become more prevalent.

The watering of fruit trees, especially in the south of England, is likely to become a necessity at times. Creating facilities for water storage and distribution will become more important. This could be something as simple as a water butt, but more sophisticated underground storage devices are now becoming available to the home user.

Planting new orchards in a changing climate

The climatic changes mentioned here are, in effect, shifting climatic areas northwards. Over the next 30 to 40 years, the climate now found in Kent is likely to become the climate experienced in Yorkshire. Up until now, the south-east of England has offered excellent conditions for growing apples and pears. This area of good growing conditions will move northwards: first the Midlands and then the north of England are likely to provide the best conditions for growing apples and pears.

Apple trees grown in the south-east of England are increasingly likely to suffer from heat and drought stress in warmer summers. The lack of sufficient winter chill might also come into play, so that fruits needing a long period of winter chill could become unviable in certain areas. (Blackcurrant growers are already facing difficulties in this respect in warm winters.) Certain varieties, such as Braeburn, which require warm summers to ripen properly, have struggled until recently, but are now being planted in commercial orchards.

There will be a mixed picture for pears: they will enjoy the increased warmth, but are likely to suffer from drought stress and more widespread fireblight.

Good plum- and cherry-growing conditions are also likely to extend further north. The more delicate types of plum, such as greengages, will succeed more widely.

Various types of fruit that have been grown speculatively, or in the most sheltered areas, are likely to become widespread in southern England. Peaches and nectarines will move out into the open, away from their protective walls, so long as the problem of peach leaf curl is addressed. Apricots, already successful in south-east England, will become more common. Scotland, Northern Ireland and

Loquats will ripen only in the warmest of summers.

increase. It is easy to imagine that we will be basking in a Mediterranean climate in years to come, but this is not what is forecast.

We are likely to see an increase in temperature, but one accompanied by high winter rainfall and increasingly unpredictability. It is this unpredictability that could cause the greatest problems. Is there really a possibility that the Gulf Stream might reverse, sending us spiralling into a sub-Arctic climate? Whither our peach trees if the glaciers return?

northern England will all benefit from more clement conditions for growing fruit, so long as extreme weather events do not intervene too regularly. Pears and plums will succeed in areas where they have struggled until now.

Persimmons, pomegranates, olives and loquats will all become worthy of speculative planting in southern areas and will provide occasional worthwhile crops, but this is not the same as the regular heavy cropping that we experience from our more normal fruit trees at the moment. These trees are all frost-hardy, but suffer from winter rainfall, particularly in the wetter western areas. Increased winter rainfall is likely to present problems if you try to grow most 'exotic' fruits, particularly on heavy soils.

So, although it might seem like a rosy picture in some respects, with increased warmth providing better conditions for fruit trees, there will also be many challenges. New opportunities will arise, but pressures from diseases and unpredictable weather will also

QUICK GUIDE TO CHOOSING THE RIGHT FRUIT TREES

By asking the right questions, you will be able to find the answers you need. Use books and/or the internet to research different varieties, and ask your local nursery or orchard group for advice. Care taken now will be repaid later.

Remember that our climate is forecast to become warmer. Are the fruits that you are choosing suitable for warmer conditions?

These are the questions that you need to ask to help you choose varieties that will flourish:

- What sort of fruit tree do I want to grow?
- What will I use the fruit for?
- When do I want the fruit to be ripe? Can I extend the season by choosing appropriate varieties?
- Are the varieties I choose suitable for the place I live?
- Which rootstock do I need?
- Will the varieties chosen pollinate each other successfully?

Chapter 5

Planning your orchard

The previous chapters will have given you an understanding of how to prepare a site for your trees and which types of fruit you will be able to grow. This chapter shows you how to fit these trees into your garden or orchard site.

Here you will find model plans for three very different sites, varying from a few trees in a back garden to a plan for a large orchard. Your space may not exactly mirror the ones modelled here, so you will need to adapt the ideas to suit your particular location. Once you have observed your site over the seasons (see Chapter 1), you will be in a position to take up pen and paper and plan where your trees will be planted.

The requirements of different fruits

Although most fruit trees enjoy similar conditions, there are subtle differences that will make one type of fruit more suited to a particular area of your site than another. Understanding these different requirements will enable you to plant your trees in the right place for them to thrive.

Apples

Apples are the most adaptable of fruit trees, tolerating a wide range of conditions. The ideal position is a sunny, sheltered site on fertile, well-drained soil, with a pH between 6 and 7. Apples will tolerate drought more than waterlogging, but attention should also be paid to the demands of the rootstock (see Chapter 2). Their tolerance of less-than-perfect conditions means that in a mixed orchard apples must surrender the best sites to those fruits that are more demanding in nature.

There are many local varieties of apple, which have developed over time to suit local conditions. If you would like to grow traditional varieties of apple, it can be worth contacting your local fruit tree nursery or orchard group to find out which trees will grow well in your area. They are usually resistant to the diseases found in their locality.

Left: Care taken when planning an orchard will ensure an abundance of fruit.

Pears

Pears are a little more demanding than apples. They will tolerate a range of soils and conditions, but dislike dry and chalky soils, which often go together. The demands of different cultivars can differ widely: a fairly tough pear such as Hessle, originating in Yorkshire, will not need as much as cosseting as Joséphine de Malines, a late-flowering French variety that needs the shelter of a warm wall to ripen well. Many pear cultivars have French names, which give a clue to the climatic conditions that they enjoy.

Plums

Plums are a little more fussy than apples and pears. Ideally they prefer a continental climate, which is one with cold winters and hot summers without too much rain. The southeast of England is the closest we come to this in Britain. Plums prefer a slightly acid, fairly heavy soil, which is also well drained. They will not tolerate chalky soils. Although they are in need of soil moisture, they detest waterlogged soils. Plums flower early in the year, so a sheltered position away from frost pockets is preferable, in order to encourage pollinating insects at a time of year when they are scarce.

There are several kinds of plums, all with different requirements. Greengages require the most cosseting, often needing the assistance of a warm wall to ripen fully. Bullaces, damsons and cherry plums are less fussy, being more at home in the wetter parts of Britain – the famous Westmoreland Damsons being good examples. Cooking plums, bullaces and damsons will tolerate some shade.

Cherries

Cherries come from the same family as plums and also prefer a continental climate, but are more tolerant of a range of soil conditions, adapting to both acid and alkaline soils. They also need good drainage, being prone to phytophthora, a disease most common in badly drained soils. They flower early, so will benefit from a sheltered position.

Sweet cherries need plenty of sun, while acid cherries such as Morellos can be grown in shady positions, even tolerating a north-facing wall, where few other fruits will grow well.

Peaches, nectarines and apricots

Peaches and apricots are grouped together here because they require similar conditions. It is only in the most favoured parts of the British Isles that these trees can be grown in bush form, out in the open. In all places they benefit from the shelter and warmth of a south- or west-facing wall. Nectarines are even more tender than peaches: they can be grown outside only in the most favoured parts of southern England. In most places they are best grown in a cool greenhouse.

Peaches, nectarines and apricots prefer a deep, fertile loam with a neutral pH – apricots preferring slightly more alkalinity than peaches. Moisture retention is important, especially bearing in mind that trees planted close to a wall tend to receive less moisture than those grown in the open.

Figs

Figs can be grown in the open but do need warmth, shelter and plenty of sun. Think of them as plants suited to a Mediterranean climate and you will not go far wrong. They prefer an alkaline soil that is well drained. Although the tree will enjoy a fertile soil, it will crop better if the roots are restricted and the soil is not too rich. Incorporating lime rubble, such as old cement, into the planting

Apricots can provide a worthwhile crop in favoured locations.

such as sandy or chalky soils. They need plenty of space, so are suitable only for the larger garden.

Sunshine requirements

It becomes apparent from these descriptions that some fruits have a greater need of sunshine than others. In most gardens there will only be only one or two really favourable spots that are south-facing or in full sun. A pecking order of fruits, with those most demanding of sun and warmth at the top, would look like this:

Peach and nectarine
Apricot and fig
Mulberry
Pear, plum and sweet cherry
Medlar
Quince
Apple
Acid cherry

hole will help to provide these conditions. The shelter of a warm wall will help and also make lime available from the mortar.

Medlars

Medlars prefer full sun and a free-draining, moisture-retentive soil, but are more tolerant of different soil conditions than are most other fruit trees. They will benefit from the application of manure or compost.

Quinces

Quince trees are content with more moisture in the soil than most fruit trees, but it is still best to avoid waterlogged soil. Light or sandy soils will be improved by the addition of organic matter.

In Scotland and the north of England, quinces will benefit from the protection of a wall to help them ripen fully; further south, they can be grown in the open.

Mulberries

Mulberries prefer a warm, sheltered site with a well-drained but moisture-retentive soil. They dislike thin soils with sharp drainage,

Soil problems

Before firming up your plan, it is important to consider two soil-borne diseases that can cause serious problems to newly planted fruit trees. These diseases are likely to be found only in the presence of mature trees, so they are largely a problem where new trees are planted into an existing orchard.

Honey fungus

Honey fungus is a serious disease that can kill trees by attacking their roots. If you find trees dying unexpectedly, particularly if they have small, yellowing leaves, it is worth suspecting honey fungus. You might also see honey-coloured toadstools in the autumn – these are the fruiting bodies of the disease. See Chapter 9, page 134, for more information on how to recognise and control honey fungus.

Replant disease

Replant disease is likely to be encountered where a fruit tree is planted very close to the site where an older tree of the same kind grows or used to grow. So, it is often found where old fruit trees are replaced by new trees, or where new trees are planted into an existing orchard. The young trees are swamped by pathogens that co-existed happily with the old trees.

The symptoms of replant disease are stunted growth and lack of vigour in young trees. These symptoms can also be caused by other problems, such as allowing grass to grow close to the trunk. See Chapter 9, page 137, for information on controlling replant disease.

Drawing a plan

You now have the knowledge required to start planning an orchard. You will be aware of the effects of soil type, aspect, sun and shade, exposure and soil-borne diseases, as well as the requirements of different fruits. It is time to apply this knowledge to the specific conditions of your site.

There is really no substitute for using pen and paper at this stage. This will involve you taking measurements of your site and making a note of the different aspects, including the amount of sun that different areas of the site receive. If your site is large, any variations in soil conditions can also be recorded at this point. What you are aiming for is an aerial view of your site that will show all the main features, such as existing trees, fences and buildings. Upon this, you can superimpose your ideas for positioning your fruit trees, bearing in mind the requirements of each type of tree.

Particularly important at this stage is the information given in Chapter 2 about rootstocks. For example, if you can allow a spread of only 3m (10') for a plum tree, is there a suitable rootstock available?

On the following pages are three different plans that demonstrate the various considerations that need to be taken into account when planning an orchard. The gardens in the first two plans are extensively planted with fruit trees; while this might seem extreme, it is laid out in this way so that all the locations in these gardens can be considered for their suitability for growing fruit.

Plan 1: The small town garden

This site is a small back garden of the kind that is commonly found with town houses. This particular plot is a courtyard garden with paving surrounded by raised beds, but the same principles would apply to a small garden behind a modern terraced or semi-detached house.

The most important consideration in such a small space is the aspect. Because the garden is so small, there are, in effect, four walls on which to grow fruit trees. The aspect governs the amount of light and shade that each wall receives. The north-facing wall receives virtually no sunshine, whereas the south-facing wall receives large amounts of sunshine, being in the shade cast by the house only during the few weeks around the winter solstice (21 December), when the sun is at its lowest.

In such a small plot, it is unlikely that there will be large differences in factors such as soil type or exposure, so we can use the varying amounts of sun and shade to determine where to site the different trees.

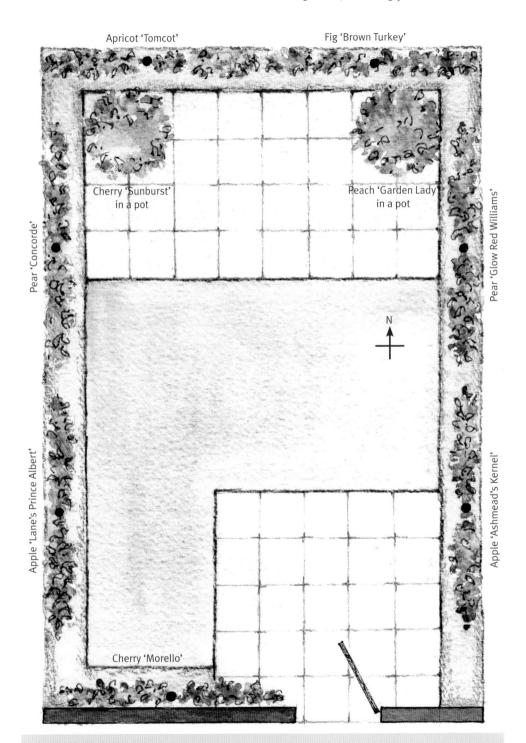

Apricot 'Tomcot'

Fig 'Brown Turkey'

Cherry 'Sunburst'
in a pot

Peach 'Garden Lady'
in a pot

Pear 'Concorde'

Pear 'Glow Red Williams'

N

Apple 'Lane's Prince Albert'

Apple 'Ashmead's Kernel'

Cherry 'Morello'

Diagram 6 Plan 1: The small town garden.

Although nearly all fruit trees prefer a sunny position, some, such as peaches, apricots and figs, are almost insistent on such a location to produce decent crops. So in this instance the peach, apricot, fig and sweet cherry gain the coveted spots on the south-facing wall. The pears gain the next-sunniest positions, at the southerly end of the two side walls. The apples will tolerate a more shaded spot nearer the house. In other words, the trees most in need of warmth and shelter are given the best locations.

The peach and the fig are given the warm, sheltered corner facing the south-west, where they will appreciate the afternoon and evening sun. The apricot and cherry will be content in the south-east-facing corner, which is almost as favourable a location.

The least favourable wall is the north-facing wall of the house. Receiving almost no sun, this might seem an unsuitable location for a fruit tree, but these conditions will be tolerated by acid cherries.

There are important differences between east- and west-facing walls. East-facing walls are sheltered from westerly gales and receive less rainfall, but are prone to cold easterly winds in the spring. They are more susceptible to frost damage, when the morning sun lands on frozen branches. Apples, sweet cherries and pears will cope well on an east-facing wall.

West-facing walls receive the warm afternoon sunshine, but also strong winds and heavy rainfall. They are sheltered from easterly winds. Peaches, apricots and figs that don't find room on a south-facing wall will find this an acceptable substitute. Apples, pears, plums and sweet cherries will all enjoy this warm situation.

In such a small site it is important to control the size of the trees, so that they do not grow too large for their location. This is achieved by choosing dwarfing or semi-dwarfing rootstocks, which will keep the trees to an appropriate size without the need for hard pruning.

Choice of varieties

Having chosen the different types of fruit to grow, we will need to consider which actual varieties to choose. For more information about the attributes of each variety, see the chapters on individual fruits in Part 3, and Appendices 2 to 4. At this stage, we are mainly concerned with choosing varieties that will produce a good range of fruit, meeting pollination requirements and making sure that we have suitable rootstocks.

Peach **Garden Lady** is ideal for pot culture, being genetically dwarf. All peaches are self-fertile, so there is no need for a second tree to ensure pollination.

Apricot **Tomcot** is an excellent variety, one of a number with the suffix 'cot' that are suitable for growing in Britain. Tomcot will produce large apricots with an intense flavour. Apricots are self-fertile, so there is no need for another apricot for pollination purposes. We could use either Torinel or St Julien A rootstocks here, though in both cases the trees will need careful training to ensure they do not grow above the height of the wall.

Fig These are also self-fertile, so one fig tree will suffice. **Brown Turkey** is the variety most suited to the British climate. Figs are grown on their own roots and are likely to produce a tree that could become too big for a small site such as this garden. Careful pruning and restricting the roots will help to keep the size of the tree under control.

Concorde, a very useful new variety of pear.

Lanes Prince Albert, a cooking apple suitable for wall training.

Pears These need pollinating by another pear tree, so we need to plant two pear trees that will flower at the same time. **Concorde**, in pollination group E, will be a good partner for **Glow (or Glou) Red Williams**, in group D. They will be ready for eating at different times, helping to prolong the season. Concorde is a deep red pear similar to Conference, while Glow Red Williams is a sport of the common Williams' Bon Chrétien pear that shows more resistance to scab. Quince A or Pyrodwarf are the most suitable rootstocks for training against a wall.

Apples I have chosen two varieties of apple that will keep for a few months beyond October, when there is usually a glut. **Ashmead's Kernel**, an excellent dessert apple in pollination group D, will pollinate and be pollinated by **Lane's Prince Albert**, a cooking apple that is also in group D. Both are fairly weak-growing cultivars, so will grow better on a more vigorous rootstock than might other-

wise be used. So, instead of an M9 rootstock, we could choose M26.

Cherries The sweet cherry **Sunburst** is ideal for growing in a pot, being self-fertile and only moderately vigorous. The best rootstock would be Gisela 5.

There are only two varieties of acid cherry that are commonly grown: **Nabella** and **Morello**. Either variety would be suitable for this location. They are only moderately vigorous, so are most often found on a Colt rootstock. Both are self-fertile.

Plan 2: The large garden

A large garden allows the enthusiastic fruit grower the scope to grow different types of fruit as well as several different forms of tree. Within this one garden, there are half standards, bushes, stepovers, archways, cordons, espaliers and fans, as well as a mature mulberry.

The back of the house faces south, allowing the house and garage walls to be adorned with pear cordons and a peach fan, taking advantage of the aspect and heat radiating from the walls. Cordons have been chosen to train against the house, because they are easier to fit amongst doors and windows than are espaliers. Elsewhere there is a small orchard of bush trees, trained apples surrounding the vegetable garden and plum fans on the east-facing wall. Three plum trees, which will be trained as half standards, are planted in the lawn. A nectarine is to be found in the shelter of the unheated greenhouse.

Choice of varieties

Peach   The peach fan trained on the garage wall is **Avalon Pride**, on St Julien A rootstock. This new variety is resistant to peach leaf curl. It is self-fertile, so does not need a pollinator.

Nectarine   Likewise, **Lord Napier**, the nectarine grown along the greenhouse wall, is also self-fertile. This is a heavy-cropping variety that originated in Hertfordshire about 1860. It suffers from peach leaf curl, but the protection of the greenhouse will keep it healthy. The rootstock is St Julien A.

Half standard plums   The plums grown as half standards are **Jefferson**, a gage-like plum, **Denniston's Superb**, a greengage, **Blaisdon Red**, a dry cooking plum and **Opal**, a good-quality early plum. All three are self-fertile and resistant to bacterial canker.

Mulberry   There is little meaningful choice between the varieties of mulberry, so any of them would be suitable. Mulberries can grow into fairly large trees, so remember to allow plenty of space for the tree to develop.

The trained pears and plums

Against the east-facing wall are two fan-trained plum trees, and on the back of the house two pear cordons. The pears need to pollinate each other, although it is likely that they would be pollinated by the pear trees in the orchard. The closer the trees are to each other, the higher the chances of successful pollination. Here two dessert pears of low vigour have been chosen – this lack of vigour helps to keep them confined as trained trees. They are both spur-bearers – that is, they produce their fruit on knobbly growth that forms along the branches. Tip-bearers, which produce fruit mostly at the end of branches, are not suited to being trained as restricted forms.

Pears   **Fondante d'Automne** is a musky-flavoured pear in pollination group D. **Olivier de Serres** is a well-flavoured pear that is ready to use from February to April; its flowering period is also group D. Both these pears ripen best with the shelter of a warm wall. Quince C or Pyrodwarf are the most suitable pear rootstocks for training against a wall.

Plums   **Cambridge Gage** is one of the more reliable varieties of greengage, while **Kirke's Blue** is a shy-cropping (i.e. doesn't produce much fruit) dessert plum with a wonderful taste. They are both in pollination group D. The rootstock is Pixy, although St Julien A would also be suitable. This position against an east-facing wall is not ideal; there is a risk of the flowers being damaged by frost, which is increased when they are exposed to the morning sun, as in this location.

The trained apples

Growing around the boundary of the vegetable garden are various forms of trained apple, which serve a decorative as well as productive

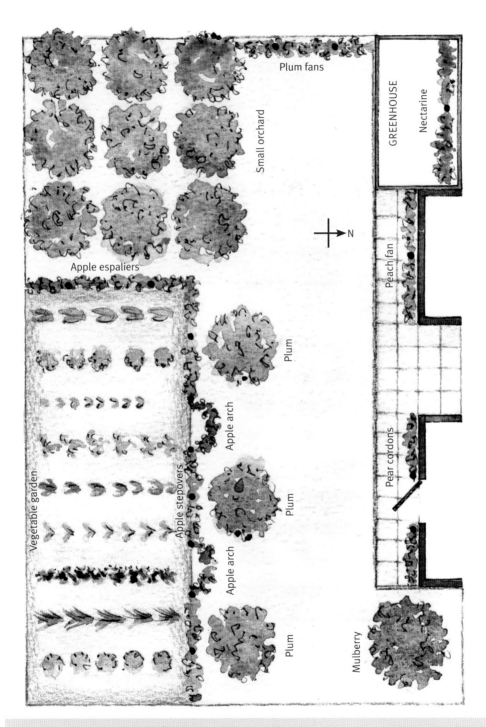

Plum fans

Small orchard

GREENHOUSE

Nectarine

N

Apple espaliers

Plum

Peach fan

Apple arch

Vegetable garden

Apple stepovers

Plum

Pear cordons

Apple arch

Plum

Mulberry

Diagram 7 Plan 2: The large garden.

Stepover apples, trained as a boundary to a vegetable garden.

purpose. As the orchard will produce the bulk of the fruit, here is a chance to experiment with some interesting apple varieties that might not otherwise gain a place when just a few varieties are chosen.

Roundway Magnum Bonum is an interesting variety, in that it tastes more like a pear than an apple. It is rather too vigorous to grow as a stepover, so it has been positioned where it can be trained over the iron archways that form the entrance to the vegetable garden. Even here, its vigour means that it will be better grown on a dwarfing M26 rootstock, as opposed to a semi-dwarfing MM106, which might otherwise be used.

Rajka and **Topaz** are two interesting and pretty dessert apples that have emerged from breeding programmes in the Czech Republic. **Beauty of Bath** will provide very early apples that are also decorative. All three varieties are suitable for stepovers, being spur-bearing and not too vigorous.

There are two espaliers on the west side of the vegetable garden. Two unusual apples have been chosen here to illustrate the wide availability of interesting cultivars. Both are early varieties that will provide useful apples before the varieties in the orchard are ready to be harvested. **Box Apple** is an old Cornish cooking apple with a season from September to November. **Red Joanetting** is an old English apple dating from the 1660s. It is a crisp, juicy dessert fruit that can be eaten straight from the tree as early as late July.

The varieties in the small orchard

Once the trees have been chosen for the main part of the garden, it is time to choose varieties to stock the small orchard in the south-west corner. The owner of this garden is keen on producing some home-made juice as well as having cooking and dessert apples available over as long a season as possible. Although any apple can be juiced, some varieties are particularly good for juicing – usually those with a strong flavour and a high

Lord Lambourne, an excellent mid-season dessert apple.

juice content. With care, it is possible to find varieties that are good for eating fresh and cooking that will also make good-quality juice. In addition, the owner is looking for a dessert and a culinary pear and one quince.

There is space in this small orchard for nine semi-dwarfing trees: these will comprise two pears, one quince and six apples. These six apples are to be divided equally between culinary and dessert varieties.

So, we are now looking for three dessert varieties of apple that are also good for juicing. There are early apples growing around the vegetable garden, so these three can be mid-season apples for eating during October and November, and late-keeping apples to extend the season through to the spring.

Dessert apples Lord Lambourne is a traditional English dessert apple that is in season from September to November, following on from the early dessert apples Red Joanetting

and Beauty of Bath. **Falstaff** (or Red Falstaff) is a good juicing and dessert apple that is in season from October to December. **Roxbury Russet**, a late-keeping aromatic apple, is in season from January to March.

All three are good juicing apples – Lord Lambourne and Falstaff being medium-sharp in nature, while Roxbury Russet is somewhat sweeter.

Cooking apples Charles Ross, a wonderful dual-purpose apple (i.e. cooking and eating fresh) is in season from September to December, producing medium-sharp juice. **Golden Noble** is perhaps the best-flavoured cooking apple, in season from October to December, producing a sharp juice. **Howgate Wonder** is a very large apple, in season from November to March, producing a full-sharp juice.

Although Golden Noble is not known as a first-quality juicing apple, it has been included because it is such a good cooking apple. **Annie Elizabeth** is another variety that could be included for its esteemed culinary qualities.

You will notice that there has been no mention of the pollination requirements of the apple varieties. When choosing a large number of varieties to be grown in a small area, it would be unusual for any variety to be lacking a pollinator, but it is worth a quick check. Here is a list of the apples chosen, together with their pollination group:

Beauty of Bath	C
Box Apple	C
Charles Ross	C
Falstaff	C
Golden Noble	E

Howgate Wonder	D
Lord Lambourne	C
Rajka	D
Red Joanetting	E
Roundway Magnum Bonum	C
Roxbury Russet	D
Topaz	D

All varieties have another variety in the same group, or in the one adjacent, so all should be pollinated successfully. There are no triploids to consider.

Pears **Louise Bonne of Jersey**, a red-flushed pear of good, slightly acid flavour, will follow on after Fondante d'Automne on the back of the house. It is in pollination group C. **Black Worcester**, a very old variety of cooking pear, also in pollination group C, is in season from December to March. It would be preferable to choose **Catillac**, which is a better-quality cooking pear, but being a triploid it does not fit in with pollination requirements. This is typical of the compromises that need to be made when choosing varieties. Often you will select your ideal varieties, only to find that pollination problems arise and a substitution needs to be made.

Quince This just leaves a quince variety to select. Here there are no pollination problems because quinces are self-fertile. **Meech's Prolific** is a good all-round variety that produces large yellow fruit suitable for quince jelly.

Varieties summary
The selection of fruit for this large garden uses various criteria, including flavour, length of season and visual interest, together with cooking and juicing qualities, to give a well-balanced range of fruit for daily use. It is also a selection of interest to the fruit connoisseur. It will be noted that no difficult climatic considerations, such as frost pockets or a wet climate, have been considered in either of these first two plans. Such conditions make the choosing of varieties more difficult, because we have to add in factors such as disease resistance and late flowering to the other criteria that we have already used. This next plan will include such difficulties.

Plan 3: The larger orchard

This is a plan for a larger orchard that will be grown in a small field of about 0.2 hectares (0.5 acres). The site is a field that slopes to the west, with a small stream and wetter ground towards the bottom of the slope. There are low hedges all around the field. It is situated in an area of high rainfall in northern England, and late frosts are often experienced.

The field's owner would like to grow a mixture of fruit trees, including a number of apple trees from which he can make cider; he would also like trees that will give him dessert and culinary fruit, including plums and pears. You can adapt these plans to suit the kind of large orchard you would like to create.

Because conditions are not ideal in this example, it is best to grow trees on vigorous rootstocks, such as M25 for apples, Brompton for plums and wild pear for pears. The resulting large trees, or standards, have been a traditional part of the landscape in many areas of the British countryside. Plums and pears are more demanding of shelter and sunlight than apples, so they are sited on the south and west sides of the orchard, where they will benefit from the shelter provided by the apple trees and the higher levels of sunlight found here.

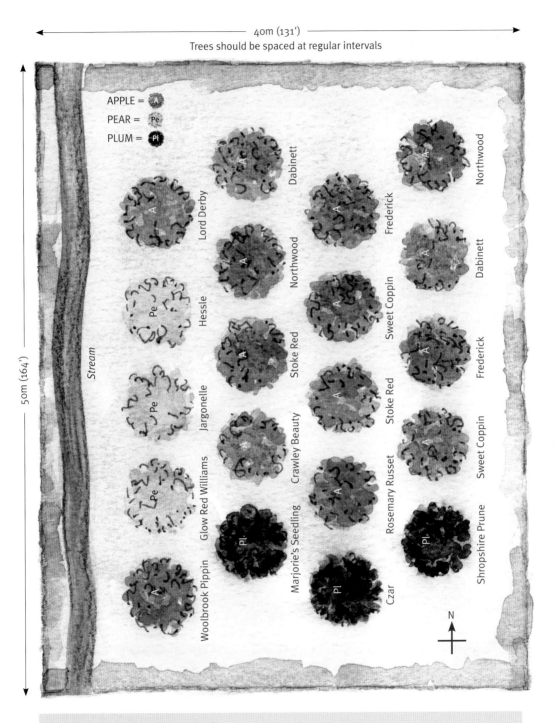

40m (131')

Trees should be spaced at regular intervals

50m (164')

APPLE = A
PEAR = Pe
PLUM = Pl

Stream

Diagram 8 Plan 3: The larger orchard.

It is possible to grow between 120 and 130 standard trees per hectare (48-52 trees per acre), depending on density, so in 0.2 hectares (half an acre) we could expect to grow 24-26 trees. We will need to leave enough room at the perimeter of the field to allow a tractor access to cut the hedges, so, taking this into account, in this field we will just be able to squeeze in 20 trees in a pattern of 4 rows of 5 trees each. Whenever you are uncertain as to spacing, you can use bamboo canes stuck in the ground to mark the position of individual trees. As a rough guide, standards are planted 10m (33') or 10 large paces apart.

Don't be tempted to plant trees too closely, because the more trees you squeeze in, the lower the levels of air movement will be. Air movement is vital for keeping fungal diseases such as scab and canker at bay. Trees planted too closely tend to grow upright to reach the light, so they have fewer horizontal branches, which bear most fruit. You might also consider the visual impact of different patterns of planting. A square pattern of planting can seem very tidy, but also regimented to the eye. Planting in staggered rows, as in this plan, can soften an otherwise rather harsh appearance.

In this example, half of our 20 trees are cider apples, leaving us with 10 other fruit trees to choose. These can be made up of three pears, three plums, two dessert apples and two cooking apples.

Choice of varieties

Cider apples   Although it is possible to produce cider from single (or vintage) varieties, most cider is made from blending a mixture of varieties, preferably all ready at the same time. There are several different kinds of cider apple to blend, known as sweets, bittersweets, bittersharps, and sharps; we are looking for a mixture of these different types. We are also looking for varieties that are resistant to scab and canker and, where possible, are late-flowering.

Varieties of all fruits that are suitable for growing in Scotland, Northern Ireland and the north of England are those that are known to tolerate cooler summers and those that are later-flowering. Sometimes this information is hard to come by, and it can be useful to contact your local nursery or orchard group to find out which varieties will do well in your locality. There is little information about cider varieties that do well in northern areas, so the safest bet is to choose later-flowering cultivars, particularly because cider varieties tend to flower early.

Dabinett is a bittersweet variety ready from mid-October to November. It is in pollination group D. **Stoke Red** is a bittersharp apple ready in November, flowering in group G. **Frederick** is a sharp, ready in mid-October and flowering in group D. **Sweet Coppin** is a sweet variety, ready in late October and early November. It is in pollination group D. **Northwood** is another sweet variety flowering in group D, ready at the same time as Sweet Coppin.

These are by no means faultless varieties, but they are among the best available for such conditions. Unlike in the other two plans, we have set ourselves tough parameters here to illustrate the kind of compromises that need to be made. You will notice that, at the moment, Stoke Red, flowering in group G, has no suitable pollinator: we will need to correct this when choosing the remaining apple varieties.

Black Dabinett, a variety of apple used solely for making cider.

Northwood, a sweet cider apple that can also be used for eating fresh and for juicing.

Dessert apples Here we are looking to choose two varieties suitable for growing in these difficult conditions, one mid-season and one late, in order to provide a supply of apples over as long a season as possible. **Woolbrook Pippin** is a very useful cultivar, originating from Devon. It is resistant to scab, canker and mildew and is in season from October to December. It is in pollination group C. **Rosemary Russet** is also resistant to the same diseases. It keeps well, being in season from November to March, and is also in pollination group C.

Cooking apples Here, we are looking for mid- and late-season varieties. Initially I chose **Lord Derby** as the earlier apple, followed by Annie Elizabeth, an excellent disease-resistant cultivar that requires little sugar when cooked. However, a check of pollination requirements showed that this choice would leave Stoke Red still without a pollination partner. In other words, we need to

change the choice of one of the apples to ensure that Stoke Red will be pollinated. In this case this is not difficult, because we can easily substitute **Crawley Beauty** for Annie Elizabeth. Unusually, Crawley Beauty has a pollination group as late as H, making it ideal for areas prone to late frosts as well as a suitable partner for Stoke Red. So the cooking apples are: Lord Derby, an excellent cooking apple that is widely grown throughout northern Britain – it is in pollination group D and in season from October to December – and Crawley Beauty, a very useful cooking apple for difficult conditions. It is in season from November to February.

Pears These are not ideal conditions in which to grow pears. Warmth and shelter encourage pears to perform best. However, if we look carefully, there are cultivars that will give worthwhile fruit in northern areas. Again, we are looking for a succession of fruits over the season. **Jargonelle** is a very

Lord Derby is a reliable mid-season cooking apple that can be grown on wetter sites.

Improved Fertility, a heavy-cropping variety of pear, suitable for northern Britain.

early pear, best eaten straight from the tree in August. It is a triploid in pollination group C. Being a triploid, it will need to be pollinated by two other cultivars.

Glow (or Glou) Red Williams is a sport of the more common Williams' Bon Chrétien. It has deep red colouring and is more resistant to scab than its parent. It is in season during September and is in pollination group D. Although not very late-flowering, it has flowers that are known to carry some resistance to damage by late frosts. **Hessle** is a hardy pear originating from Yorkshire. It is in season during October and is in pollination group D. It is not a first-rate dessert pear, but it is a useful variety because it can also be used for cooking and it crops reliably in cooler areas. **Improved Fertility** and **Louise Bonne of Jersey** are two other cultivars that are suitable for northern areas of Britain. All the pears can be grown on a wild pear rootstock in order to produce a large tree.

These varieties have been chosen for their resistance to scab and canker and their ability to cope with late frosts and cool summers. Fireblight resistance has not been considered here because it is rarely encountered in the north of England.

Plums   The conditions in this particular example are not ideal for plums. Damsons, mirabelles and bullaces are all tougher trees than plums, so are more suitable for growing in difficult conditions. By contrast, greengages are the most demanding of warmth and shelter. **Czar** is a blue plum usually thought of as a cooking plum, but also acceptable for eating when fully ripe. It is ripe in August, self-fertile and in pollination group D. Its only drawback is that it is susceptible to silverleaf. **Shropshire Prune** is an excellent-flavoured large damson. It is ready in early September and is in pollination group D. It is self-fertile. **Marjorie's Seedling** is a dual-purpose plum ready in late September. It is

Marjorie's Seedling, an excellent variety of plum, cropping late in the season.

in pollination group E and is partially self-fertile. This is the only plum of the three that requires pollinating by another cultivar; the Shropshire Prune in the adjoining pollination group will fulfil this role.

Positioning the trees in the orchard

Because all trees are growing on rootstocks that will produce large (or standard) trees, our main concern is siting the more demanding plums and pears where they will receive most sun and shelter. Both Brompton and wild pear rootstocks are fairly tolerant of the wetter soils found at the bottom of the slope, so the pears can be planted on the western or lower side of the orchard because they flower later than the plums. The plums will therefore be away from the lower slopes, which are most susceptible to any late frosts. They are to be placed on the southern boundary, where they will also benefit from high levels of sunshine.

So, while the plums and pears are along the sunny southern and western boundaries of the orchard, the cider apples can be planted in the north-east section because they are least in need of sun to ripen the fruit. In a mixed orchard like this, any smaller trees should be planted to the south or west sides, where they won't be shaded by the larger trees.

Chapter 6

Buying and planting trees

The most crucial stage in a tree's life is its planting. Selecting a suitable tree for your site and then planting it correctly are vital to growing a healthy tree that will go on to produce plentiful crops of delicious fruit. On the other hand, mistakes made now will continue to affect your tree for the rest of its life.

Buying trees

Before you order your fruit trees, it is worth reviewing the information that you will need to place an order. There are four different questions that you will need to answer, as follows.

Young trees planted and guarded correctly will produce plentiful crops for years to come.

- Which type of fruit do I want to order? (Pears, plums, etc?)
- Which varieties of each fruit do I want to order? (Bramley's Seedling, Victoria, etc?) See Chapter 4, the chapters on individual fruits in Part 3, and Appendices 2-4 for more information on choosing the right variety.
- Which rootstock would I like my trees to be grown on? See Chapter 2 for information on rootstocks.
- What age and form of tree would I like to plant?

From the preceding chapters of this book, you should now have the information needed to answer the first three questions. Now let's look at the age and form of tree to plant.

The age of tree at planting

In essence, this is a very simple question – do you want to plant a one-, two- or three-year-old tree? – but the water is muddied by some rather confusing terms used by nurseries, which relate to both the age and the form of the tree.

Maiden

This is a one-year-old tree that has not been trained in the nursery. The term **feathered maiden** is usually used to refer to a two-year-old tree that has not been pruned. In the second year, the tree has grown some 'feather' or small side branches. Confusion sets in because some nurseries use this term to refer to a one-year-old tree that has some 'feather'.

Bush

This is a tree that is two or three years old and has been trained in the nursery into an open-centred or goblet-shaped tree, with a clear trunk of 0.7-1.3m (2'4"-4'4"). This form

of tree is found on dwarfing or semi-dwarfing rootstocks.

Half standard

This is a tree that is two or three years old, that has been trained to produce a clear trunk of 1.5-1.7m (5'-5'7"). Traditionally this was a method of formative pruning that produced a tree suitable for an orchard grazed by sheep. For this purpose, the first branches would arise at about 1.7m (5'7") from the ground, in order to keep them clear of sheep intent on nibbling them. This is a form of tree found only on more vigorous rootstocks; more dwarfing rootstocks are unable to sustain such a length of clear trunk. Sometimes the leader (the main stem heading upwards) will be present; at other times it will have been removed to form a goblet-shaped tree.

Standard

This is a tree with a clear trunk of around 1.8m (6'). This form was used in traditional orchards that were grazed by sheep or cattle. Only vigorous rootstocks such as M25 or MM111 for apples, wild pear for pears, and Brompton for plums, are suitable for training as standards. Again, the leader may, or may not, be present, depending on the pruning technique used.

Some nurseries will use the terms **light standard** or **full standard**. A full standard is more developed in the growth of its crown and, at three or four years old, will usually be a year older than a light standard.

Because of the confusion caused by the use of these different terms, it can be useful to ask the nursery how old a tree is, if it is not made clear. For example, as noted, a feathered maiden could be a one- or two-year-old tree, depending on the nursery.

It is preferable to plant one-year-old trees: they establish better than older trees because they have a good proportion of roots compared with top growth. Older trees, with larger root systems, tend to suffer more from the shock of being transplanted. They are also more expensive and likely to need robust staking.

However, fruit trees can take several years before bearing a decent crop, so there is often a temptation to plant older trees so as to bring forward the time of cropping. This is fine, so long as you realise that there are drawbacks as well as advantages, and that a younger tree will catch up with an older tree in time.

Pot-grown versus bare-rooted

The choice of pot-grown versus bare-rooted trees has implications for where you will buy your trees. Garden centres tend to stock fruit trees in pots, because they are easily manageable and they can be sold at any time of

the year. The convenience of pot-grown trees is for the benefit of the garden centre rather than the customer. Eager customers can see the trees looking tempting with leaves and, on older trees, even flowers and fruits. Garden centres know that ignorant customers can be seduced into impulse buys that will be regretted later on. Growing fruit trees needs careful planning rather than the instant satisfaction promised by garden-centre buying.

Specialist fruit tree nurseries sell their trees bare-rooted during the winter months when they are dormant. Although the trees do not look tempting in the same way that they do in the summer, they are sold and planted during the winter because that way they establish much better. A tree that is planted when dormant can settle into the ground without the demands of growth and transpiration that occur if it is planted during the growing season.

A bare-rooted tree prior to planting.

A pot-bound apple tree.

A pot-grown tree planted during the spring or summer will need constant attention to see that it receives enough water during its first growing season. Trees kept in pots at the garden centre are also prone to soil exhaustion and becoming pot-bound if they are kept too long. If you do choose to buy a pot-grown tree, remove the pot so that you can check the condition of the roots and avoid any tree where the roots are developing a circular pattern around the inside of the pot.

Buying from a specialist nursery

Although there are a few enlightened garden centres, the level of advice that you will find about subjects such as pollination requirements or suitable varieties is likely to be minimal. Specialist nurseries, by contrast, can be a fount of knowledge for the uninitiated. The most usual limitation to such knowledge is the nurseryman's time, because for him (or her), time is money. This is where the internet has become such a valuable tool. Many nurseries use their websites to convey their knowledge to potential customers. Some nurseries – for example, Keepers Nursery in Kent (see Resources) – even have search engines that will allow you to factor in your particular requirements when choosing trees.

Some specialist fruit tree nurseries also stock a vast range of trees – apple tree ranges that run into hundreds of different varieties. While this may seem daunting to the uninitiated, the information is available to help customers choose something suitable. It is well worth supporting such nurseries, because they are helping to keep rare and unusual varieties in cultivation. Many will specialise in varieties that are local to their area.

Most people buy by mail order from specialist nurseries, owing to the distances generally involved. The two drawbacks to ordering from specialist nurseries are the costs of delivery and your inability to inspect the trees before delivery. It is worth checking the delivery costs before ordering your trees – some nurseries will add on a third of the invoice total in delivery charges. If you are buying a number of trees, this can be a substantial cost. If you are not happy, negotiate with the nursery.

Many nurseries run open days where you can visit the nursery, ask questions and see the quality of trees available.

Trees trained in the nursery

Aside from older trees that may have received some formative pruning in the nursery, you might come across two- or three-year-old

A young apple tree that has been trained while still in its pot.

trees that have been trained as espaliers, fans, cordons or stepovers. You can form a tree like this yourself, starting with a maiden, but trees formed in the nursery, although they can be expensive, can give you a useful head start.

You might also come across family trees. These are trees where two or three compatible varieties are grafted on to the same rootstock, which has the advantage that you will have no worries about pollination requirements. This can be useful if you only have room for one tree, but they do have drawbacks as well. Often, one of the varieties will be more vigorous and tend to outgrow the others. I would suggest growing a family tree only if you are really short of room; otherwise you would be better off growing several trees on more dwarfing rootstocks, or as cordons.

Planting

There a few simple techniques for planting a bare-rooted tree, and care taken at this time will reward you later on. More fruit trees die from mistakes made at planting time than from any other cause.

Planting bare-rooted trees

Bare-rooted trees are grown at the nursery and then dug up or lifted from November onwards for sale to the public. Because they are dormant at this time, they can be kept out of the ground for a week or so, as long as the roots do not dry out. For this reason, they will usually be wrapped in a plastic sack, often with damp straw around the roots to aid moisture retention.

If the trees are well packed, so that the roots don't dry out, they can be kept in their packaging for up to a week. Damp leaves or straw can be added around the roots to keep them damp. They should be kept in a cool but frost-free environment.

Bare-rooted trees can be planted from late November until early March, while they are still dormant. Planting earlier in this season is ideal, so that the roots have time to establish before winter frosts cool the soil down, but planting at any time during the winter is fine. When the trees arrive from the nursery, they can be planted straight away, as long as the soil is not waterlogged or heavily frosted. If the soil sticks to your boots, wait for it to dry out further, as planting in these conditions will usually result in damage to the soil structure.

CHECKLIST OF EQUIPMENT FOR TREE PLANTING

- Trees, in a sack large enough to cover the roots adequately
- Spade and fork
- Straight piece of wood (optional)
- Secateurs
- Wooden stakes (3cm x 3cm x 1-1.25m [approx 1" x 1" x 3-4'] is ideal)
- Lump or sledge hammer (if needed)
- Iron bar (if needed)
- Tree tie (if needed)
- Rabbit guard
- Mulch mats and staples for securing (optional)
- Bonemeal or mycorrhizal fungi (if used)

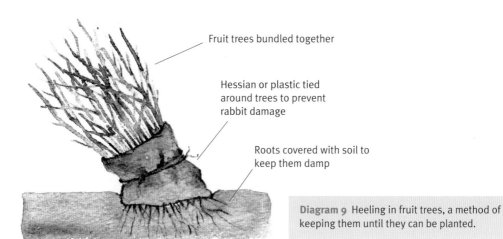

Fruit trees bundled together

Hessian or plastic tied
around trees to prevent
rabbit damage

Roots covered with soil to
keep them damp

Diagram 9 Heeling in fruit trees, a method of
keeping them until they can be planted.

Keeping bare-rooted trees for longer than a week

If you wish to keep the trees for longer than a week before planting, you can heel them in. This involves loosely planting the trees in bundles in prepared holes or trenches.

They can be kept for months like this, providing the soil is well packed around the roots. If you need to keep the trees into the early spring, a shady position will help to keep them dormant for longer. Remember that you will need to protect the trees from rabbits, either by using individual rabbit guards, or, if the trees are bundled together, by tying sacking or a similar material around the lower trunks (see page 80) for more information on rabbit protection). Rabbits can kill a tree in one night, so do protect them straight away.

Planting a bare-rooted tree with a stake

Most fruit trees will benefit from the stability that a stake provides while the roots become established. If trees on vigorous rootstocks are staked, the stake can be removed after one or two years. Trees grown on more dwarfing rootstocks require the support of a permanent stake, while trees on semi-vigorous rootstocks, such as MM106 or Quince A and C, can have their stake removed once the roots have established, usually after about five years.

Tree stakes need only reach 0.5m (1'8") above ground level. This allows most of the tree to flex in the wind, which encourages root formation. If too tall a stake is used, the tree can become reliant on the stake for support instead of developing strong roots. The exceptions to this are trees trained as pyramids or spindlebushes, which have a permanent tall stake.

For planting, you should preferably choose a damp, overcast day without too much wind. On a cold, windy day the roots can dry out very quickly. Tree roots should not be left uncovered for more than two minutes in such conditions. If the roots are at all dry, it is a good idea to soak them in water for one or two hours before planting.

The planting hole should always be dug on the same day as planting. Digging holes in

PLANTING A BARE-ROOTED TREE WITH A STAKE

1. The planting hole dug, with the turf stripped and the soil stacked neatly next to the hole.

2. The planting hole, with the stake inserted on the side of the hole from which the prevailing winds blow.

3. The tree placed in the planting hole, with the roots fitted around the stake.

4. The roots covered with soil, and the tree trunk positioned close to the stake.

5. The rabbit guard has been fitted and the tree tied to the top of the stake.

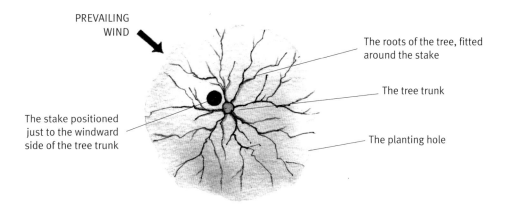

PREVAILING
WIND

The roots of the tree, fitted
around the stake

The tree trunk

The stake positioned
just to the windward
side of the tree trunk

The planting hole

Diagram 10 The planting hole from above.

advance risks them filling with water on heavy soils, and can compromise the soil structure. Dig a hole a little deeper than the depth of the roots and twice the width. If you are planting into grass, you can dig the hole slightly deeper, and bury the turf underneath the tree. This will help to feed the tree as the turf decays. Always keep the good-quality topsoil separate from turf or subsoil. If you are planting on a slope, it is best to keep the excavated soil on the up side of the planting hole, because it is much easier to replace the soil from above the hole.

Now present the tree to the planting hole. You should be planting the tree at the same depth as it was planted in the nursery – or, in other words, the soil around the tree should be at the same height as the soil mark on the trunk. If you are not familiar with this proc-ess, it will help to place a straight piece of wood from one side of the hole to the other. Look to see that the soil mark from the nursery planting is at the same height as the wood. Some nurseries keep their trees in mulch once lifted, which can make a false mark on the trunk of the tree. Another way to check is

to ensure that all the roots will be covered by soil, together with a few centimetres (one inch) of the trunk.

What is most important is that the union (see photo on page 29 / Diagram 15 on page 100) is well above the level of the soil around the tree.

If the union is at soil level or below, the scion can form roots – definitely something to avoid. Also, check at this stage to see if there is any damage to the roots; if so, prune this out with secateurs, back to healthy roots, just as you would prune growth above ground.

Once you have checked to see whether the tree fits correctly in the planting hole, place it back into the sack while you finish preparing the hole. With a fork, loosen the bottom and sides of the hole. This will help the roots to establish more quickly. This is particularly important on clay soils, where there is a danger of the clay puddling to form a sump, where the water will fail to drain properly.

Next, use an iron bar to begin the hole for the stake in the base of the planting hole, near the middle but slightly towards the direction of the prevailing wind. Use a lump hammer or sledgehammer to hit a wooden stake vertically into this hole. The stake should protrude around 0.5m (1'8") above the ground. Now take the tree out of the sack and place the roots into the hole, so that they fit well around the stake, with the trunk vertical and close to the stake.

If you choose to use bonemeal or mycorrhizal fungi (see page 82), add this to the excavated soil at this stage.

Now place the tree in the planting hole and, while holding the tree upright, replace the good-quality soil around the roots. This can be tricky for one person, as using a spade needs two hands, so the careful use of your boot, or the help of a friend, are helpful tactics. Shaking the tree will help to spread the soil evenly around the roots, avoiding air pockets. When the hole is full, gently compact the soil with your foot.

The danger of poor staking. This tree has been allowed to blow against the stake, creating a wound on the trunk, where disease can enter.

Once the tree is planted, fix the tree to the stake with a tree tie. There are various types available: those with a high rubber content are ideal because they stretch as the tree grows. There must be some form of collar to keep the trunk away from the stake. For the same reason, the tree should be tied tightly to the top of the stake. This avoids the risk of the tree blowing around and being damaged by the stake. Where this happens, a wound will occur, which can become an entry point for diseases such as canker. More trees die from incorrect staking than from any other cause. Old stockings can make acceptable tree ties, but do not be tempted to use materials such as rope, which will cut into the trunk of the tree.

Lastly, fit a rabbit guard. Even if you think that you don't have rabbits in your garden, it is worth fitting one, because a rabbit can kill a tree in one night by removing the bark around the trunk. Plastic spiral guards are cheap and effective devices to prevent rabbit damage, but guards can also be made from chicken wire.

Planting a bare-rooted tree without a stake

If you are planting a tree without a stake, follow the preceding guidelines, missing out the directions for staking. Instead of positioning the tree close to the stake, you should simply position it in the middle of the planting hole and backfill around it with soil.

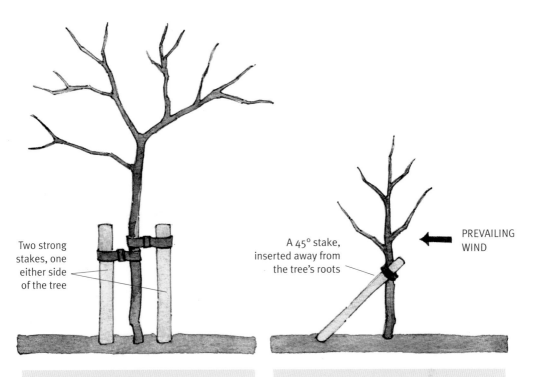

Two strong stakes, one either side of the tree

A 45° stake, inserted away from the tree's roots

PREVAILING WIND

Diagram 11 Double-staking a large tree.

Diagram 12 Staking at 45 degrees.

Planting large bare-rooted trees

If you are planting a large standard tree, you will require a more substantial stake because the roots are likely to be small compared with the size of tree above ground. Alternatively, two, or even three stakes can be used to support large trees, particularly in exposed sites, as shown in Diagram 11.

Planting pot-grown trees

If you do decide to plant a pot-grown tree, you can use the method for bare-rooted trees with a few alterations. Firstly, you will not be able to use a vertical stake because it will not be possible to fit the roots around the stake. Instead, you can use a stake at a 45-degree angle, as in Diagram 12. When you remove the tree from the pot, tease out the roots if they have started to develop a spiral pattern in the pot.

This method can also be used where it is necessary to fit a stake after a tree has been planted – usually when strong winds have caused a tree to shift. It is preferable to have a helping hand to hold the tree out of harm's way when you hit the stake into the ground.

Planting trained trees

There are various restricted forms of tree, such as fans or espaliers, that are trained on a permanent framework of wires, either against a wall or between posts. It is sensible to construct the means of support before planting, because of the risk of damaging the tree during construction.

The planting methods are the same as those for planting bare-rooted trees, except that the support will already be in place. If you are

Young cordon trees growing on a framework of wires.

planting a tree that is to be trained against a wall, plant it at least 50cm (1'8") from the wall, because the soil is drier close to the wall. You are also likely to find that the soil close to the wall is more alkaline, because of the mortar used in its construction.

Spindlebush and pyramid trees (see pages 110-11) are planted close to a tall stake, which should be inserted before the tree is planted.

Feeding trees at planting time

If you have good soil that has been prepared well, you will not need to add anything to it at planting time. However, there are several materials that can be added, particularly if your soil conditions are less than ideal.

Bonemeal, being rich in phosphorus, is useful for stimulating root growth. A couple of handfuls mixed into the soil excavated from the planting hole will help the tree establish a good root system.

Mycorrhizal fungi are fungi that form a symbiotic relationship with plants. They form a secondary root system that channels nutrients and water to the tree, while obtaining sugars from the tree's roots, which they use as a food. Mycorrhizal fungi are naturally present in soil, but can be depleted by regular cultivation, fungicide application and intensive farming. It is also thought that the use of these fungi can help to counteract the effects of replant disease (see page 137).

Although it is only recently that research has been conducted into mycorrhizal fungi, initial results show that they have a beneficial effect on the establishment of trees after planting. As with bonemeal, the granules should be added to the soil that is used for backfilling when planting.

Many experts advocate planting into a luxury pit where the soil is 'improved' by the addition of fertiliser, manure and other soil improvers. This is not necessary, and can even hinder successful establishment of the tree, as the roots become used to the rich soil in the planting hole and are less disposed to venturing into the unimproved soil beyond.

Figs benefit from having their roots restricted: if there are no natural restrictions, such as walls, it might be necessary to incorporate material such as builder's rubble.

Mulching trees at planting time

In order to help successful establishment of the tree, it is important to keep an area of soil, about 1m x 1m (3' x 3') around the tree, free from grass and weeds. This can be achieved by hand-weeding or the use of mulches.

In my experience, it is rare that hand-weeding is kept up during those busy summer months. Applying organic mulches such as compost can be an effective way of keeping down weeds, so long as application is regular and the mulch not full of weed seeds ready to germinate. A mulch used on top of damp soil will also help to preserve soil moisture.

The most effective way of keeping down grass and weeds is to use a mulch mat. These are available in various different materials. Some are biodegradable, made from wool or flax; others more permanent, made from woven polypropylene. They are sold pre-cut with a slit to fit around the trunk of the tree after planting. They can also be made from landscape fabric or other second-hand materials, so long as the material is permeable, allowing water to reach the tree's roots.

The woven polypropylene mats can be chopped into the turf with a spade. There is a knack to this, usually perfected by the time you get to the last tree. Alternatively, the mulch mat can be anchored with staples designed for this purpose. One disadvantage of mulch mats is that voles are attracted by the warmth and shelter that such a mat provides. Voles can cause substantial damage to tree roots; if this happens, it can be better to lift the mats and consider using an alternative method.

A woven polypropylene mulch mat, fitted after planting, to prevent the growth of vegetation around the tree.

Other mulches, such as compost or manure, can be placed on top of the mulch mat, where the nutrients will slowly be washed into the soil by rainfall. Where looks are important, a decorative mulch, such as bark chips or cocoa shells, can be used to hide the mulch mat.

If you prefer, herbicides such as glyphosate can be used to keep an area free from grass, so long as the manufacturer's instructions are followed carefully.

Watering trees after planting

In general, most bare-rooted trees will not need watering after planting, particularly in the wetter areas towards the west of Britain. However, shortage of water, shown by yellowing and drooping foliage, can be fatal to trees in the years immediately following planting. In dry areas of Britain, on free-draining soils, or where large trees or pot-grown trees have been planted, particular attention will need to be paid to water provision.

Trees need a good soaking when they are watered. The water needs to reach the roots low down in the soil. Watering little and often will cause the tree to establish roots close to the surface, which are then even more prone to suffering in dry spells. If you are planting a tree that is likely to need regular watering, it is good practice to incorporate vertical plastic pipes close to the trunk of the tree, extending 20-30cm (8-12") into the soil, into which a hosepipe can be inserted.

Protecting fruit trees

Unfortunately, many types of animal, both wild and domesticated, are also interested in your fruit trees, either to nibble or to lean on, or to use as a scratching post. As already noted, it is good practice to fit a rabbit guard

at planting time, but you might also need to guard your trees against other animals. In a garden situation you will generally not need to provide extra protection for your trees, because you will be keeping grass short with a mower and wild animals such as deer will be too shy to come close to the house.

In a larger orchard, or with trees further away from the house, you might want to use grazing animals to keep the grass under control. If you don't own your own animals, a local farmer will often be grateful for the extra grazing, so long as the orchard is securely fenced. It is really only sheep that are suitable for grazing an orchard; cattle and horses are sometimes used but they tend to 'poach', or compact, the soil and have a long reach, meaning that more substantial guards need to be built.

You might find that deer encroach into an orchard further away from the house. They can cause considerable damage to fruit trees. The size of guard needed to protect the trees (pictured on page 86) will depend on the type of deer found in your locality. Another option is to build a deer-proof fence all around the orchard. If you suspect that deer will be a problem, make sure that the trees are protected straight after planting – leaving them unprotected overnight could be fatal.

A four-post guard suitable for sheep is illustrated opposite and pictured on page 86. Some sheep are much more adventurous than others, so the design of guard can be varied accordingly. The use of barbed wire, although annoying for humans attempting to access the trees, allows the use of a less substantial guard than would otherwise be needed. It is important to facilitate human access to the trees when constructing a tree

Poached soil where cows have been allowed to graze close to apple trees.

guard, so that pruning and weeding can be carried out easily – the most practical method is to staple the first three sides of netting to the posts, but tightly hook the fourth side over strong nails, so that it can be unhooked to allow access.

Pig or sheep netting made from galvanised wire can be used to construct the guard, but proprietary plastic mesh is also effective, so long as it is strong enough and tightly fitted.

Weed growth inside the guard can be controlled by fitting a mulch mat the same size as the inside of the guard. This is best kept in place with staples or pegs.

Similar guards with three posts are often suggested. They save on the cost of materials, but are not as effective, because they are too close to the tree. The tree is likely to hit the guard in strong winds, causing damage to the trunk. Animals are also able to get closer to the tree – sometimes too close!

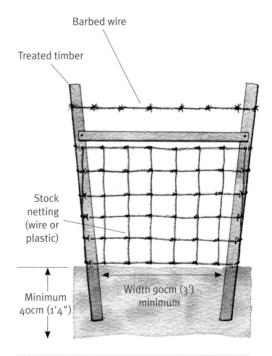

Barbed wire

Treated timber

Stock netting (wire or plastic)

Minimum 40cm (1'4")

Width 90cm (3') minimum

Diagram 13 A four-post guard designed to protect fruit trees from sheep or small deer.

A robust four-post guard, suitable for protecting trees from sheep.

A strong, tall guard that will protect trees from deer and cattle.

A cheap, basic tree guard, built with wood and plastic mesh, providing a low level of protection.

A guard made of chicken wire – tempting to use, but it carries a high risk of damage to the tree.

There are disadvantages even to four-post guards, which could mean that other types of guards are worth considering. They are time-consuming to build and expensive, usually costing considerably more than the tree they are guarding; they are also difficult to build on steep slopes.

Where necessary, pre-formed guards made of wire mesh can be fitted. These are not ideal because they are very close to the tree, with the attendant danger of damage to the trunk (see photo below), but they are considerably cheaper and easier to construct than four-post guards. If they are used, it is necessary to inspect the trees regularly in order to avoid damage – wounds on the trunk can give rise to potentially fatal infections of canker. Trees will usually need to be tied to the guard to prevent rubbing. Pre-formed guards 1.5m (5') high are usually sufficient to deter sheep.

Damage cause by the trunk rubbing against a wire mesh guard.

Growing fruit trees in pots

Most types of fruit trees can be grown in pots with care and attention. Growing them in pots allows gardeners with only a patio, or even a balcony, the pleasure of growing and harvesting their own fruit. If a greenhouse is available for winter protection, fruits can be grown that would not otherwise be possible in colder areas. It is, however, important to realise that growing trees in pots is not just a question of planting a tree and waiting for the fruit. Constant care is needed to overcome the challenges of container growing.

Choosing varieties for growing in pots

A tree that will grow successfully in a pot will usually be one of low vigour, spur bearing where this appropriate, and grafted on to a dwarfing rootstock. Some recommended varieties are as follows.

Dessert apples Adam's Pearmain, Claygate Pearmain, Egremont Russet and Sunset
Cooking apples Arthur Turner, Bountiful and Howgate Wonder
Pears Concorde, Conference, Glou Morceau, Gorham and Louise Bonne of Jersey
Plums Blue Tit, Opal and Victoria
Cherries Lapins, Stella and Sunburst
Apricots Delicot, Moorpark and Tomcot
Peaches Avalon Pride, Duke of York, Garden Lady, Peregrine and Rochester
Nectarines Early Rivers and Nectarella
Fig Brown Turkey and Brunswick

Suitable rootstocks for pot culture

A more dwarfing rootstock, such as the following, will help to control the tree's vigour.

Apples M9 and M26. It is best not to use M27 as it prefers perfect soil conditions, which are not found in pots.

Pears Quince C and Pyrodwarf

Plums Pixy

Cherries Gisela 5

Apricots Torinel or St Julien A

Peaches and nectarines Pixy or Montclaire. There are also genetically dwarf varieties of peach and nectarine that are ideal for pot culture. Being naturally dwarf, they do not need the dwarfing influence of the rootstock.

Remember that you will still need to attend to the pollination requirements of varieties that you choose. This can be particularly important when growing in pots, when you are likely to be growing fewer trees.

Suitable containers for pot culture

Any container can be used, so long as it is a suitable size with holes in the bottom to aid the drainage, although metal pots are best avoided because they can get too hot on sunny days in the summer. Plastic pots are lighter if you are planning to move the tree into a greenhouse for the winter. A tray on wheels can also help with the moving of heavy plants! The weight of clay pots can, however, be an advantage in stopping the pots blowing over in windy weather.

For the tree's first pot, choose a size that the roots will comfortably fit into, but no more than 8cm (3") wider than the size of the

Fruit trees grown in pots. The nearest one is a pear, Black Worcester.

roots. Place crocks or grit in the bottom to allow good drainage.

Suitable growing media for pot culture

Although peat-based composts can be a good medium for long-term growing in pots, now that the environmental damage from harvesting peat – both locally and from CO_2 emissions – is firmly established, we need to look for alternatives. If you still want to use peat, it is now possible to buy peat composts that are made from peat that has been filtered from streams. Moorland Gold from West Riding Organics is one such product. Soil-based composts such as John Innes No.3 are ideal for growing fruit trees in pots, although they do contain some peat. Peat-free composts are available, but they are not ideal for the long-term growing of fruit trees in pots. So, some compromise is needed, which could be a soil-based compost that contains a reduced amount of peat.

One of the benefits of growing trees in pots is that you have complete control over the growing medium, in a way that is not possible with trees growing in the open. You can easily control variables such as the pH or the drainage, which can otherwise be difficult. Whichever compost is used, there will be a need to replenish nutrients that are used up as the tree grows. See Chapter 7, page 97 for information on the maintenance of pot-grown trees.

Planting trees in pots

Before planting, soak bare-rooted trees in water for an hour or so if they are at all dry. Large, thick roots or damaged ones can be cut back at this stage. This will encourage the production of fibrous roots.

Place some compost in the bottom of the pot, balancing the tree on this. Add further compost, shaking the tree every so often, to help the compost settle around the roots. Plant the tree firmly, allowing at least 3cm (1") gap between the compost and the top of the pot. Stand the pot on pot feet or bricks to allow good drainage. Water well.

QUICK GUIDE TO BUYING AND PLANTING TREES

- Ideally, buy bare-rooted trees from a specialist nursery.
- One-year-old (or maiden) trees will establish best and are cheaper to buy.
- Plant bare-rooted trees within the first week after they arrive from the nursery, or heel them in the ground to keep the roots moist.
- Make sure that the roots do not dry out at any stage, especially when planting on a cold, windy day.
- Most fruit trees will need staking. A stake 1-1.25m (3-4') is usually sufficient; 0.5m (1'8") should protrude above ground.
- Grass and weeds will need to be kept clear around the trunk. Mulching or mulch mats are effective ways of achieving this.
- Fit a rabbit guard.
- Small fruit trees can also be grown in pots.
- Consider how you will keep grass and weeds under control and whether you will need to protect the trees from grazing animals or deer. If so, construct appropriate tree guards.

Part 2

Fruit tree management

Chapter 7

Caring for your trees

Once you have planted your trees, there is a sense of sitting back and waiting for fruit production to begin, but this is not a time for doing nothing. The first years of a tree's life are the most important: formative pruning, feeding and watering will all ensure that the young tree gets off to a good start. There is a host of pests and diseases that can potentially threaten your tree, and regular inspection of your trees will allow you to nip these problems in the bud.

The principles of pruning are examined in Chapter 8, while pests, diseases and other problems, and the means of combating them, are dealt with in Chapter 9.

This chapter covers the other aspects of caring for fruit trees, which are often overlooked, such as ensuring a good water supply for the roots, paying attention to feeding requirements and preventing heavy crops from causing problems further down the line.

Heavy crops can bend branches down to the ground, as seen here on a Bramley's Seedling apple tree.

Watering fruit trees

It is only during the first year or two after planting that most trees will need to be watered. This time can be stressful for trees: their roots have been chopped when they are lifted from the ground in the nursery and they suffer from the shock of being transplanted. The roots can struggle to take up all the moisture that the tree needs.

Symptoms of drought stress are: leaves failing to open well all the way along branches in the late spring, followed by foliage yellowing and dropping off during the summer. Fruit can be small and drop off early.

Watering may also be necessary on free-draining soils, in areas where rainfall is particularly low and where a tree is planted close to a wall. In these situations, it is useful to insert a vertical section of pipe when planting to ensure that water can get down to the roots. It is important to add water in sufficient quantity, so that it reaches down into the soil rather than wetting the surface. If this is the case, roots will be attracted to the surface to find moisture.

Where a number of trees need watering, it can be useful to fit a trickle irrigation system – a hose with small holes in it so that water gradually permeates the soil, rather than running off when it is applied suddenly. Benefits will also be seen from mulching with organic matter in the spring when the soil is damp; this helps to conserve soil moisture over the growing season.

Feeding fruit trees

Most fruit trees do not require high levels of feeding. If the soil has been prepared well

Keeping an area around the tree free from grass allows it to establish without competition for water and nutrients.

before planting time, and attention paid to any deficiencies found, this will go a long way to providing the trees with the nutrients that they require. However, if trees are to perform well, some supplementary feeding is likely to be necessary. Before feeding your trees, ensure that they are not being starved of nutrients by grass or weeds growing close to the trunk. A circle of approximately 50cm (1'8") radius around the tree should be kept clear of vegetation.

Like all plants, trees are able to convert sunlight, water and carbon dioxide into the sugars that are needed to enable plant growth. However, additional nutrients are needed to keep the tree healthy and fruiting well. These nutrients are discussed in Chapter 1 (page 20).

Nitrogen (for growth) and potassium, or potash (for fruit formation and development), are the two most important nutrients for fruit trees. A deficiency of either of these will lead to a tree becoming starved and unproductive, but it is also important not to feed a tree too heavily. Excess nitrogen leads to soft, sappy growth that is prone to disease, while excess potassium can lead to problems with bitter pit and with trace-element absorption.

Phosphorus, magnesium and trace elements such as sulphur and copper are also needed. So, unless you are trying to correct an imbalance of a particular nutrient, you will be looking to apply a balanced fertiliser with a high level of potash.

Non-organic and commercial growers have the luxury of choosing fertilisers with specific N (nitrogen), P (phosphorus) and K (potassium) levels. Organic growers, looking to use more natural sources of plant food, often find it harder to obtain the exact constituents of particular plant foods. Organically based fertilisers designed for fruit trees are now appearing on the market, but they are still few and far between.

Seaweed contains low levels of the NPK nutrients normally found in synthetic fertilisers, but does contain high levels of all the trace elements and minerals that are important for plant growth. It also contains plant hormones, including cytokinins, which are thought to regulate plant growth. Seaweed is an excellent plant food for fruit trees, although regular use can be expensive; it is available as a liquid that can be used as a foliar feed, or as seaweed meal for adding to the soil. A study in 2008* found that seaweed, sprayed five times during the growing season, "stimulated the growth of shoots and leaves, [and] caused an improvement in flower quality . . ." There was also evidence to show that seaweed "improved the fruit set and size of apples".

Animal manure and **compost** are both excellent mulches to place around fruit trees. They contain the major nutrients in small quantities, as well as good levels of trace elements. They also add humus to the soil. Take care to keep manure and compost away from direct contact with the trunk.

Pelleted chicken manure is a useful, organically acceptable fertiliser with a well-balanced supply of nutrients. **Wood ash**, either from a fire in the house or from a bonfire, is a good source of potassium. It is, however, highly water soluble, so ash from a bonfire must be used before rain washes away the useful nutrients. Liquid feeds made from **comfrey** or **nettles** can be used on fruit trees. Nettles are higher in nitrogen; comfrey in potassium.

Management techniques

Aside from pruning (see Chapter 8), there are several methods of manipulating fruit trees to help achieve the required balance between growth and fruiting.

Correcting biennial cropping

Biennial cropping is the tendency of certain trees, usually apples and pears, to crop heavily in one year and lightly in the next. Although certain varieties have a tendency towards biennial cropping, it can also be induced by frost damage or an over-heavy crop. Once biennial cropping sets in, it can become an established pattern unless something is done to correct it. The simplest way is by not allowing the tree to carry a heavy

* Alina Basak (2008) 'Effect of preharvest treatment with seaweed products, Kelpak® and Goëmar BM86®, on fruit quality in apple'. *International Journal of Fruit Science*, 8(1&2): 1-14.

crop in the year that it would normally do so. This can be achieved by thinning the blossom or young fruit in the heavy-cropping year, or by pruning out some of the fruit buds in the winter before the heavy crop is expected. I prefer thinning the young fruit, because by the time that the young fruits have formed it is possible to see how heavy a crop the tree is likely to bear, and consequently how hard the thinning needs to be.

It can be helpful to see a fruit tree as having only a limited amount of energy. This energy can be used for various functions in the tree, such as putting on growth and fruiting, or for fruit bud development. Fruit buds begin to form in the summer before they will become fruit. If, at this point, the tree is carrying a heavy crop, there will be less energy available for the initiation of fruit buds. So limiting the heavy crop means that the tree is more likely to have energy to form fruit buds, which will carry fruit in what would otherwise be the quiet year.

Fruit thinning

Fruit thinning is also used to ensure that a tree carries an optimum amount of fruit, and fruit of good quality, in the current year. A heavy crop can be a strain for the tree, as well as increasing the likelihood of small, malformed fruits that are more prone to disease. Thinning the fruit means removing some of a cluster of a fruit, leaving individual fruits with plenty of room to develop.

Some varieties, such as Victoria plum, are prone to constant heavy cropping. Although this might seem desirable, it can lead to broken branches, which are then open to disease such as silver leaf. Thinning the young fruits, once a heavy crop is apparent, helps to avoid this. Thinning can be supplemented by supporting heavy branches with a prop or stake, usually made from wood with a forked branch at the top. Branches can also be supported from a central stake – a process known as maypoling, as shown in Diagram 14 overleaf.

Part of a pear tree before and after the fruit has been thinned in the spring.

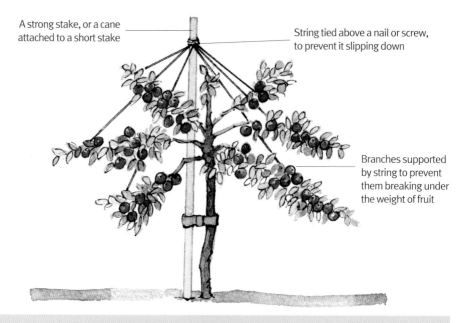

A strong stake, or a cane attached to a short stake

String tied above a nail or screw, to prevent it slipping down

Branches supported by string to prevent them breaking under the weight of fruit

Diagram 14 Maypoling, used to support branches that are heavy with fruit.

Other varieties, such as the apple Falstaff, tend to carry a heavy crop while tree is still young; although this might seem to be desirable, it can lead to the tree becoming stunted at an early stage, because there is little energy left over for growing as opposed to fruiting.

Altering branch angles

The more upright a branch is, the more vigorous it will be and the more likely it is to be largely vegetative in nature. Conversely, a horizontal branch is less vigorous and more likely to bear fruit.

We can use this knowledge to alter a tree's habits. For example, some varieties tend to grow in an upright shape, especially when they are young. Tying down the branches will bring them into fruiting more quickly as well as reducing the vigour of the tree. Ties, usually of twine, can be attached to heavy

stones or metal hoops inserted into the ground. Once a branch remains in position when the tie is taken off, the tie can be removed altogether.

The danger with this technique is of overdoing it. The branches of fruit trees tend to become more horizontal with age, so if they have been tied down when young they can end up dragging on the ground, particularly with the weight of heavy crops. So, this technique is best applied to trees that are unfruitful and upright in their growth, rather than indiscriminately because you are impatient for a tree to bear fruit.

The same technique can be applied to wall-trained trees while they are establishing. Vigorous, more upright shoots can be brought down towards the horizontal to reduce their vigour, while weak horizontal growth can be tied up to increase its vigour. This can be useful to correct uneven growth on a fan-trained tree.

Caring for fruit trees in pots

Planting fruit trees in pots is covered in Chapter 6, but once you have planted the tree, there is still maintenance to carry out, which can be rather different from looking after trees planted in the ground.

Siting

The beauty of growing fruit trees in pots is that you can move them around to take advantage of different situations. For most of the year a warm, sunny position is ideal, preferably sheltered from strong winds. It is a good idea to tie the tree loosely to a wall or post so that it cannot blow over.

For the winter, some of the more tender trees, such as peaches or apricots, will appreciate the shelter of an unheated greenhouse. Don't place them in a heated greenhouse, because, like most fruit, they have a need for a certain amount of chilling in the winter. A greenhouse will also give protection against spring frosts, which can damage blossom, although the trees will need to be accessed by pollinating insects. Alternatively, you can pollinate the blossom by hand (see Chapter 3, page 39).

In cold areas, it is worth wrapping the pot in bubble wrap – partly, in the case of clay pots, to prevent cracking, but also to protect the tree's roots from hard frosts.

Watering and feeding

Paying careful attention to watering and feeding is vital for pot-grown trees. The soil should be kept moist, which means watering daily at the height of summer, reducing to very little watering during the winter. It is important to avoid the extremes of waterlogging and drought, both of which can result in the tree shedding fruit.

The nutrients in the compost at planting time will soon be used up, necessitating additional feeding. Every spring, a top dressing can be applied to enrich and refresh the compost. Manure and compost make good top dressings, but the best material is homemade worm compost, a very concentrated source of nutrients.

Liquid feeds will also be needed, particularly those high in potassium, such as tomato food or comfrey liquid. Seaweed is also helpful in alleviating the potentially stressful conditions of growing in a pot. You can tailor the feeding to the requirements of different trees: stone fruit, for example, will need more nitrogen, particularly at the beginning of the growing season. Fruit trees will benefit from feeding every 7-10 days while the fruit is swelling. The feeding can be stopped once the fruit has been harvested.

Re-potting

The tree will need re-potting every year until it reaches maturity. Late autumn to early winter is the best time for this. Carefully remove the tree from the old pot, partly by tipping the pot and partly by pulling on the trunk. Once the tree has been removed, tease out the roots and trim back the protruding ones. Thick roots without much fibrous growth can be cut back harder. Removing some of the old compost allows room for new, nutrient-rich compost when the tree is re-potted.

Chapter 8

Pruning fruit trees

The art of pruning holds an air of mystique for many people; indeed, it can even put people off growing fruit trees, because they imagine that they will have to learn complicated techniques and spend hours putting them into practice. These techniques certainly exist, but it is more important to understand why fruit trees are pruned and what happens when you make a pruning cut.

This chapter examines the reasons for pruning fruit trees and looks at the principles behind pruning. Formative pruning and the various forms of fruit trees are also discussed. Specific information on pruning individual fruits is contained in the chapters in Part 3.

A five-year-old plum tree that has never been pruned.

Why prune fruit trees?

One way to find out why fruit trees are pruned is to look at what happens when a tree is not pruned. The photograph on the right shows a plum tree that is only five years old; it has never been pruned and, despite its tender years, it already has a number of branches growing in an unruly fashion that will hit each other as soon as a strong wind blows. As the tree grows, it is likely to become a mass of tangled branches; it will still fruit, but little sunlight will find its way to much of the tree where it is needed to ripen the fruit. Long, unpruned branches will break in the wind or through the weight of a heavy crop, and disease is likely to enter when broken branches are not pruned back to leave a clean cut. Over time, fruit on an unpruned tree tends to become smaller and suffer from fungal diseases, which thrive in the moist environment that arises when there is little airflow through the tree.

There are many reasons for pruning:
- Forming a sound framework of branches that will provide a strong base for the tree during the rest of its life. This is known as formative pruning.
- Maintaining a balance between the vegetative growth and fruit production.
- Stimulating new growth of healthy young wood.
- Ensuring that the tree is stable and not prone to blow over or lose branches in strong winds.
- Increasing fruit production by allowing sunlight to reach the fruit and wood. Both the fruit and the wood need sunlight for ripening.
- Replacing exhausted growth with new branches.
- Removing dead, diseased and damaged wood. Fungal canker is a good example of a disease that can be controlled by pruning.
- Encouraging the tree to grow into a form that is desired, such as an espalier, spindlebush or standard.

The principles of pruning

Pruning fruit trees is a subject that seems to be shrouded in mystery. Many people, not really knowing where to start, are afraid of damaging their trees; others complain that their trees don't look like 'the trees in the book'. There is some truth behind these remarks: it is possible to harm fruit trees, either by pruning too hard, or pruning at the wrong time of year, but clear instructions and an understanding of the principles of pruning will allow you to make judicious cuts that will help your trees to prosper.

It *is* very likely that your trees will not look like those 'in the book' – the directions given for pruning aim to give clear instructions for all situations, but each tree is an individual; rather than following detailed advice slavishly, it is much better to gain an understanding of the principles involved, so that you can work with your own unique tree rather than trying to impose a system on it. To some knowledgeable people, the advice on pruning in this book will seem oversimplified. This is deliberate, because it is better to understand the basic principles than to become confused by dogmatic and complicated instructions.

The photo below shows fruit and leaf buds on a branch of a plum tree. The fruit buds are swollen, slightly pointed, and protrude from

A plum tree branch, showing the fruit and leaf buds.

GLOSSARY OF THE DIFFERENT PARTS OF A FRUIT TREE

Diagram 15 shows the constituent parts of an apple tree, but most fruit trees are similar, except that the fruiting spurs are particularly pro-nounced on apples and pears.

The **trunk** is the main woody stem that emerges from the ground.
The **union** is a swelling, usually low down on the trunk, where the **scion** was grafted on to the **rootstock** when the tree was formed.
A **framework branch** is a large branch growing from the trunk. This is one of the branches that are selected during formative pruning.
A **lateral** is a branch growing from a framework (or main) branch, or from the trunk.
A **sublateral** is a side shoot growing from a lateral.
A **fruiting spur** is a shoot on which fruit buds form.
The **central leader** is the upright growth at the top of the trunk.
A **branch leader** is the new (or exten-sion) growth at the end of the branch.

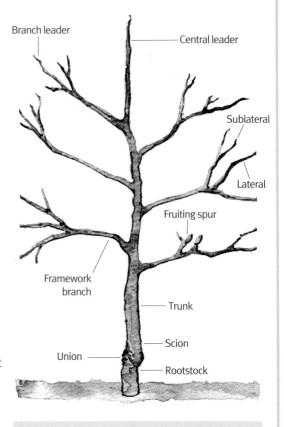

Branch leader

Central leader

Sublateral

Lateral

Fruiting spur

Framework branch

Trunk

Scion

Union

Rootstock

Diagram 15 The different parts of a grafted fruit tree.

the branch (most of those in the photo are fruit buds), whereas the leaf buds are more rounded and tight into the wood that they spring from. They emerge as leaves when growth commences, whereas fruit buds turn into flowers, and will eventually fruit if they are pollinated. It can be important to differ-entiate between the two when pruning.

It is also important to be able to identify the current year's growth (or extension growth) when pruning. Often you will be asked to remove a proportion of the current year's growth. You can identify this by finding the rings that form between each year's growth (see Diagram 17, page 102) and by looking for subtle changes in the colour of the bark.

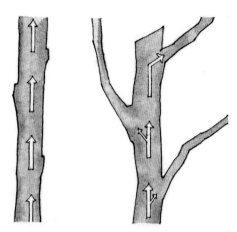

(a) Before pruning
The tree's vigour is directed primarily upwards towards the terminal bud

(b) After pruning
The tree's vigour is directed into the lateral buds, causing them to grow strongly, particularly the top one

Diagram 16 The effect of pruning on apical dominance.

Apical dominance

Apical dominance is the tendency of a shoot to continue strong upright growth. Diagram 16 shows how the apical dominance present in (a) is broken when a pruning cut is made: the growth that was strongly upwards through the terminal bud is now changed, so that the side shoots (or lateral buds) now grow more strongly. When you make a pruning cut, you are not only removing unwanted growth but also causing a change in the growth pattern of the branch that remains.

This principle can be used when forming a young tree into a goblet shape. The cut made in (b) will encourage the laterals to grow strongly, helping to produce a more spreading tree.

Pruning lightly or hard

Every time we make a cut, the tree will try to respond by sending out more growth – either from close to the cut, or further down the remaining branch. You can use this principle

to help create more growth or fruiting shoots in a place where you would like them. Successful fruit tree pruning involves creating the right balance between fruiting and vegetative growth. Vigorous growth is usually vegetative (although it can become fruitful later on). The balance is achieved by pruning vigorous growth lightly and weaker growth harder. This is something that can be difficult for the beginner to grasp, as it can be tempting to cut the strongest growth the hardest. In the same fashion, a vigorous tree needs only light pruning, whereas pruning a weak tree a little harder will encourage stronger growth.

To gain an understanding of the vigour of the tree, look at the new growth at the top of it. Look to see how much the tree has grown in the last year. Is this new growth strong and vigorous, or weak and spindly? Diagram 17 overleaf shows how to spot the growth rings that enable you to see the last year's growth.

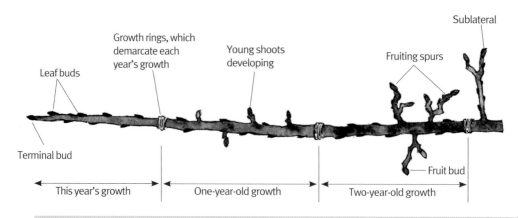

Sublateral

Growth rings, which
demarcate each
year's growth

Young shoots
developing

Fruiting spurs

Leaf buds

Terminal bud

Fruit bud

This year's growth   One-year-old growth   Two-year-old growth

Diagram 17 The features of a young apple or pear branch.

However, if you prune a tree too hard it will try to send out more growth to compensate. The harder you prune, the more vigorous the regrowth will be. If you continue this process over a few years, you will end up with a tree like the one in the photo below. Unfortunately, the upright shoots produced are vegetative rather than fruiting growth, so the end result is a congested tree without much fruit. Overpruning is the most common cause of fruit trees bearing small crops. It is difficult to limit a tree's size through pruning; instead, the size of the tree should be determined by the rootstock on which it is grown. Pruning lightly is much less likely to harm a tree, so it is always a good maxim to be sure that you

This apple tree has been pruned too hard, resulting in vigorous upright regrowth that bears little fruit.

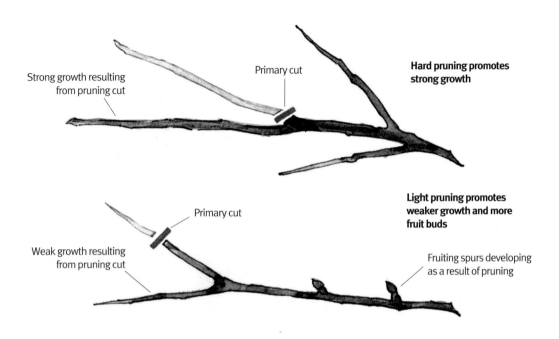

Strong growth resulting from pruning cut

Primary cut

Hard pruning promotes strong growth

Light pruning promotes weaker growth and more fruit buds

Primary cut

Weak growth resulting from pruning cut

Fruiting spurs developing as a result of pruning

Diagram 18 The growth resulting from pruning cuts made in the previous winter.

know why you are making any particular cut – that way you are less likely to damage the tree by heavy pruning. It is much better to prune a tree lightly every year than to prune it more heavily every few years. A maximum of 15 per cent of the growth should be pruned off in any one year. This can be extended to 20 per cent when renovating a crowded tree. These figures do not apply to formative pruning (see page 108) or pruning restricted tree forms.

Achieving the correct balance between fruiting and vegetative growth is something that comes with experience. You might not get it right first time, but watching how the tree responds to your pruning will enable you to refine your techniques over time (see Diagram 18). In order to learn, you can take a photo of a particular branch before and after pruning and then return a year later to see how the tree has responded. (Tying a ribbon on the branch will enable you to find it again in a year's time.)

Pruning at the correct time of year

It is vital to prune fruit trees at the right time of year, both to have the desired effect on growth and to prevent diseases that can become established if pruning is done at the wrong time.

The pome fruits (apple, pear, quince and medlar) are normally pruned in the winter, which encourages more growth, but there are exceptions to this rule, as follows.

- Trees grown in a restricted form, e.g. cordons, fans and espaliers, are pruned in late summer because summer pruning keeps growth compact.
- Trees that have been pruned too hard are best pruned in the summer until the imbalance has been corrected (see page 142).
- Summer pruning of pome fruits is also an effective way of letting light and air into the tree, particularly when fruits have become shaded by congested growth.

Stone fruits (plums, peaches, nectarines, cherries and apricots) are pruned during the spring and summer, when they are actively growing, in order to prevent disease problems that could arise from winter pruning. Formative pruning of stone fruits can be carried out in the spring, just after bud burst, whereas mature trees are normally pruned during the summer.

Some trees, such as mulberries, will weep sap if pruned at the wrong time of year. The correct time of year for pruning all fruit trees can be found in the chapters on individual fruits in Part 3.

It is always best to prune on a dry day. Some fruit tree diseases are spread by wind and rain. Pruning wounds are the ideal surface for these diseases to establish and find their way into the tree. It is also worth avoiding days when the temperature is below freezing.

Pruning techniques

Learning how to make pruning cuts in the correct fashion will ensure that your pruning has the desired effect, rather than opening the tree up to disease and potential structural weakness.

Using secateurs to prune to an outward-facing bud.

Small pruning cuts

Small cuts are those made with secateurs, usually to a particular bud whose growth you want to encourage.

When cutting to a bud, the cut should be gently sloping, slightly above the bud. Cutting to a bud will encourage that bud to grow on, so the direction that the bud is facing will determine the future direction that the branch takes. For this reason, pruning is usually to an outward-facing bud, encouraging growth towards the outside of the tree (see Diagram 19). However, it is not only the topmost bud that will shoot after pruning; the first two or three buds are likely to form strong shoots. A bud that is likely to form a shoot heading in the 'wrong' direction, usually inwards, towards the middle of the tree, can be rubbed out with your finger at the time of pruning.

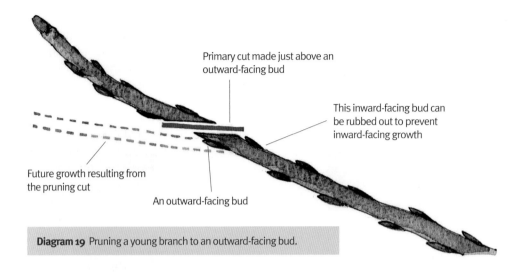

Primary cut made just above an outward-facing bud

This inward-facing bud can be rubbed out to prevent inward-facing growth

Future growth resulting from the pruning cut

An outward-facing bud

Diagram 19 Pruning a young branch to an outward-facing bud.

Larger pruning cuts

Larger cuts are those that need to be made with loppers or a pruning saw. While it is all right for smaller branches to be cut to a bud in the middle of the branch, larger branches should be cut to a junction with another branch, as in Diagram 20, or to the trunk of the tree. The branch that you cut to is known as the replacement branch: this is usually a younger branch that will replace the growth that is being cut. Avoid leaving a stub when cutting larger branches: this stub will either put on new growth in an inappropriate way, or die back.

If you are cutting back to a replacement branch, this should be at least a third of the size of the branch that you are cutting, to ensure that the replacement branch is able to take up the vigour of the main branch. Alternatively, a large branch can be cut back to its origin from the trunk of the tree.

Where it is necessary to cut back to the trunk, trying to remove a branch with just one cut

Removing the whole branch back to the branch collar

Cutting in the middle of the branch, leaving a stub

C   B

A

Cutting to a replacement branch

Cuts at A or B are good practice. Cutting at C will either produce weak shoots or the stub will die back

Diagram 20 Cutting back to a replacement branch or to the trunk.

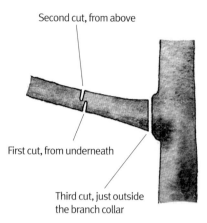

Second cut, from above

First cut, from underneath

Third cut, just outside
the branch collar

Diagram 21 Removing a large branch.

Nicking and notching

Although not strictly pruning, nicking and notching are related and useful techniques, used to manipulate the growth habits of individual fruit buds. A small V-shaped piece of wood is removed with a sharp knife, either just above or just below a bud. Late spring is the best time to carry out nicking or notching. These techniques are usually used only on apple and pear trees. They should not be used on stone fruits, because of the danger of introducing silver leaf and bacterial canker.

Nicking – removing wood from just below a bud – weakens any growth from that bud. This technique is often used in formative pruning, when removing the leader. Where the leader is removed, there are usually

can lead to the weight of the branch tearing the bark on the trunk of the tree. Diagram 21 shows the correct technique for removing a large branch, by making several cuts. Firstly, an undercut should be made about 40cm (1'4") away from the final cut. This cut should be around a third of the way into the branch. This is followed by a downward cut, slightly further away, which will remove the branch without any tearing of the bark. What remains is a small section of branch that can be supported while the final cut is made. This final cut should be just outside the branch collar. Like all pruning cuts, it should leave a clean surface without any tearing or roughness. Any imperfections can be cleaned up with a sharp pruning knife.

The use of wound paints to protect a cut from disease is now recommended only for the stone fruits – plums, cherries, peaches, nectarines and apricots. See page 140 for more information on wound paints.

Nicking – removing a small piece of wood from below a bud – weakens any growth from that bud.

several new shoots, all competing to be the new leader. This results in branches emerging from the trunk at a steep angle, which makes them prone to breaking later in their life. If nicking is carried out below these topmost buds, they will only grow weakly. The following winter, this weak growth can be cut back to the laterals further down that developed at a wider angle as a result of the nicking. Alternatively, unwanted growth can be rubbed out with your fingers, as it grows.

Notching is the process of removing a small piece of wood just above a bud. This encourages growth from that bud. This technique can be useful in formative training, particularly on restricted forms, such as espaliers, where you wish to fill in a gap by encouraging a new branch to grow.

Notching – removing a small piece of wood from just above a bud – encourages strong growth from that bud.

ASSESSING THE TREE

It is tempting to start pruning straight away, but it is vital to spend a few minutes assessing the present condition of the tree and what you hope to achieve by pruning it.

This assessment is the most important stage in pruning. Ask yourself the following questions.

- Is the tree healthy? Are there any diseases, such as canker, that can be pruned out to improve the health of the tree?

- Are there any branches that have been damaged, perhaps by wind or animals?

- Is the tree stable, growing evenly on all sides, or is it leaning to one side?

- How vigorous is the tree? Do you therefore need to prune lightly or harder?

- Is the growth congested and therefore in need of thinning out?

- Is the tree likely to bear a heavy crop? This can be ascertained by looking at the number of fruit buds on it.

- Are there branches that are becoming too long or heavy for the good of the tree?

By considering these factors you are building up a picture of the tree and how to correct any problems by pruning.

Formative pruning

Formative pruning is the process of shaping a young tree for the rest of its life. It is vitally important to build up a strong, evenly spaced framework of branches that will serve the tree well in the long term. Although the actual pruning techniques will vary according to the form of tree grown, the principles of formative pruning are shown in Diagram 22 below.

Nearly all tree forms require a certain length of clear trunk before the first branches arise. (The exception is stepovers, but this form is unusual.) Forming this clear trunk involves removing the laterals that form below this point. It is good practice to do this over a two-year period, as illustrated – leaving stubs to grow on for a year helps the trunk to strengthen.

Above the clear trunk, there should be a selection of well-spaced laterals growing at a wide angle to the trunk. Shoots growing at a narrow angle will always be weak, often splitting from the trunk later in the tree's life, and should be removed.

A young tree will often try to form more than one leader. If a leader is being retained, it is vital that there is only one, otherwise you will be left with a weak point that is likely to split later in the tree's life. It is best to remove

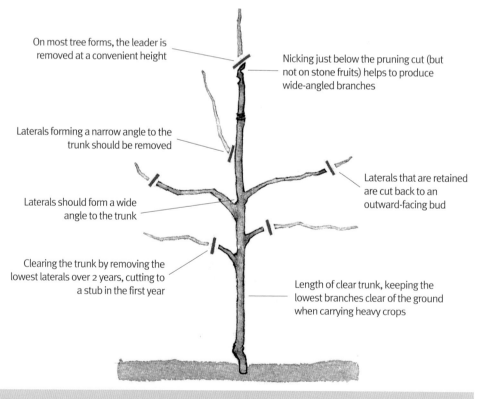

On most tree forms, the leader is removed at a convenient height

Nicking just below the pruning cut (but not on stone fruits) helps to produce wide-angled branches

Laterals forming a narrow angle to the trunk should be removed

Laterals that are retained are cut back to an outward-facing bud

Laterals should form a wide angle to the trunk

Clearing the trunk by removing the lowest laterals over 2 years, cutting to a stub in the first year

Length of clear trunk, keeping the lowest branches clear of the ground when carrying heavy crops

Diagram 22 The principles of formative pruning.

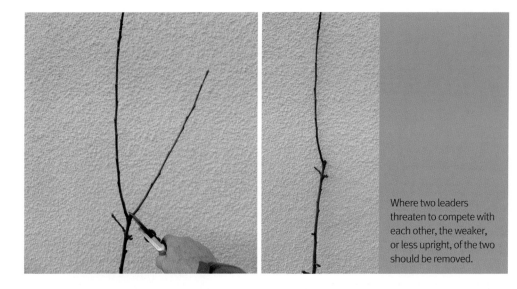

Where two leaders threaten to compete with each other, the weaker, or less upright, of the two should be removed.

whichever is the weaker, or less upright, of the two leaders. Where a leader is pruned, it is likely that one or more shoots will grow back from buds just underneath this pruning cut. If a replacement leader is desired, the strongest and most upright of these shoots can be retained.

The pruning that follows on from this will depend upon the form of tree you desire. During the early years of a tree's life, the emphasis should be on developing strong growth rather than encouraging fruiting. Although it is fine to allow a few fruits to develop, heavy crops at a young age can cause the tree to become stunted (see Chapter 3, page 42).

Fruit tree forms

There are many different forms of tree that can be used. The most popular ones are described below, together with their suitability for different fruits. Further information about pruning methods for each form can be found in the chapters on individual fruits in Part 3.

The trained forms – espalier, fan, cordon and stepover – are normally grown on the less vigorous rootstocks, because their size is restricted to fit the wall or supporting wires. Most pruning is carried out in the summer, because this encourages weaker growth.

Wall-trained trees need a strong system of support wires. These can either be suspended between wooden posts or fixed against a wall or fence. It is preferable to keep the wires a little way out from walls and fences, in order to increase the air circulation around the tree.

Bush

This is the most common form of tree and one that arises almost by default if little pruning is undertaken. It is suitable for most types of fruit and is easy to maintain. Framework branches emerge from a short trunk (60-90cm [2-3']) to produce an open-centred tree.

Bush

Standard

This is a large tree, suitable for traditional orchards and large gardens. It is a large version of the bush tree, grown on a clear trunk of around 1.8m (6'). It is suitable for all fruit trees that can be grown on vigorous rootstocks, as well as mulberries, which naturally form a large tree. Harvesting and pruning can be difficult on such a large tree, requiring access by ladder or long-handled pruning tools.

Half standard

This is a similar tree to a bush, but with a longer trunk. The first branches usually emerge about 1.5m (5') from the ground. Half standards can be grown only on the more vigorous rootstocks. They were traditionally grown in orchards grazed by sheep, but are also suitable for specimen trees in gardens. The height of the first branches allows easy mowing underneath.

Standard

Half standard

Spindlebush

This is a broad, cone-shaped tree with the leader retained, supported by a tall stake inserted at planting time. Most suited to apples and pears, it is a form that is designed to allow maximum sun to reach all parts of the tree. The spindlebush is an efficient way of growing fruit, but it needs skilful pruning to keep it in shape.

Espalier

This is a form of tree with horizontal branches, or arms, suitable for cultivars of apples and pears that form spurs easily. It is a decorative form for growing on a garden wall or creating boundaries in a garden. The number of tiers can be varied to suit the space available and the vigour of the rootstock.

Spindlebush

Espalier

Pyramid

This form is a more slender cone shape than the spindlebush, and is also supported by a permanent stake. It is usually used for plums, or, in more dwarf form, for apples and pears. Summer pruning can be used to keep the size of the tree small. Again, it is an efficient shape for allowing sunlight to reach all parts of the tree.

Fan

This is a form of tree most suited to the stone fruits (plums, cherries, peaches, nectarines and apricots), as well as figs. It is usually grown against a wall. The short trunk splits into two wide-angled arms, from which the rest of the branches spread. When forming, the middle is filled in last.

Pyramid

Fan

Cordon

The cordon is a fairly upright form of trained tree, most suited to apples and pears. Oblique cordons are most common, because the angle of the trunk encourages heavier fruiting, but upright cordons can be grown, either as a double cordon, or even with three or four arms. Where space is limited, cordons training can enable a number of cultivars to be grown in a small area. The side branches are restricted by summer pruning. A wire framework is needed to support cordons.

Cordon

Stepover

The stepover is usually grown as a decorative edging to a bed. It is suited to spurbearing apples on more dwarfing rootstocks. The support of wires is needed to hold it in place.

Stepover

ORNATE TREE SHAPES FROM THE PAST

In the eighteenth and nineteenth centuries the French took the training of fruit trees to the level of an art form. All kinds of fancy shapes were created, not because they produced more fruit but because they fitted with the formal, fussy style that was all the rage at that time.

Ever more intricate shapes were produced before the bubble burst at the start of the twentieth century.

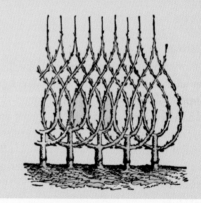

An example of the intricately shaped trees that were formed by grafting.

Pruning mature trees

There are several complicated systems of pruning fruit trees, which can serve to perplex the fruit tree grower. Poring over a book, trying to work out which is the fourth bud on a sublateral before making a cut, can be a source of confusion and disillusionment. Fruit tree pruning doesn't need to be too technical. After all, most people grow fruit trees for fun and to harvest a worthwhile crop – they don't have the pressure of a commercial

A hedge of fruit trees, providing fruit – despite being pruned with a hedgetrimmer!

grower desperate to achieve the maximum crop from every tree. Although learning to prune can seem daunting, it is worth doing. Once you understand the principles involved, it seems much easier.

It is also not worth worrying too much about exact techniques. I have inherited a hedge of apple and pear trees that, due to time pressures, I prune with a hedgetrimmer, and it still provides a worthwhile harvest each year. Follow a few golden rules when pruning and you will not go far wrong.

One system of pruning, known as regulated pruning, is simple enough for the amateur to grasp and effective enough to improve the health and cropping potential of most fruit trees. For this reason regulated pruning is explained in this general chapter on pruning, while its adaptation for particular fruits is covered in the chapters in Part 3. Other types of pruning suited to particular fruits are also covered in those chapters.

Regulated pruning

Regulated pruning is a method that involves opening up the tree to sun and light, renewing growth that has become exhausted and keeping well-spaced branches growing in a radial pattern.

Growth to be considered for pruning out will fall into one of the following categories.

Dead, diseased and damaged wood (sometimes called the 3Ds). Although dead wood might be left on where management for wildlife is important, it is generally good practice to remove it. The removal of diseased wood is important to remove the potential source of infection. The pruning out of diseased wood can take place at any time of year. Examples of diseases controlled by pruning are apple and pear canker and mulberry canker.

Crossing and rubbing branches. Where branches are rubbing against each other, it

The wound caused by a broken branch is an ideal place for disease to enter.

is likely that the growth is congested, leading to lack of air flow and the increased risk of fungal diseases. Branches hitting each other in strong winds can cause wounds, which are a potential site for spores to lodge and diseases to become established. The photographs below show the thinning out of a congested area of growth on an apple tree. When faced with an extremely dense area of growth, it can be daunting to know where to start – but the only answer really is to start. Once a few cuts have been made, the picture will become clearer.

Misplaced branches. If viewed from above, a tree would ideally resemble a bicycle wheel, with branches radiating out from a central trunk in a regular pattern. Branches that deviate sharply from this pattern are candidates for removal, as shown in Diagram 23. This particularly applies to branches growing back in towards the centre of the tree. Also in this category are branches

These photos show a congested area of an apple tree, before and after pruning.

that emerge from the trunk in a weak manner, as illustrated in the diagram.

Vigorous upright growth. Some trees contain over-vigorous upright branches that emerge from a horizontal branch. These are best removed, because it is preferable to encourage horizontal growth that is more likely to fruit. Vigorous upright growth that emerges from a horizontal branch is also likely to be growing through more desirable branches.

Branches that have become too heavy or long. Such branches are liable to break under the weight of a heavy crop, or in strong winds. These branches will either look too long for the size of tree, move more than might be expected, or bow down under the weight of a heavy crop. There is no need to remove such a branch, especially if it is bearing well; instead, it can be cut back to a replacement branch, as shown in Diagram 24 overleaf.

It is important to be guided by the shape and habit of the tree that you are pruning. Each variety of fruit tree has its own particular growth habit: some will be spreading; others will be upright. Although the principles of pruning are the same, you will not be able to prune both in the same way. Spreading trees

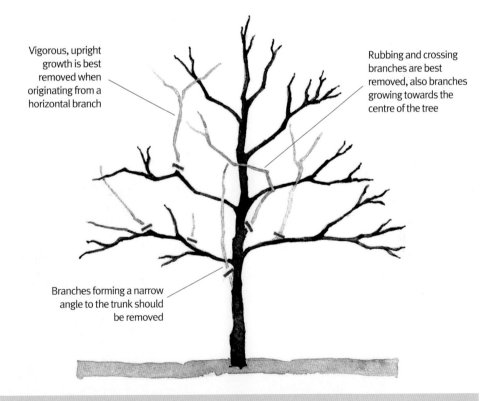

Vigorous, upright growth is best removed when originating from a horizontal branch

Rubbing and crossing branches are best removed, also branches growing towards the centre of the tree

Branches forming a narrow angle to the trunk should be removed

Diagram 23 Regulated pruning: removing misplaced growth from a young tree.

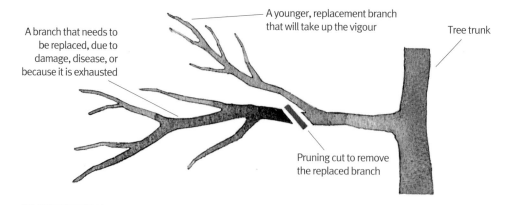

A younger, replacement branch that will take up the vigour

A branch that needs to be replaced, due to damage, disease, or because it is exhausted

Tree trunk

Pruning cut to remove the replaced branch

Diagram 24 Cutting back to a replacement branch.

can be encouraged to grow in a more upright fashion by pruning to upward-facing buds or growth, while on upright trees it is important to encourage more lateral growth by pruning to outward-facing buds or growth.

Leaning trees

The photograph below shows a leaning fruit tree in need of pruning that will make it more stable. The first thing to ascertain when encountering a leaning tree is whether the cause of the lean can be remedied. Fruit trees are sensitive to light and will often grow away from a tree or building that is causing heavy shade. While removing a building might seem a bit drastic, trees that are causing shade can be reduced in size or crown-thinned, or overgrown hedges can be laid to reduce the shadow cast by them.

A leaning tree. Pruning can help to correct the problem, but this tree has been planted too close to a large tree on its right, so it will always want to grow to the light on the left-hand side.

Removing large branches on this side of the tree will reduce the imbalance, making the tree more stable

Many smaller cuts on this side of the tree will stimulate growth

Diagram 25 Pruning a leaning tree.

Once this has been considered, there are further beneficial effects that can be conferred by pruning. What is needed, unsurprisingly, is to remove some of the weight from the 'heavy' side of the tree – usually the one that is receiving more light. It is important, though, to remember that pruning stimulates more growth. If normal pruning was carried out on this side, in a few years the situation could be even worse because pruning encourages growth. Instead, the weight can be removed by making a few major cuts, possibly even removing branches back to the trunk, where regrowth is unlikely. Conversely, it is good to encourage growth on the 'light' side (the one with less growth) of the tree. This is achieved by making lots of small pruning cuts, each one encouraging more growth. (See Diagram 25.)

Pruning tools

It is always worth buying good-quality tools if you can afford them. They give better results and last longer. The steel used in the blades will be of better quality, holding a sharp edge for longer. Where you have a choice, it is always worth buying brightly coloured tools that will show up well against a green background.

Brightly coloured tools show up well in grass.

Secateurs

These are used for the smallest cuts, but a good-quality pair will cut surprisingly large stems. In fact, secateurs and a pruning saw should be sufficient for pruning all easy-to-reach branches. There is a choice of bypass or anvil types of secateurs. Bypass secateurs

These large secateurs are capable of cutting thicker branches than most.

cut rather like scissors, whereas anvil secateurs have a blade that cuts more like a knife on a chopping board. Although this is largely a matter of personal choice, bypass secateurs are usually reckoned to give the best cut. There are also secateurs with such useful innovations as a rotating handle for those with a weak grip, left-handed secateurs and mini-loppers, which will cut thicker stems.

Loppers

Loppers are useful for cutting thicker stems and for gaining extra reach, since they have longer handles than secateurs. Again, there is a choice of bypass and anvil heads. Many loppers have extendable handles, useful for reaching higher branches. Bear in mind that unless loppers are sharp and well adjusted, they have a tendency to crush branches, leaving a torn cut where disease can enter.

Long-handled loppers

These are useful tools for cutting small branches high up in a tree. There are various

Pruning with bypass loppers.

Long-handled loppers reaching high into a young tree.

types available, the old wooden types having been largely superseded by those with aluminium or fibreglass handles. Those with a small head can be useful in the congested crown of a fruit tree. Some long-handled tools have attachments that enable fruit to be picked high up in a tree.

Pruning saw

This is such a commonly used tool when pruning fruit trees that it is worth buying a good-quality one. Modern saws that cut on the pull stroke can be expensive, but are generally worth paying for if you are doing a fair amount of pruning.

A sharp pruning saw will produce clean cuts.

Pole saw

When you need to cut higher branches, a pole saw can be invaluable. It is safer to cut high branches with long-handled tools than by accessing the tree with a ladder. On the other hand, a ladder allows you to get closer to the branch that you are cutting, which often enables you to make a cleaner cut.

Pruning knife

You can use a pruning knife to tidy up any ragged cuts caused by loppers or pruning saws – worthwhile to help prevent disease.

Ladder

A ladder can be useful for reaching into large

A pole saw allows you to cut large branches from ground level.

fruit trees, but it is always worth considering whether this is the safest way to carry out a job. See the box on page 315 about ladder safety. It is possible to buy ladders with a back leg to support them, often advertised for use while pruning hedges. They can be useful for pruning tall trees that are not strong enough to support a ladder. It is also possible to buy ladders with a narrow top, which are designed to fit well between branches.

Disinfectant

This can be a useful aid when pruning diseased wood. The blades of pruning tools can be dipped into a bucket of dilute disinfectant (one that is recommended for garden use), or wiped with a rag soaked in disinfectant, especially when moving on to prune a new tree.

Tools should be cleaned and dried after use and sharpened regularly, where appropriate.

QUICK GUIDE TO PRUNING

- Make sure that you are pruning at the right time of year – apples and pears (non-restricted forms) in the winter; stone fruits and restricted forms in the late summer.
- Prune only when the weather is dry.
- Step back and assess the tree before pruning.
- Don't prune too hard. Most damage is caused by hard pruning. You should have a reason for each cut you make. It is better to prune a tree lightly each year than to make hard cuts every so often. Prune a maximum of 15 per cent of the growth in any one year (except when carrying out formative pruning).
- If you learn nothing else, learn the principles of regulated pruning. This system of pruning provides the basic knowledge that will allow you to prune most fruit trees.
- Thinning heavy crops encourages good-quality fruit, counters biennial cropping and helps prevent broken branches.
- Decide what forms you will use for your trees, so that you can begin the appropriate formative pruning.
- Formative pruning, in the first years after planting, is vital for producing a strong tree in the future.
- Do not allow too much fruit in the early years. Remove all fruit that forms in the first year after planting.
- Buy good-quality tools and consider safety when pruning.

Chapter 9

Problems of fruit trees

Through regular inspection of your trees, subtle changes will become apparent. Some, such as leaves yellowing and falling off in the autumn, are completely normal, while others are the harbingers of diseases.

Knowing which is which requires some knowledge of the major diseases that affect fruit trees. Particular vigilance is needed in late spring and early summer, when many pests and diseases first show their hand.

Cherry leaves yellowing in autumn. Leaves turning yellow earlier in the year can be a symptom of disease.

The first part of this chapter covers those disorders that are common to most types of fruit trees. Those specific to one type of fruit, such as apple sawfly or plum moth, are covered later in the chapter.

Inspecting fruit trees

Fruit trees do not thrive on neglect. They thrive when looked at and looked after on a regular basis. Many of the problems incurred by fruit trees develop quickly and can soon become damaging if left unchecked.

One example is aphids, which infest fruit trees over the late spring and summer months. Initially, just a few aphids will be present – so few that you will be able to squash them with your fingers – but they breed rapidly and, before you know it, you have a tree covered in aphids, causing weak and distorted branch formation. Likewise, fungal canker is a potentially fatal disease that can be controlled, by cutting it out, so long as it is caught early.

As well as looking for pests and diseases, keep your eyes open for damage caused by animals, branches broken by the wind and crops that are becoming too heavy for a branch to bear. Check that the tree is well anchored in the ground and that stakes are still firm and tree ties secure. Over time, tree ties can become loose, so that they drop down the stake, allowing the trunk of the tree to rub against the stake, causing damage (see photo on page 80). If a tree tie is securely fixed, it is worth checking that it is not strangling the tree – loosen it if necessary.

If a tree is loose in the ground, try to find out the reason, so that the correct remedy can be applied. If the tree is staked, is the stake doing its job, or has it become loose or rotten? If a new stake is needed, use a sledgehammer to insert one at a 45-degree angle, so as not to damage the tree's roots. It is useful to have someone hold the tree to one side while you are hitting the stake, to ensure you don't damage the tree.

Sometimes voles and moles can undermine tree roots, raising the soil by digging tunnels. Often, compacting the soil with your foot is all that is needed, but in severe cases further action might be needed. Sonar devices can be used to move them on, while placing dog hair in their tunnels is a folk remedy that is reported to have the same effect.

This regular inspection of your trees, preferably at least monthly, need not be seen as a chore. Inspecting your trees for potential problems can also broaden your understanding of the processes at work, from fruit bud formation through pollination to ripening of the fruit. Instead of being another task to fulfil in the garden, it can be a time to enjoy the beauty of the blossom and to appreciate the fruit swelling and ripening.

Nutrient deficiencies

Like all plants, fruit trees require sufficient nutrients to enable to them to be strong and healthy. Deficiencies of a particular nutrient will affect the tree adversely and will also produce a particular set of symptoms, which provide a clue to the remedial action needed.

Nitrogen deficiency
Symptoms: The leaves become smaller, losing their dark green colour and healthy sheen. The tree appears dull and lifeless. Fruit yields may decline and the fruit become smaller and more brightly coloured.

Iron deficiency.

Magnesium deficiency.

Control: Nitrogen deficiency is found particularly in light soils lacking in organic content. Apply plant food with a good level of nitrogen. In extreme cases, dried blood can be used to give an immediate boost to nitrogen levels. Leguminous green manures, such as clover or tares, can be grown around small trees: they 'fix' nitrogen from the air, making it available in the soil.

Iron deficiency

Symptoms: Inter-veinal chlorosis, a yellowing between the veins, turning into brown patches that start at the leaf margins. Young leaves are usually affected first.

Control: Iron is not usually lacking in the soil, but it can be unavailable to the tree's roots, particularly on alkaline soils. So any material that acidifies the soil, such as manure, composted bracken or pine needles, will help. Sulphur sprayed against scab will also help. The application of seaweed meal is also an effective control.

Magnesium deficiency

Symptoms: Similar chlorosis to that found in iron deficiency, except that symptoms are usually seen in older leaves first. The brown patches usually affect the centre of the leaves.

Control: This problem is often found on acid soils in areas of high rainfall, where the magnesium is leached away. High potash levels can make the problem worse. The application of seaweed products will help, or Epsom salts as a foliar spray at a dilution of 20g per litre (1oz per 2 pints).

Potassium deficiency

Symptoms: Trees have a stunted look with small flowers and fruit. Leaves become yellow around the edge, followed by a brown scorching.

Control: A dressing of rock potash will redress the problem.

Phosphorus deficiency

Symptoms: Growth can be stunted, but the most distinguishing feature is a blue or blue-green colour to the tree, particularly on the older leaves.

Control: Apply bonemeal, which is high in phosphorus.

Other deficiencies

The deficiencies listed on the previous pages are those most likely to have a harmful effect on your trees. A deficiency of any trace element will have an effect, but not so marked as with those just described. Most other deficiencies can be remedied by the application of manure or seaweed meal.

Pests of fruit trees

Some pests – the pear midge, for example – are specific to certain fruits, while others, such as birds and wasps, affect various different fruit trees. These more general pests

CREATING AN ECOSYSTEM TO ENCOURAGE BENEFICIAL WILDLIFE

If you read a list of the various pests that can affect fruit trees, you might think that it wouldn't be worth growing them. You might imagine a host of aphids, moths, caterpillars, weevils and mites ready to descend on your trees the moment your back is turned – and that's before we look at diseases. It's easy to see how, encouraged by the manufacturers of chemical sprays, we can become fearful gardeners, standing on guard with our spray of 'bugattack' in hand, ready to pounce and fight the enemy in hand-to-hand conflict. Often, we will even be fighting an enemy that doesn't exist, just in case it shows up!

We don't need to be fearful gardeners; we can co-exist with nature most of the time, only responding to a problem when it is persistent and damaging. Nature will often lend a helping hand, if we allow it to – ladybirds or hoverflies will keep the aphid numbers to an acceptable level, for example. We can even encourage beneficial insects by creating habitats that suit them.

Lacewings devour large quantities of aphids.

Creating a habitat that encourages such insects, and other wildlife, is mostly a matter of creating rich and diverse habitats in which they can flourish. In addition, certain plants that are known to be helpful can be planted to encourage the process. Honesty and poached egg plant, for example, are known to attract hoverflies and lacewings, which will feed on aphids. Red clover, grown around fruit trees as a green manure, will add nitrogen to the soil, but will also encourage bees and predatory insects.

are described in the following pages, while the pests that particularly affect specific fruit trees are detailed later in this chapter.

As to finding a remedy for these problems, wherever possible the answer provided is using methods that are in harmony with nature. Regular and careful observation is your most important ally. All pests and diseases are countered more easily if they are caught early.

Aphids

There are many types of aphid, some of which live only on specific host plants. Woolly aphids, for example, mostly affect apples, and are distinctive enough to have their own section below (see page 148). Pears are particularly affected by the pear bedstraw aphid (see page 151). Mealy plum aphid and plum leaf-curling aphid (see page 153) are specific to plums, while cherries suffer from cherry blackfly (see page 156).

Symptoms: Aphids feed by sucking the sap of the host plant, often causing leaves to curl and shoots to become weak and distorted. In addition to noticing the insects, which come in various, usually dull, colours, you might see the whitish outer skins of the nymphs, which are deposited on the leaf surface as the insects grow larger. You will also see a sticky honeydew deposit on the leaves. In time, this will blacken with the growth of a sooty mould.

Control: Because they proliferate rapidly, it is important to control aphids before they become widespread. When only a few are present it is possible to reduce their numbers by squashing them between your fingers, although this can be difficult when they are hiding in curled-up leaves.

A large aphid colony on a pear tree.

Aphids have many natural predators, which you can encourage to your garden. Lacewings, hoverflies and ladybirds can be attracted by growing flowers such as poached egg plant and buckwheat. A 'lacewing hotel'

Ladybirds are capable of keeping aphids under control if they arrive in time.

(available from garden centres and wildlife product suppliers) will provide a site for these insects to hibernate in the winter. They can also be made at home from bamboo or other dried stems placed in a container such as a section of pipe. Both ladybirds and lacewings can be bought as biological controls to be introduced to the garden. Biological controls can be expensive, but they are effective if the simple instructions are followed carefully. Blue tits are another predator of aphids; they can be encouraged by hanging fat balls in fruit trees.

A strong jet of water from a hose can be used to wash aphids from an affected tree, but, if numbers still increase rapidly, there are also organically approved insecticides to control aphids. These include pyrethrum, soft soap and sprays based on rapeseed oil. They are contact insecticides that need to be sprayed directly on to the aphids to be effective. Be aware that they can also be harmful to beneficial insects such as bees. Spraying late in the day, when bees are not active, is safer. Winter washes of horticultural oil give some protection where aphids are known to overwinter, usually in egg form.

Birds

Symptoms: Bullfinches are the birds most likely to damage fruit trees. They can strip a tree of many of its buds during the winter. Although their numbers are now much reduced, their effect can still be devastating. Birds can also cause serious damage to ripening fruit, especially cherries (see page 256).

Control: Prompt action is necessary. There is no simple answer, but a combination of methods can be effective. Netting can be used to cover small trees. CDs and black netting hanging in trees can have good results, but when they are after food, birds soon get used to devices designed to scare them. In extreme circumstances (and in isolated locations!), noisy bird scarers could be used.

Bullfinches can decimate crops on fruit trees by stripping the fruit buds in winter.

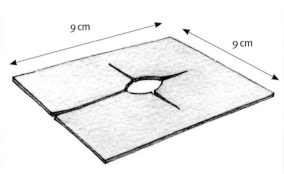

Diagram 26 A piece of cardboard with a hole in the middle can protect fruits such as pears.

Leaf damage caused by the light brown apple moth. The silky web of the caterpillars is also apparent.

A piece of cardboard with a hole in the middle (see Diagram 26), placed over individual fruits, can deter birds when they try to land on it and find it unstable. This is time-consuming, but can be worthwhile for valued fruits, such as prized pears.

Light brown apple moth

Despite its name, this is an increasingly serious pest of cherries, mostly in southern England.

Symptoms: This tortrix moth was first discovered in Britain in Cornwall in the 1930s. It lived in a small area near Newquay until the 1980s, when it started to spread across southern England. It is now becoming a widespread pest, particularly troublesome on cherries, but also on apples and plums. It is the caterpillars that cause the damage: they are around 18mm (0.7") long with green longitudinal stripes. They spin silky webs and roll leaves to protect themselves, at the same time as feeding on the leaves and developing fruit. Other tortrix moth caterpillars also attack fruit in a similar way.

Control: These are difficult pests to control, because they breed quickly and protect themselves inside rolled-up leaves and webbing. Spraying has a limited effect because the caterpillars are well protected. Their mating patterns can be disrupted with pheromone traps, but research on this is still limited. On a small scale, the caterpillars can be controlled by squashing the leaves they are hiding inside. Rolled-up corrugated cardboard, hung in the tree, will attract caterpillars that can be taken away.

Pear and cherry slugworm

Symptoms: The leaves of pear and cherry trees are eaten by the larvae of a sawfly known as slugworm because it resembles a small black slug. The leaves show a skeletonised pattern where they have been eaten. Damage occurs usually in two bursts, from May to June and from July to August.

Control: Contact insecticides, including soft soap, vegetable oil and pyrethrum, will deal with this pest effectively. Poultry kept under the trees is another method of control.

A slugworm eating its way through a leaf, causing the skeletonised pattern that characterises the damage of this pest.

Damage caused by red spider mite. The bronzed mottling on the leaves betrays their presence.

Red spider mite

Symptoms: Apple, plum and apricot trees can be affected by fruit tree red spider mite. These are tiny, dark red mites less than 1mm long. They are difficult to spot with the naked eye, so a magnifying glass can be useful. The mites are usually found on the underside of leaves. A pale mottling on the upper surface of the leaves gives a bronzed appearance to sections of the tree. Premature leaf fall may follow.

Control: Red spider mites tend to be much more of a problem when chemical insecticides have been used, because these destroy natural predators such as *Typhlodromus pyri* (known as typhs). The main organic control is the application of insecticidal soap, used after flowering. Sulphur, if used against scab, will also have some effect. Some people have claimed that seaweed applied as a foliar spray is helpful. Red spider mites thrive in dry conditions, so spraying the trees with water, particularly from low down to reach the underside of leaves, will help.

Wasps and hornets

Symptoms: Wasps and hornets will eat ripe fruit, particularly soft-skinned fruit such as plums. They have difficulty attacking tougher-skinned fruit such as apples and pears, but they will feed on these fruits if the skin has been punctured by birds.

Control: The traditional remedy is to hang jars of sugary water or syrup from the tree to give the wasps or hornet an alternative food source, in which they will drown. Clusters of fruit can be netted, but this can be time-consuming. The nets used to sell onion and other vegetables can be used for this.

Winter moth

Symptoms: Winter moths emerge from pupae in the soil between October and January. The almost wingless females enter the tree by climbing up the trunk. They lay eggs in the tree, from which the larvae emerge in

The caterpillar of the winter moth.

Wasps (and a ladybird) enjoying an apple. The initial damage has been caused by a bird.

the spring. These light green caterpillars feed on the leaves and blossom. They are easily identified because they have only five pairs of legs in total, which makes them walk with a looping action. They will also eat developing fruitlets, causing them to become distorted or to drop from the tree. Sometimes, leaves will be bound together by silky threads. Various fruit trees are affected, especially apples.

Control: Because the females have to climb the trunk to gain access to the tree, the main control is the application of grease or grease bands in early autumn. The female moths are unable to pass over the sticky surface. If control is necessary once the caterpillars are present, pyrethrum can be used, but remember that it can also be harmful to beneficial insects. *Bacillus thuringiensis* (Bt) is a biological control that is effective against young caterpillars, but it must be applied between

pink bud stage (just before flowers open) and petal fall. Hanging fat balls in trees will attract insect-eating birds, such as great, blue and long-tailed tits, which will help to keep the numbers of winter moths (and other insect pests) under control.

Diseases of fruit trees

As with the pests described in the previous pages, the diseases described here are common to a range of different fruit trees. Diseases specific to particular fruit trees are detailed later in this chapter.

Growing strong, healthy trees is the best protection against many diseases. Remember that good orchard practice will lead to less disease. Of primary importance is choosing varieties that are resistant to the diseases that are most common in your area (see Chapter 4, pages 45-6). Also important are good pruning techniques – for example, pruning to allow good airflow through trees, which will lessen the incidence of scab and canker. Where possible, ensure that you are not contributing to conditions that encourage the spread of disease. So, for example, either burn all prunings or remove them from your orchard or garden, as they may be harbouring disease that can spread to other fruit trees.

Although providing good cultural conditions will promote the health of trees, beware of over-feeding, particularly with nitrogen, because the resulting soft, sappy growth will be more susceptible to some diseases.

Bacterial canker

Symptoms: This is a disease that can affect all the stone fruits, but is particularly troublesome on plums and cherries. There are many symptoms of bacterial canker. The actual cankers are elliptical-shaped wounds on the bark, often depressed and sometimes exuding an amber-coloured gum. The gum can be a sign of a stressed tree – from drought, for example – but gum from bacterial canker usually oozes from the side of a canker. Branch dieback is caused when the canker girdles the branch, interrupting the supply of sap to it.

One of the most characteristic symptoms is branches with long areas where leaves have yellowed and fallen from the tree, but foliage still remains on the ends of the branch. Flowers and young shoots may open in the spring, only to shrivel and die a few weeks later. The leaves can develop 'shotholes' – small brown spots on the leaves that later fall out to leave a hole, usually surrounded by a small brown ring.

Control: Bacterial canker spreads mostly in damp weather in the early spring and autumn. For this reason, carrying out the regular pruning of plums and cherries during the summer and in dry conditions is prefer-

Yellowing leaves on the tips of branches and gaps where leaves have fallen are signs of bacterial canker.

able. Healthy trees will often shrug off an attack of bacterial canker, so paying attention to good cultural practices can help. Planting varieties resistant to bacterial canker is important, particularly in the wetter climates found in the west of Britain, where the disease is most troublesome (see Appendix 4.3). The rootstock used can also play a part: Pixy shows some resistance to bacterial canker, whereas St Julien A is more susceptible.

Pruning out infected branches is one means of control: cut back well beyond the diseased area to a replacement branch, remember to avoid pruning from September to May, and apply a wound paint to larger wounds.

Bordeaux mixture, a copper-based fungicide, will also give some control. It is best sprayed after the fruit has been harvested. Up to three sprays can be applied on a monthly basis. Bordeaux mixture can cause a little damage to the foliage, but this is not too serious because the leaves will soon be falling from the tree. Although copper-based sprays are permitted organically, it is preferable not to spray them on a prolonged basis because they can leave a copper residue in the soil, which inhibits earthworm activity.

It is important to pay attention to the feeding of nitrogen to plum trees. Too little nitrogen will stress them, making them more prone to bacterial canker, while too much nitrogen, particularly at the end of summer, can lead to soft, sappy growth, which is highly prone to infection in the autumn. So a balanced level of feeding needs to be achieved.

Blossom wilt

Symptoms: Blossom wilt is caused by a fungus that is very similar to the one that causes brown rot (see overleaf). Most fruit trees can be affected. The initial signs are the blossom wilting and dying. This can be followed by the dieback of shoots and leaves in the same vicinity. As the disease spreads, it can form a patchwork pattern on the tree, with dieback of young shoots spreading seemingly at random over the crown of the tree. Small white- or cream-coloured pustules can be seen on close inspection. The fruit can also be affected, particularly plums.

Control: Where blossom wilt is known to be a problem, Bordeaux mixture applied just before flowering will give some control. Infected shoots can be pruned out. The cultural controls suggested for brown rot will help to break the cycle of infection. Seaweed applied as a foliar spray is said to help control blossom wilt; it should be applied when the flower buds are first appearing, before the colour of the petals can be seen, and every two weeks between petal fall and early August.

Some varieties of fruit are resistant to blossom wilt, although information can be hard to come by. Czar and Jefferson, for example, are resistant varieties of plum.

The characteristic early signs of blossom wilt.

Brown rot

Symptoms: This is caused by a fungus which attacks the fruit through holes in the skin, such as those caused by birds, or the exit holes of the codling moth. It starts as a brown mark on the surface. This rot quickly spreads to infect the whole fruit, which will either drop from the tree or become mummified. This mummified fruit often develops cream-coloured pustules, usually formed into rings. Infected fruit placed into storage can spread the infection quickly to other fruits.

Control: The main method of control is the removal of infected fruits from the tree, as well as any remaining on the ground, thus preventing the spread of infection. These fruits should be removed from the garden or burnt. Controlling problems that cause holes in the fruit, such as codling moth or scab, will help to lessen the disease. Storing apples in plastic bags (see Chapter 10, page 199)

Brown rot on a pear.

will limit the spread of any storage rot. Bordeaux mixture and sulphur-based sprays used for other diseases can also give incidental control of this problem. Seaweed applied as a foliar spray is reputed to help. Planting resistant varieties can be helpful where brown rot is troublesome, although, again, information can be hard to come by. Czar and Jefferson are resistant varieties of plum.

Canker

This is a serious fungal disease that affects pears as well as apples, particularly in wetter regions of Britain.

Symptoms: The early signs of canker are a flaking of the bark, followed by cracks in the bark, often forming in rings around the branch. This can be followed by a warty appearance to the bark, which is sometimes sunken, yet with swollen tissue around it.

If the canker girdles all the way around a branch, the growth beyond the canker will die. White fungal pustules can develop around the canker during the summer. During the winter, bright red fruiting bodies are displayed. Canker usually affects young growth, particularly where excess nutrients have been applied, resulting in soft, sappy growth.

Control: Many varieties of apple and pear are almost completely resistant to canker. As with scab (see page 137), planting resistant varieties is the most important method of control. Where scab is a problem, it is likely that canker will also be present. There are a number of varieties resistant to both scab and canker (see Appendices 2.3 and 3.3), and planting these varieties will go a long way towards successful cultivation of apples and pears in wetter parts of the UK.

The advanced stage of canker, where the disease has girdled the branch.

The characteristic orange pustules of coral spot.

The methods of preventing a damp microclimate listed under scab (see page 138) also apply to canker. Bordeaux mixture and sulphur-based sprays (see pages 138-9) provide a limited amount of control against canker.

The main method of controlling canker is removing it by pruning. It can easily be seen when carrying out winter pruning. It is necessary to prune back well beyond the place of infection, preferably to another branch that will replace the infected one. If a tree is badly affected, think about removing it, so that you prevent the disease from spreading to other trees.

Take care not to apply too much nitrogen when feeding apple and pear trees. Damp soil and excess nitrogen exacerbate the spread of canker.

Coral spot

Symptoms: The first noticeable sign is the dieback of branches, followed by the appearance of small, bright orange pustules. Coral spot is more of a problem on ornamental trees, but fig trees are quite susceptible and apples can also be affected. It is caused by a fungus, which is spread by rain splash all year round.

Control: Prune out all affected growth well back into healthy growth. All affected wood should be removed from the garden or burnt.

Fireblight

Symptoms: Fireblight is a bacterial disease that affects only pome fruits. It is particularly common on pears. The first sign is the blossom wilting and dying; this can be confused with other diseases, such as blossom wilt, but the rapid onset of other symptoms will point firmly towards fireblight. As the disease progresses, shoots and branches will shrivel and die, taking on the appearance of branches that have been in a fire. The ends of young shoots will be shaped like a shepherd's crook. Healthy growth can be seen next to infected branches in the early stages.

The blackened stems and leaves symptomatic of fireblight.

The fruiting bodies of honey fungus.

Dark cankers, particularly at the junction of branches, and a fox-coloured stain under the bark, are further symptoms that *may* be present. A white slimy liquid can ooze from affected areas. Fireblight thrives in warm, humid conditions. It is found in southern England, but is less common further north. As the climate warms, this disease is likely to become more widespread, so it is worth considering planting varieties that show some resistance, especially with pears (see Appendix 3.4).

Control: The only control is to remove affected wood, cutting back around 30cm (1') into clean wood on small branches and up to 60cm (2') on large branches. Tools should be disinfected between cuts to avoid spreading the disease. Citrox is an organically acceptable disinfectant, but Jeyes Fluid and methylated spirits can also be used. Prompt action is necessary because the disease spreads rapidly: a whole orchard can be destroyed in one season if it is left unchecked. All prunings should be burnt on site if possible. Removal of the branches is another

option, but this carries the risk of spreading the disease elsewhere.

Fireblight can easily spread from rogue flowers that appear on a fruit tree during the summer. These should be removed as soon as they are seen. The disease also affects other trees, including hawthorn, from which it can spread. Where possible, avoid planting susceptible fruit near hawthorn hedges that are allowed to flower, or trim hedges before flowering.

Honey fungus

Honey fungus (also known as bootlace fungus) is a fungal disease that has the ability to kill many kinds of trees and shrubs, including most fruit trees. It can be a serious disease in orchards, slowly killing one tree after another as the fungus spreads.

Symptoms:
- Trees slowly dying, although the eventual demise can be sudden.
- Leaves can be small and yellow.
- Sometimes there will be an intense dis-

play of flowers in the season before death.
- Honey-coloured toadstools (or fruiting bodies) that appear in the autumn close to infected wood or roots. They have a small ring underneath the cap. Although they are the easiest symptom to spot, they will not always be present.

At the base of the trunk, or below the ground, you will find:
- A white mycelium (or fungal growth) spreading around the base of the trunk underneath the bark, which will often be peeling back from the tree. This mycelium smells strongly of mushrooms.
- Rhizomorphs that resemble black or brown bootlaces. These rhizomorphs are the means that the fungus uses to colonise new areas. Although they give their name to the fungus, they are rarely seen, especially in the more aggressive and damaging species.

Control: Although the white mycelium on the trunk is the most reliable indicator of the presence of honey fungus, there is no single symptom that you can use to be sure of the diagnosis. If you suspect that you have honey fungus, the next step is to conduct a spore print. Collect a mature toadstool and place it indoors on a dark, flat surface. After about two hours, you should be able to see the white spores on the dark paper. The presence of these spores is another indicator of the existence of honey fungus – sometimes you will be able to see them coating the surface of other toadstools, where they are growing in a clump.

There is no chemical control for honey fungus – the only means of controlling its spread are physical ones. If you have honey fungus in your garden or orchard, you can stop it spreading by inserting a barrier, such as strong polythene or pond liner, into the soil to a depth of at least 50cm (1'8"). This is the maximum depth that the rhizomorphs will penetrate to. If you want to plant a tree in an area known to be at risk from honey fungus, you can also remove the topsoil to this depth and replace it with clean topsoil.

Where possible, the roots of trees that have died from honey fungus should be removed completely. If the roots are sizeable, you will need to employ a professional with a stump grinder. Good garden hygiene is also important. Don't leave wood lying around the garden, as you may unwittingly be helping to spread honey fungus. These methods of control can be time-consuming and expensive, but they can halt the spread of a deadly disease.

St Julien A, wild pear and hawthorn rootstocks are thought to have some resistance to honey fungus, so can be planted in areas affected by the disease.

Phytophthora

Symptoms: Phytophthora, also known as crown rot, is a soil- or water-borne fungus that causes rotting of tree roots, particularly in poorly drained soils. The first signs of phytophthora are sparse foliage that can also become discoloured. As the disease develops, whole branches can die, potentially leading to the death of the tree. Inspection of the roots will show that the finer roots have died and larger roots have a blackish colour. A similar discolouration, often with reddish tones, can be seen underneath the bark at the base of the trunk.

Control: There is no effective control for phytophthora once it has become established.

Discoloured and flaking bark caused by phytophthora.

Powdery mildew on apple foliage.

Dead wood, together with the roots and accompanying soil, should be removed from the garden. Before planting fruit trees in a damp area, it is worth considering improving the drainage, or using another location where the drainage is better. Some rootstocks, such as Quince A, have a degree of resistance to phytophthora. Amongst apple rootstocks, MM106 is the most susceptible.

Powdery mildew

This is a serious disease of apples and pears, but it can also affect other fruits.

Symptoms: Powdery mildew is a serious fungal disease of fruit trees, particularly damaging on apples. The upper surface of the leaves is covered with a white powdery coating, formed of the fungal spores. Affected leaves can become distorted, fail to reach full size, and eventually fall from the tree. Blossom can also be affected.

Control: The fungus overwinters on the tree and then reinfects leaves and blossom as they appear, and these primary infections give rise to secondary infections during the growing season. Breaking this cycle of infection is the key to halting the spread of the disease. Affected shoots can be pruned out during the summer. Pruning techniques that maintain an open canopy, allowing good air flow through the tree, help to keep powdery mildew under control. It is worst when the soil is dry and the air is warm and humid. Watering during dry spells and the application of a mulch will help to keep soil moisture levels high. Some varieties of fruit are resistant to powdery mildew (see Appendix 2.4 for apple varieties), and these should be planted where mildew is known to be a problem (more in the drier east of England than in the wetter and cooler regions of the British Isles).

If preventative and cultural methods are not effective, one to three applications of sulphur, between the time when pink buds are seen and small fruitlets are forming, will provide some control. This is particularly applicable to peaches and nectarines, which are vulnerable to a strain of mildew that affects the fruit more than the leaves. Seaweed, regularly applied through the summer, is also said to give some control of mildew.

Replant disease

Replant disease is known by many names, such as specific apple replant disease (or SARD for short), sick soil syndrome, specific replant disease, etc. Although it is often known as *apple* replant disease, it is not specific to apples, affecting most fruit trees to some extent. Replant disease is likely to be found when a fruit tree is planted very close to the site where an existing tree of the same kind grows or used to grow.

Symptoms: It is thought that replant disease is not really a disease at all, but a collection of fungi, bacteria and nematodes that live in the soil and co-exist quite happily with mature trees. When these trees die or are cut down, these pathogens continue to live on and around the decaying roots. When a new tree is planted in the same place, the pathogens can overwhelm its small roots, which are already under stress from being dug up and replanted. The result is a tree that never really establishes well, suffering from stunted growth and poor root development.

There is no effective cure once the tree has been planted. Fruit trees grafted on to dwarfing rootstocks are more likely to suffer heavily as a result of replant disease, because of their lack of vigour.

Control: Replant disease can remain in the soil for up to 15 years, gradually declining in effect, but there are various measures that can be taken to counteract the problem.

- Removing the roots of old trees. As with honey fungus (see page 134), this will remove the conditions that enable replant disease to perpetuate.
- Planting new trees as far away as possible from the site where an old tree grew.
- Planting different types of fruit tree. Consider whether you really need to plant an apple tree in the same place as the original one. Could you plant it somewhere else, or plant a cherry or a plum in that spot instead? Replacing pome fruits (apples, pears, medlars and quinces) with stone fruits (plums, cherries, peaches, apricots and nectarines), and vice versa, is good practice.
- Planting fruit trees in pots. This can be worthwhile, even if it is a temporary measure while the replant disease subsides. After a few years, the tree can be planted into the open ground.
- Changing the soil. If you really do need to plant in the same place, you can change the soil for clean uninfected soil. Although this might sound easy, it is likely to take longer than you think because of the amount of soil that you need to replace. The clean soil needs to extend well beyond the planting hole in both depth and breadth.
- Adding mycorrhizal fungi to the soil at planting time. This is thought to lessen the effects of replant disease.

Scab

Scab is a potentially serious disease of apples and pears.

Symptoms: This disease is easily recognisable by the black-brown spots that develop on both the leaves and fruit. These spots start to develop early in the growing season. In a serious infection, the spots will coalesce, causing severe damage to leaves, which may fall prematurely. Likewise, the spots on the fruit can merge to form lesions that can split and provide a site for other diseases to infect. Lesions can also develop on the bark: these are known as wood scab. The disease is particularly prevalent in the wetter areas of the UK and in damp summers.

Control: The most effective way of dealing with scab is to use resistant varieties. Even in susceptible areas, scab-free apples can be grown if the right varieties are planted. Local varieties of apple will often carry more resistance than nationally known ones.

Scab overwinters on fallen leaves beneath the trees. In spring, the infection is transferred from the decaying leaves on the ground to the young leaves unfurling on the tree. Interrupting this cycle of infection can reduce the incidence of disease – so, for example, collecting the fallen leaves in the autumn will remove the source of infection. A mower that collects the mowings is the most efficient way to do this, although raking up the leaves can be just as effective. Alternatively, a rotary mower that chops up the leaves will help, because they are in a form more able to be incorporated into the soil by worms and other invertebrates, although it won't prevent infection.

Avoiding a damp microclimate helps to prevent scab. Long grass holds a lot more moisture than short grass. Tall hedges and surrounding trees can inhibit air flow. Laying a hedge surrounding an orchard can make a surprising difference, by reducing both shade and moisture in an orchard. Correct pruning techniques will allow plenty of air movement through a tree. Wood scab can be removed by pruning.

If all else fails, there are organic sprays that inhibit the spread of scab. Bordeaux mixture and sulphur-based fungicides are effective

A bad case of scab, seen here on Brown's Apple.

against scab and will also give some incidental control against canker. However, these sprays are not without their problems. Some varieties of apple are known to be 'sulphur-shy', that is, they react badly to sulphur sprays. Copper sprays can cause a build-up of copper in the soil, and copper is a heavy metal that is harmful to worms and other soil life. As a result, it is allowed organically only on a restricted basis. More detailed information about using copper and sulphur sprays can be found in *Organic Apple Production* by Garden Organic (see Resources).

There have been reports that seaweed, used as a foliar spray, reduces the incidence of scab. Seaweed also provides trace elements essential for healthy growth.

Silver leaf

Silver leaf is a serious disease of the stone fruits (plums, peaches, nectarines, cherries and apricots), but it can also affect apples.

Symptoms: Unsurprisingly, the main symptom of silver leaf is the leaves of a tree taking on a silvery hue. The culprit is a fungal disease that particularly affects members of the *Prunus* genus, including apricots and cherries, and is especially troublesome on plums. It can, however, affect apples as well. Whole orchards have been grubbed up because of silver leaf.

The silvering of leaves starts in one small area of a tree, but spreads fairly quickly to other parts of the same tree. It is quickly followed by the dieback of affected branches. In most cases, this dying back of branches will continue across the tree if no control measures are taken, often resulting in the death of the tree. Infected branches will show a foxy brown stain in the wood, which is revealed if they are cut with a pruning saw.

Dead or dying wood can play host to the fruiting bodies of the fungus: these are like overlapping tiles, 2.5-10cm (1-4") across, starting off dark purple in colour, and later becoming brown.

Silver leaf, seen here on a plum tree.

The silvering of leaves and dieback can be confused with other problems of plum trees if found in isolation, but when found together they can be taken as indicators of silver leaf disease. The silvering of leaves may also be diagnosed as false silver leaf – whereby the symptom is caused by drought stress, malnutrition or particularly hot weather. False silver leaf will not show the signs of branch dieback or fruiting bodies.

The dieback of branches can also be attributed to bacterial canker, but in this case the symptoms of silver leaves and fruiting bodies will be absent.

Control: The fungus that causes silver leaf disease is spread by wind and rain splash and on pruning tools. Where silver leaf is present, careful hygiene when pruning is crucial. All cuts should be left as clean as possible. Large cuts that are not entirely smooth should have any jagged parts removed with a sharp pruning knife, and wound paint should be painted on the wounds as soon as possible after the cuts are made.

Most wound paints act by sealing the pruning cut against spores, as well as having a fungicidal effect. There has been much debate on this matter in recent times, because it was realised that although they offer protection, wound paints could also seal in pathogens. There are also products based on seaweed that do not seal the cut, but also have fungicidal properties. If you do use a wound paint, it is vital to apply it as soon as you have made the pruning cut – don't wait until you have finished pruning the whole tree.

Pruning tools should be disinfected regularly, particularly while pruning infected trees. Dip the blades of tools in garden disinfectant, or, where this is difficult, wipe with a rag soaked in disinfectant. Also, all pruning should take place between May and September, with the exception of removing broken branches. These should be removed as soon as they are seen, cutting back to a junction with another branch.

Some varieties show resistance to silver leaf, and the rootstock Pixy also has some resistance to the disease. In some areas where silver leaf is known to be a problem, it is worth planting resistant varieties on Pixy rootstock to gain the highest level of resistance. In such areas, with a high level of spores in the air, more care should be taken to keep the disease at bay.

Although careful orchard hygiene is important in preventing the spread of the disease, once it has been found on your trees, cutting out infected branches is the only means of control. You will need to cut back 10-15cm (4-6") beneath the point where no further staining is seen in the wood, preferably to a junction with another branch. It is important to remove all infected wood from the site, or burn it as soon as possible. Once silver leaf has been found, it is vital to act swiftly: this is a disease that can easily spread from tree to tree if care is not taken to prevent its spread.

A fungus called *Trichoderma viride* has successfully been used as a biological control for silver leaf, but is not widely available. See Appendix 4.3 for details of resistant plum cultivars.

Other problems with fruit trees

Aside from pests and disease, there are other factors that can cause fruit trees to perform poorly. The weather often plays its part, but cultural problems can also be significant.

Frost damage

While fruit trees are normally hardy, frost can cause significant damage to fruit tree blossom. Early-flowering fruits, such as peaches and plums, are particularly at risk of frost damage. Pears flower during April and early May, so are likely to suffer from frost damage in some years, especially in locations prone to late frost. In colder regions or frost pockets, it may be necessary to take preventative action – covering the blossom with fleece or other material to protect it. The warmth of a wall, especially where the heat of a house comes into play, can make a big difference in preventing frost damage. Temperatures usually need to be below -1.5°C (29°F) to cause significant damage, depending on the stage of blossom. In the early stages of blossom opening, however, it will take lower temperatures to cause harm. Where late frosts are likely, varieties that flower late or have frost-resistant flowers can be planted in order to improve the chance of success (see Appendices 2.1, 3.1 and 4.2). Apples such as Falstaff or Worcester Pearmain, plums such as Czar or Belle de Louvain and pears such as Beurré Hardy or Jargonelle have flowers resistant to frost damage. In colder areas of the UK, some fruit may need to be grown in pots, which can be placed under cover during the coldest parts of the winter. If frost damage is suspected, look for the tell-tale signs of black or brown tissue that indicate where damage has occurred. Fruitlets affected by a late frost

Damage to blossom, caused by frost.

may develop a russetted appearance, with the skin becoming distorted or corky.

Trees that are not fruiting

If you have a tree that is not fruiting, the way to discover where the problem lies is to observe the tree carefully over the course of the year – watching the process that starts with the blossom, then moves on through pollination and the development of the fruit. Ask yourself the following questions.

- Are there flowers on the tree in the spring?
- Are the flowers successfully pollinated? (See Chapter 3.)
- Are young fruitlets formed?
- Do these fruitlets continue their successful development?

Once you have identified which stage of the process is failing, you can continue your detective work. For example, if you find that the fruitlets are falling from the tree, open them up to see if there is an insect pest inside. There is usually a simple reason why a tree doesn't fruit, which can easily be remedied, but correct diagnosis is vital.

The first question is whether the tree has sufficient flowers to produce a worthwhile crop. There can be several reasons why a tree might not have many flowers.

The over-pruned tree

Pruning too hard can encourage a lot of vegetative growth at the expense of fruiting potential. This is one of the most common causes of poor fruiting. If your tree looks something like the one in the photo below, where excessive upright growth begins to dominate, then over-hard pruning is the likely cause.

Unfortunately, this kind of neglect is not easy to correct. Patience is necessary in order to break the cycle of overstimulation producing vegetative growth. It is best to prune such trees in the summer, because summer pruning stimulates less growth. The upright vegetative shoots will, in time, become normal fruiting growth, but at this stage there are far too many of them. Between a third and a half can be removed each year

until you are left with a few that can be allowed to grow on to form new branches. This process will take several years. It is preferable to make just a few larger cuts when pruning in this way, rather than many smaller ones, because each new cut will result in more new shoots emerging. Cuts should be made low down on each branch so as to remove them entirely.

The over-vigorous tree

If you have a tree that is vigorous and unproductive, but not as a result of hard pruning, there are other remedies to consider.

- Root pruning and bark ringing were once commonly used but have now gone out of fashion. This may be because they are either time-consuming or potentially harmful. They are methods of shocking the tree into production.
- Stop using any high-nitrogen feed.
- Grow grass right up to the trunk of the tree. It might seem strange, but grass can compete with a tree for nutrients and

Strong upright growth like this is usually a sign of pruning a tree too hard.

water to such an extent that it can interfere with the tree's vigour, particularly in the case of smaller trees.

- Move to summer rather than winter pruning. Winter pruning has the effect of encouraging growth, whereas summer pruning is more likely to encourage fruit production.
- Use a feed high in potash, such as wood ash or comfrey – feeding with nitrogen encourages leaf growth, while potash encourages flowering.

The starved, unproductive tree

The starved tree is almost the opposite of the over-vigorous tree: looking spindly and putting on little new growth, it will often be found growing in grass, which is competing for water and nutrients. Young trees and those growing on dwarfing rootstocks are

An stunted pear tree, with grass growing up to the trunk.

particularly susceptible to competition from grass and weeds. Ideally, an area around the base of the tree, approaching the size of the crown of the tree, should be kept clear of grass. This can be achieved by the use of a mulch such as compost or bark chippings, or a systemic herbicide such as glyphosate applied with care during the growing season. Hand weeding can be effective, but in my experience is not usually kept up well enough. If this is the case, a mulch mat is a suitable alternative. These are now available in a range of different materials, including biodegradable ones such as wool or linseed fibre, or more permanent ones such as woven polypropylene. You can buy these ready-made in a suitable shape to fix around a tree, or cut them yourself from a roll of landscape fabric. It is best to avoid impermeable materials such as polythene (black plastic), because they will not allow the passage of water or plant feed to the roots. See Chapter 6, page 83, for more about mulch mats.

Having removed the grass, attention can be paid to feeding the tree. A balanced, general-purpose fertiliser, such as chicken pellets or manure, will assist the tree in putting on more growth.

See Chapter 17, page 314, for details of how to prune older, neglected trees.

Other reasons for a lack of flowers

Bullfinches (see page 126) are particularly fond of eating fruit buds during the winter, when food is scarce. They can reportedly eat over 30 buds per minute. Fortunately for the fruit grower, bullfinches have become scarcer over the last few decades, and what was once a common problem is much less so now. If your trees are troubled by them, there is no easy solution. As with many problems, the most effective remedy is a combination of visual deterrents, such as CDs, and physical barriers, such as black cotton or netting. If you use netting, be aware that birds can become trapped inside the net.

Heavy shade can also reduce the number of flowers. Keeping hedges or other trees under control can help, whereas if the shade comes from a building, it may just be that your tree was planted in the wrong place.

With a few exceptions, fruit trees do need a sunny position.

Canker is a fungal or bacterial disease (see pages 130 and 132) that kills branches by girdling them and halting the flow of sap. It can reduce the number of flowers when it affects the young growth on which the flowers would normally occur. Planting varieties resistant to canker is important, while subsequent control is normally by pruning.

COMMON FEATURES THAT ARE NOT PROBLEMATIC

There are some common features of fruit trees that can be mistaken for problems. The most frequently encountered are lichens. It is perfectly normal for these to be found on trees, particularly in damp locations. In fact, you should be pleased, as abundant lichens are a sign of clean air. The only drawback is that they can harbour overwintering pests or eggs – but then these will find nooks and crannies on your trees to hide in anyway.

The other 'symptom' that you are likely to come across is adventitious roots. These form where the tree attempts to grow roots from the trunk. The young roots start to form, but soon die back when it is realised that this is not actually a suitable place to grow. However, they can look like a worrying disease to if you have not seen them before. They are most often found on apple trees and are completely harmless.

Lichen growing on an apple tree.

Adventitious roots on an apple tree.

Problems affecting blossom

Returning to your observation of the tree during the spring and summer, once you have seen that the tree does have sufficient flowers that are being pollinated by bees, there still various other problems that can interfere with pollination.

Blossom wilt (see page 131): This is a fungal disease that can affect most fruit trees; the symptoms are the flowers and surrounding leaves wilting and turning brown.

Apple blossom weevil (see right): The larvae of this weevil hatch inside the flower and eat the fruit bud, which fails to develop properly and has a 'capped' appearance.

Frost (see page 141): Frost can cause significant damage to fruit tree blossom. If the blossom is severely damaged by frost, young fruitlets will not develop. If the damage is less severe, the fruit will develop but, in the case of pears, will be distorted; in apples, russeted and cracked. The planting of late flowering cultivars or those with frost-resistant blossoms can help significantly (see Appendices 2.1, 3.1 and 4.2).

Problems of the developing fruit

Once pollination has occurred, and the fruit is developing, there are still many pitfalls that can occur.

Insects such as the pear midge (see page 151) or apple sawfly (see page 147) can still cause fruitlets to drop off the tree.

Fungi such as mildew (see page 136) or scab (see page 137) can cause damage to the developing fruit, but careful observation will enable you to spot such problems and apply the appropriate control to nip it in the bud.

Although the possibilities for failure can appear daunting, it is important to remember that most fruits make it through unscathed, and, where a problem is discovered, there is usually a remedy for it.

Problems of apple trees

Apple trees play host to a variety of different pests and diseases, some of which can cause serious problems. Vigilance is the key to keeping your trees healthy. Most problems are easy to overcome if you catch them early.

Pests of apple trees

The **apple sawfly**, **codling moth** (see page 147) and **winter moth** (see page 128) are perhaps the most damaging of the insect pests, but the severity of an attack will vary from year to year and place to place.

By pecking ripening fruit, **birds** (see page 126) cause damage that other pests and diseases can exploit. **Aphids** (see page 125), the **light brown apple moth** (see page 127) and **red spider mite** (see page 128) can also cause problems.

The pests that are specific to apples are detailed below.

Apple blossom weevil

Symptoms: The apple blossom weevil spends the winter months hidden under leaf debris or in hedges or trees, becoming active on warm days from February onwards, when it goes looking for the buds of apple blossom. The adult weevil injects an egg through the side of a developing bud. The larvae hatch and eat the fruit bud, which fails to develop properly. The blossom becomes 'capped', i.e. the flowers remain closed and the petals turn brown. If you pull the blossom

Damage to blossom caused by the apple blossom weevil.

Corky scars on a developing apple, caused by the apple capsid bug.

apart, you will find a creamy-white bug around 5mm (0.2") long inside. A severe infestation can cause a considerable loss of yield, particularly in a year when there is not a lot of blossom.

Control: Control is not easy. Picking off infected buds can be helpful if you have small trees. Pyrethrum applied between bud break and mouse ear (the early stages of fruit bud development) can be effective, but the difficulty is in knowing that the weevils are present in order to make it worth spraying. Spraying is only worthwhile to disrupt a cycle of heavy infestations. Tying sacking or cardboard around branches in early summer is said to trap weevils, which can then be destroyed. Good winter hygiene in the garden, such as clearing up leaves can help; this can also help to reduce scab reinfection.

Apple capsid bug
Symptoms: The nymphs of the capsid bug feed on the young leaves and fruitlets, lead-

ing to small holes on the leaves and fruits. These are like puncture marks and can be surrounded by reddish markings. The fruits can develop raised corky scars. Severely affected shoots will be distorted and will not open properly. Regular inspections, particularly in late spring, can reveal infestations at an early stage.

Control: Maintaining a balanced ecosystem that includes habitats to encourage natural predators can be helpful; for example, wildflower margins will encourage insect-eating birds. While light attacks of this pest will cause little damage and can be tolerated, spraying with pyrethrum can help control more serious attacks. However, this can also kill beneficial insects, so it is important to spray in a targeted fashion. Pyrethrum is best applied at pink bud stage or at petal fall. Spraying for capsid bugs is more likely to be necessary if there has been a problem in the previous year. Removing suckers and long grass from the base of trees helps to reduce the favoured nesting sites of capsid bugs.

Apple sawfly

Symptoms: Apple sawfly is a serious pest of apple trees. The most characteristic symptom is the ribbon-like scars to be found around the bottom of affected apples. These are caused by the larvae of the apple sawfly burrowing under the skin of the apple to feed on the flesh. The eggs are laid on the blossoms in late spring, and the larvae hatch from these eggs and burrow into the developing fruit. Affected fruits will often drop from the tree during June and July. The larvae then burrow into the soil, where they overwinter, emerging again to pupate the following spring. It is possible to observe the eggs and the development of the larvae with the aid of a magnifying glass.

The ribbon-like scar produced by the apple sawfly, together with its frass (droppings) on the leaf below.

Control: Maintaining a diverse and healthy ecosystem will encourage the natural predators of apple sawfly. Long grass and wood piles are specific habitats of, for example, ground beetles, which will help this process. Picking up the affected fruitlets when they fall will remove the larvae that are contained within them. However, the larvae soon leave the apple to take up home in the soil, so covering the soil with a tarpaulin is a more efficient way of interrupting the lifecycle of this pest.

If you want to spray because of a heavy infestation the previous year, pyrethrum sprayed when the petals are falling will give some control. A second spray can be applied one week later. Once this window of opportunity has passed, spraying will be ineffective because the larvae will be inside the developing fruitlets. Spraying in the evening or in cloudy conditions will help to avoid damaging bees.

Codling moth

Symptoms: Like apple sawfly, codling moth is a grub that bores into the flesh of developing fruit, eating as it goes. The damage caused by the codling moth is not as obvious as that caused by the apple sawfly, lacking the tell-tale ribbon scars. Sometimes it is only when the apple is cut open that the codling moth larva, a small white caterpillar with a brown head, is detected. Careful observation can reveal a small hole with a red or purple discolouration; this is where the larva has eaten its way out. After leaving the apple, the caterpillar will look for loose bark or another hiding place to overwinter. The codling moth is most common in southern England and the Midlands, and most active in warm, dry conditions.

An apple damaged by a codling moth larva. The visible damage is the exit hole of the larva, surrounded by its frass.

Control: It is possible to spray against the codling moth, using pyrethrum or *Bacillus thuringiensis* (Bt), but control is limited, partly because of the critical importance of spraying at the right time. As a result, most gardeners opt for the limited control that is achieved by using pheromone traps. These are sticky traps, sold as codling moth traps, which contain the pheromone scent that attracts the male moths. They can be used to monitor the moths' population, so that the right time to spray can be chosen, but they also trap enough male moths to reduce breeding and control their numbers. Adult moths are most active during June and July, but can be found throughout the summer. Codling moth is a difficult pest to control – whether traps or spraying is your chosen method, it is vital to follow the manufacturer's instructions carefully to ensure that it is effective.

Woolly aphid

Symptoms: The woolly aphid is an easy pest to spot during the summer months – think cotton wool. The woolly coating is excreted by the pink aphids in order to protect them. During the spring, they are usually seen on rough bark at the base of branches. As summer comes, they move to feed on the sap of young shoots. Where they congregate, galls can form; these can then split to let in fungal diseases, such as canker.

Control: Woolly aphids multiply rapidly during the spring and summer, so early control is vital in reducing numbers. Because they are easily spotted and not very mobile, spot treatment is usually effective. Brushing colonies with a paintbrush dipped in water and detergent will keep them under control.

The methods discussed on pages 125-6 for dealing with aphids, such as attracting natural predators and encouraging a healthy ecosystem, are equally relevant for woolly aphids. Ladybirds, lacewings and hoverflies are all natural predators of woolly aphids.

The distinctive woolly coating that woolly aphids use to protect themselves.

Diseases of apple trees

In addition to the minor diseases specific to apples mentioned below, apples are susceptible to nearly all the general diseases of fruit trees described earlier in this chapter. Some of these can cause serious problems that will adversely affect both growth and yields. **Powdery mildew** (see page 136) and **canker** (see page 132) can cause severe damage to the foliage, while **brown rot** (see page 132) can ruin fruit, either on the tree or in storage. **Scab** (see page 137) is capable of causing widespread damage to the fruit and the leaves, particularly in wetter areas and on susceptible varieties. Fortunately it is possible to avoid the worst effects of these disease by planting resistant varieties (see Appendices 2.3, 2.4 and 3.3). Apples can contract **fireblight** (see page 133) and **silver leaf** (see page 139), but the effect is less devastating than it can be on plums or pears. In addition, **blossom wilt** (see page 131), **coral spot** (see page 133), **honey fungus** (see page 134), **phytophthora** (see page 135) and **replant disease** (see page 137) can all affect apple trees.

Apple sooty mould and fly speck

Symptoms: Both of these diseases are fungi that cause superficial discolouration of the skin of apples. Apple sooty mould is characterised by black blotches, while fly speck looks like sooty fingerprints on the surface of the apple. These two diseases are grouped together here because they both cause superficial marks that can look alarming; however, they are not serious because they can be wiped off to leave clean fruit.

Control: Both fungi thrive in cool, damp conditions. Encouraging good airflow through the orchard and through individual trees will help to keep these diseases under control. Wiping apples with a damp cloth will remove the surface marks. It is worth doing this at harvest time if the apples are going to be stored, because the fungus will continue to develop during storage.

Other problems of apple trees

There are two cultural problems that apple trees suffer from. Both are linked to the supply of water to the tree.

Apple fruit split

Symptoms: The fruit develops splits in the skin that can also penetrate into the flesh of the apple. If this occurs when the fruit is still young, the damage may heal over, leaving a corky patch on the surface. If the fruit is older, it is likely that secondary infection will occur, particularly caused by brown rot (see page 132).

Control: Splitting is caused by sudden growth when rain follows a dry spell. Mulching trees and keeping them watered during dry spells will help to mitigate the problem.

Apple fruit split.

Bitter pit

Symptoms: Bitter pit is characterised by ginger-to-brown spots in the flesh of the apple. These can also show as small round, sunken spots on the surface of affected apples. As the name implies, they can give a bitter taste to the fruit. Sometimes the symptoms will only develop during storage. Some varieties, such as Newton Wonder, are more susceptible to bitter pit; it is usually found in large apples and on trees that are cropping heavily.

Control: This problem is caused by a deficiency of calcium in the apple. There may not be a deficiency of calcium in the soil, but a difficulty for trees with large apples and heavy crops to take up calcium during dry conditions. Avoid feeding with high-nitrogen feeds and mulch trees well in order to preserve soil moisture. Spraying with calcium chloride is an organically acceptable method of providing calcium for the tree to absorb. This should be carried out from June to September.

Problems of pear trees

Pears are susceptible to many of the same diseases as apples, but fortunately these can be largely overcome by planting resistant varieties or using natural methods. There are a number of different insect pests that are specific to pears, with pear midge being one of the most damaging.

Pests of pear trees

Pears share some pests with apple trees, such as the **codling moth** (see page 147) and **winter moth** (see page 128), but these tend to effect pears less severely. **Pear and cherry slugworm** (see page 127) is also a less serious problem on pears than it is on cherries.

Some **birds** will eat pears as they approach ripening. They can be deterred with pieces of cardboard placed over individual fruits (see page 126). **Wasps and hornets** (see page 128) are also tempted by the ripening fruits.

The following pests are specific to pears.

Damage to an apple caused by bitter pit.

A large colony of the pear bedstraw aphid.

Pear bedstraw aphid

Symptoms: These are large pink-grey aphids that can colonise pear trees in large numbers, causing leaf-curl and discolouration of the leaves. In midsummer they retreat to bedstraw plants, a native wildflower.

Control:. Spraying a winter wash (see page 126) can be helpful if this aphid is persistent.

Pear leaf blister mite

Symptoms: From mid- to late spring, pear leaves develop yellow or dark pink blotches or blisters that group together either side of the midrib. By midsummer, these blotches become darker. They are much smaller than the blackish lesions caused by scab (see page 137), which tend to coalesce, becoming large markings on the leaf. Pear leaf blister mite is caused by a microscopic gall mite that lives within the leaves. A severe attack can cause premature leaf fall.

Control: Affected leaves can be picked off and removed from small trees. Luckily, this pest, although unsightly, does not have a major impact, so tolerating it is usually the best approach.

Pear midge

Symptoms: The young fruitlets appear healthy while first developing, but soon start to turn black from the bottom of the fruit upwards. Before long, the affected fruits will drop from the tree; inside are white and orange maggots about 2mm long. They emerge from the fruit, making their way into the soil.

Control: The individual fruitlets can be picked off, but an easier approach is to lay a tarpaulin under the tree to catch the fruits as they drop. They can then be removed. Keeping poultry under the trees will keep this pest (and others) under control.

A leaf affected by pear leaf blister mite.

A pear fruitlet damaged by pear midges.

Pear sucker
Symptoms: This insect is similar to a small aphid, both in appearance and effect. It is dark green and about 2mm long and excretes honeydew, which in turn gives rise to sooty mould.

Control: As for aphids (see page 125).

Diseases of pear trees

Scab (see page 137) and **canker** (see page 132) are serious problems, particularly in wetter regions and on susceptible varieties. Choosing resistant cultivars is the most effective method of combating these diseases. **Fireblight** (see page 133) is a severe problem in parts of southern England, where it is best to plant resistant varieties. The following diseases can also affect pears: **blossom wilt** (see page 131), **coral spot** (see page 133), **brown rot** (see page 132), **honey fungus** (see page 134) and **replant disease** (see page 137).

The diseases specific to pear trees are as follows.

The adult pear sucker and its eggs.

Stony pit virus on a pear.

Pear stony pit virus
Symptoms: Affected fruits appear knobbly on the outside. Inside are areas of hard flesh caused by dead stone cells. The symptoms are usually confined to one branch of a tree. The symptoms can be confused with boron deficiency (see below), but this is characterised by brown spots in the flesh and is not confined to just one branch.

Control: There is no cultural control, but some cultivars are more susceptible than others. Beurré Hardy, Doyenné du Comice and Winter Nellis are all susceptible, while Williams' Bon Chrétien has some resistance.

Other problems

There is one nutrient deficiency – boron – to which pears are particularly susceptible. (For general information about nutrient deficiencies, see page 122.)

Boron deficiency
Symptoms: Fruits are distorted, with an unpleasant texture caused by dead cells that are brown in colour. The tree may lack vigour and even show dieback.

A pear affected by boron deficiency.

that is nearly ripe can suffer from rain damage caused by heavy rain and hail. Aside from covering the fruit, there is little that can be done.

Pests of plum trees

Wasps and hornets (see page 128) can be particularly troublesome on plums. Providing alternative food sources hanging in the tree is the only effective control. **Winter moth** (see page 128) is less troublesome on plums than it is on apples.

Red spider mite (see page 128) can be a problem in dry summers. **Bullfinches** (see Birds, page 126) can also be a nuisance, eating the buds in the winter. The **light brown apple moth** (see page 127) can also affect plum trees.

Control: Boron is a trace element that is easily leached from the soil by heavy rainfall, particularly on light soils. A deficiency can be corrected by the use of borax; it can be added to the soil before planting or sprayed on to trees with a wetting agent. The use of compost, manure or seaweed as a mulch will help to retain minerals in the soil.

Problems of plum trees

Although a range of pests and diseases affect plum trees, bacterial canker and silver leaf are by far the most serious. Both can cause severe problems if left unchecked. However, careful hygiene in the orchard will make the spread of these diseases less likely. Pruning in the summer months is vital to keeping disease at bay.

Frost damage (see page 141) can be a major problem in cold springs, because plums flower comparatively early in the year. Fruit

The following pests are specific to plum trees.

Aphids

There are two types of aphid specific to plums: the **plum leaf-curling aphid** and the **mealy plum aphid**. Plum leaf-curling aphids are 2mm-long green insects with white skins, which can be seen on the bark after they have been discarded. These aphids cause damage in the spring before migrating to other plants. Mealy plum aphids are lighter in colour and are present from late spring onwards. Both types can cause significant damage to young trees if not controlled.

The methods described on pages 125-6 should prove sufficient to control them; a winter wash will be worthwhile for aphid species whose eggs overwinter on the trees. Some varieties of plum, such as Anna Spath and Victoria, are resistant to plum leaf-curling aphid.

Mealy plum aphids, together with their skins that have been sloughed.

Plum leaf gall mite

Symptoms: Light green swellings or galls appear on the leaves of the plum family, particularly towards the edges, in early summer.

Control: These swellings are caused by tiny gall mites, which suck sap from the leaves. There is no effective control, but fortunately the mites cause little damage.

Plum moth

Symptoms: It is the caterpillars of the plum moth that cause the problem, by eating their way into maturing plums. These pinky-white caterpillars, with brown heads, feed on the flesh of the plum, leaving their brown excrement behind, before leaving the plum to hide elsewhere on the tree. Flattened portions of a plum often point to where the caterpillar has

The swellings caused by plum leaf gall mite.

A plum damaged by the plum moth caterpillar.

left the fruit. Affected fruits tend to ripen early and drop from the tree. Plum moth caterpillars are most common in the south of England.

Control: Pheromone traps hung from every third tree will give some degree of control by interrupting breeding habits. The traps should be put out in June and left up until August.

Plum sawfly

Symptoms: Plum sawfly is a similar pest to plum moth, except that it feeds on the developing plums earlier in the season. The larvae, which look similar to plum moth caterpillars, eat their way into the developing fruits in the spring, leaving round holes on the surface. Black excrement may also be present. The plums fall from the tree during May and June.

Control: Placing a sheet or tarpaulin under the tree will catch the fruitlets that drop, together with some of the larvae before they head for the soil, where they overwinter.

Diseases of plum trees

Although **silver leaf** (see page 139) and **bacterial canker** (see page 130) pose the most serious problems, other diseases are also worth paying attention to. **Blossom wilt** (see page 131) can be a serious problem on plums. Some varieties are resistant to this disease – Czar and Jefferson being the most well known. **Brown rot** (see page 132) is a very common disease of plums; as with blossom wilt, Czar and Jefferson are resistant varieties.

Powdery mildew (see page 136) is less of a problem on plums than on apple and pear trees, but can still be troublesome in dry

areas, or where plum trees are under stress. As with most fruit trees, **honey fungus** (see page 134) can cause serious problems. The plum rootstock St Julien A shows some resistance to this disease. **Replant disease** (see page 137) and **phytophthora** (see page 135) may also cause problems.

The following diseases are specific to plum trees.

Plum rust

Symptoms: The upper surfaces of leaves are covered in yellow spots during late summer, while the undersides of the same leaves are home to the rust-coloured spores. In severe cases, the spots coalesce, the spores blacken and the affected leaves fall prematurely from the tree.

Control: These symptoms are caused by a fungus that is worse in damp conditions. Usually, this is not a serious disease, but it can build up over a few seasons if left uncontrolled. Where the problem is severe, interrupting the life cycle of the fungus will give some control. One method of doing this is to rake up and remove the fallen leaves in order to prevent reinfection the following year. It's also worth looking out for the same disease on anemones – removing the anemones can help lessen the problem on plum trees. Victoria is a cultivar that is particularly susceptible to this disease.

Problems of cherry trees

Although cherries, like other members of the *Prunus* genus, are susceptible to bacterial canker and silver leaf, they are not usually badly affected. It is birds, blackfly and the weather that pose the biggest threats.

Pests of cherry trees

The light brown apple moth (see page 127) is a major pest of cherry trees, and **birds** (see page 126) can also cause significant damage, necessitating control with netting. **Pear and cherry slugworm** (see page 127) can damage the leaves of cherry trees. The caterpillars of the **winter moth** (see page 128) eat the leaves, blossom and developing fruits.

The only pest specific to cherry trees is **cherry blackfly**.

Cherry blackfly

Symptoms: This is a particularly troublesome form of aphid. These small black insects colonise the underside of cherry leaves in late spring. They cause the leaves to curl, which helps to protect them from predators and sprays. Later in the summer, leaves will turn brown and shrivel. Repeated cycles of infection can cause dieback on young branches.

Control: Cherry blackfly is a difficult pest to control, because it is fairly resistant to soft soap sprays, so it might also need a winter wash to provide effective control (see page 126).

Diseases of cherry trees

Bacterial canker (see page 130) and **silver leaf** (see page 139) can cause problems on cherries, although they are not as serious on cherries as they are on plums. In wetter areas, it is worth planting resistant varieties. **Phytophthora** (see page 135) can also be a problem in wetter areas and on poorly drained soils.

The following diseases can affect cherry trees: **Honey fungus** (see page 134), **blossom wilt** (see page 131), **brown rot** (see page 132) and **replant disease** (see page 137).

Other problems of cherry trees

Cherries are sensitive to imbalances of cultural conditions. Poor drainage or soil structure can cause problems, as can nutritional excesses. Climatic conditions can also affect cherries adversely, with cold winds and frost affecting pollination, and heavy rain and hail leading to the risk of **fruit split**.

Fruit split

Symptoms: Cherries are particularly prone to splitting as they ripen, often leading to the fruit going mouldy.

Control: Ensuring a regular supply of water to the roots helps to keep this problem under control. However, heavy rain or hail, just before harvest time, can break the skin of cherries. Placing a cover, such as tarpaulin, over the fruit is the only way to prevent this, so it is worth keeping a close eye on the weather forecast. Some varieties, including Lapins and Noir de Guben, are resistant to splitting.

The early stages of cherry blackfly infestation.

Problems of peaches and nectarines

Frost damage (see page 141) is likely to be a problem, but by far the biggest nuisance on peaches and nectarines is peach leaf curl. Fortunately, winter protection helps protect against both these problems.

Pests of peach and nectarine trees

Insect pests are not usually troubling; the main problems are likely to come from **birds** (see page 126) and **wasps and hornets** (see page 128), which are, understandably, fond of peaches. **Aphids** (see page 125) can occasionally cause problems.

Earwigs can also be troublesome on peach and nectarine trees.

Earwigs
Symptoms: These creatures can burrow into the fruit, particularly when it has split.

Control: The simplest method of control is to make alternative homes for the earwigs.

Screwed-up balls of newspaper, hung in the tree and kept moist, will attract them. Rolled-up corrugated cardboard will have the same effect. Every so often, remove the earwigs from their habitat, or remove the habitat and start again.

Diseases of peach and nectarine trees

Although peaches and nectarines are susceptible to other diseases, keeping **peach leaf curl** (see below) at bay is likely to be the main difficulty. If it is not kept under control, the infection will slowly worsen, to the stage where the tree may have to be removed. Peaches and nectarines can also be affected by **honey fungus** (see page 134), **phytophthora** (see page 135), **replant disease** (see page 137), **powdery mildew** (see page 136) and **silver leaf** (see page 139).

Peach leaf curl
Symptoms: This is a fungal disease that causes serious damage to peach and nectarine trees. In the spring, affected leaves begin to take on a puckered or blistered appearance.

An earwig on a peach.

The red blisters characteristic of peach leaf curl.

The blistered areas soon become pinky-red. Later on, the fungal threads break through the blister, revealing a grey, felty surface, from which the spores spread. The most affected leaves turn brown and fall from the tree. A second flush of foliage usually develops, remaining free of the symptoms. The skin of nectarines can become infected, showing rough, bumpy batches. The vigour of trees can become severely weakened by repeated infections.

Control: Once a tree has become infected, it is too late to control the course of the infection for that season. The only thing that can be done is to remove the infected leaves from the garden. In the longer term, there are two main methods of controlling peach leaf curl: covering the tree during the winter (see Chapter 14, page 261) and spraying with Bordeaux mixture.

Covering the tree is the preferable method, partly because it is the most effective and also because it avoids the need to spray. It is difficult to control the disease by spraying alone, but it can be a useful adjunct to covering the tree. The timing of spraying is important: it should be done in late autumn and late winter, just before the flowers open.

Feeding trees and keeping them in good health will make them less susceptible to attack. Seaweed sprays can be useful for this. Some people swear by planting garlic near their trees as a means of keeping peach leaf curl away. Garlic sprays have also been reported to have an ameliorative effect.

Some varieties show resistance to peach leaf curl. Avalon Pride is a new introduction that is more resistant than any other. However, it is not immune to the disease, so don't make the mistake of thinking that you won't need to take any precautions.

Problems of apricot trees

Apricots are relatively untroubled by pests and diseases. They are prone to **frost damage** (see page 141), because they flower so early, so providing protection early in the year is important.

They suffer little damage from insect pests, but **birds** (see page 126) and **wasps and hornets** (see page 128) can be troublesome. **Aphids** (see page 125) are mostly a problem on young trees.

Bacterial canker (see page 130), **blossom wilt** (see page 131) and **brown rot** (see page 132) can all be troublesome on apricots. Goldcot and Moorpark are varieties that show some resistance to brown rot. **Peach leaf curl** (see page 157) is sometimes found on apricots, but is much less of a problem than it is on peaches and nectarines. Apricots can also be affected by **honey fungus** (see page 134), **phytophthora** (see page 135), **replant disease** (see page 137), **powdery mildew** (see page 136) and **silver leaf** (see page 139).

The only disease specific to apricots is **dieback**.

Dieback

Symptoms: Leaves wilt and turn yellow, followed by the death of the branch.

Control: This condition is thought to be caused by a combination of different fungi that usually attack a tree that is stressed in some way. The immediate solution is to cut out affected branches, until the brown-coloured stain in the wood is no longer

Dieback on an apricot tree.

The dark red spots caused by quince leaf blight.

visible. Preferably, cut back to the junction with another branch, painting the cut with wound paint. In the longer term, take steps to ensure that the tree is not troubled by drought or malnutrition. Applying a foliar feed of liquid seaweed is likely to help.

Problems of quince trees

Quince trees are remarkably free from attack by pests. Even **wasps and hornets** (see page 128) and **birds** (see page 126) leave the fruit alone for a long time because of their tough skins. The only pests that do sometimes trouble quince trees are **codling moth** (see page 147) and **winter moth** (see page 128).

There are two diseases that are particularly troublesome on quince trees. One of them is **quince leaf blight** (see right), which not only affects fruit production but also disfigures the tree. The other is **brown rot** (see page 132), common to many fruits, but especially problematic on quince trees. Quinces can also be affected by **honey fungus** (see page 134), **replant disease** (see page 137), **powdery mildew** (see page 136) and **silver leaf** (see page 139).

Quince leaf blight

Symptoms: Numerous dark red spots appear on affected leaves soon after growth starts in the spring. These soon coalesce and turn black. The leaves can turn yellow and fall from the tree, and in severe cases localised dieback of shoots can occur. The infection can affect the fruit in some cases, showing as small spots. Fruiting can be seriously affected because the places where fruit buds would develop are infected.

Control: Removal of the infected leaves, either by raking or mowing, will provide a measure of control. Spraying with Bordeaux mixture, once in the autumn and once when the leaves unfurl, is the most effective form of control, but this is a disease that can become entrenched, returning year after year. Garlic spray (see box overleaf) is also said to keep quince leaf blight under control.

GARLIC SPRAY

Garlic has antifungal properties that are said to counteract quince leaf blight and peach leaf curl. However, care must be taken in using it because it can harm beneficial insects. The easiest way to make garlic spray is to use garlic purée, which can be bought in supermarkets. Use a 10cm (4") squirt of the purée per litre of water. Whisk or blend the garlic into the water and add a squirt of washing-up liquid. This helps to keep the spray on the leaves rather than running off them. Spraying in early spring is the most effective, continuing as needed into the summer. Garlic is also used to deter many insect pests, keeping them at bay with its pungent smell. Garlic sprays can also be bought ready-made from good garden centres or organic suppliers.

Problems of medlar trees

Medlars are normally healthy trees, suffering little from the pests and diseases that affect most fruit trees. Aside from **hawthorn leaf spot** (see below), there are no problems specific to medlars, although they can still be affected by more general diseases, including **honey fungus** (see page 134), **replant disease** (see page 137) and **powdery mildew** (see page 136).

Hawthorn leaf spot
Symptoms: Hawthorn leaf spot is the only disease that has a particular affinity to medlars. It is characterised by multiple brown or purple spots, 1-2mm across, appearing on the leaves. In severe cases the leaves will turn yellow and fall from the tree.

Control: The only method of control is to pick up the infected leaves and either burn them or remove them from the garden. Pruning out areas of overcrowded growth to allow good air circulation will also help to keep this disease under control.

Problems of fig trees

Fig trees are largely free from troublesome pests and diseases, but **birds** (see page 126), **wasps and hornets** (see page 128) can cause a problem, as they all enjoy eating your figs. Providing alternative food near your fig tree might lure them away; otherwise, pick the figs a day or two before they are completely ripe. Netting can be an effective way to keep birds away from fan-trained trees.

Fig trees can suffer from **fig rust** (see below), and can also be affected by **coral spot** (see page 133), **honey fungus** (see page 134) and **replant disease** (see page 137).

Fig rust
Symptoms: This is a fungal disease that produces small yellow-orange spots on the leaves. Left alone, these spots coalesce, leading to leaf fall. The disease is more prevalent in wet seasons.

Control: Spraying with Bordeaux mixture can mitigate the effects of fig rust.

Problems of mulberry trees

Mulberries are largely free from the pests and diseases that affect other fruit trees, and are resistant to honey fungus. The main problem is **mulberry canker** (see above right). This can be a serious disease of young trees, causing severe dieback of young shoots if it is not controlled.

Mulberry canker

Symptoms: The first symptoms that are usually noticed are the appearance of yellow leaves, followed by leaf fall and dieback. Closer inspection will reveal a flattened wound or canker on the bark of young shoots. Where this girdles the stem, it interrupts the flow of sap, killing the shoot above the canker. These cankers are usually noticed in the summer, because they can spread quickly.

Control: It is best to break the rule of pruning in the winter in order to halt the spread of the disease. Remove the canker by pruning at least 5cm (2") away from the wound. The prunings should be promptly burnt or removed from the garden.

Wilting leaves and cankered stems are the early signs of mulberry canker.

The more advanced stage of mulberry canker, with dieback on numerous branches.

QUICK GUIDE TO GROWING HEALTHY TREES

- Pests and diseases are most likely to colonise unhealthy trees. Provide good growing conditions for your trees and they are likely to ward off minor attacks.

- Ensure that newly planted trees are well watered in times of drought. Mulches of manure or compost in the early years will provide nutrients and help to preserve soil moisture.

- Encourage natural predators. A wildlife-friendly garden will contain pests, but also their predators. Growing plants to attract lacewings or providing fat balls for insect-eating birds will help to control pests.

- Regular inspection of your trees will enable you to nip many problems in the bud. When a potential problem is seen, take care to identify it accurately and take remedial action promptly.

- Learn to live with a few 'pests' in your orchard. Ask yourself whether you might be prepared to share a little of your harvest in order to have a richness of biodiversity in your garden. If not, take action.

- Ensure that your soil contains all the nutrients required by a particular fruit tree. Feed if necessary, and look out for signs of any deficiencies.

Part 3

The fruits

Chapter 10

Apples

"There is no kind of Fruit better known in England than the Apple, or more generally cultivated. It is that Used that I hold it almost impossible for the English to live without it, whether it be employed for that excellent Drink we call Cider, or for the many dainties, which are made of it in the Kitchen. In short, were all other fruit wanting us, Apples would make amends."

Richard Bradley, *New Improvements of Planting and Gardening* (1718)

The history of apple growing in Britain

Apples are etched deep in the British psyche. Apple blossom, apple pie, apple bobbing and scrumping are enshrined in the memories of many a youngster growing up in Britain.

Although the modern apple originated from wild apples found in Asia Minor, it is thought that this fruit has been grown here since Roman times. Court Pendu Plat, a variety of dessert apple still grown today, probably dates back to this time. For a thousand years after the Romans left Britain, there was little development in the art of apple growing. It was largely in monasteries that the techniques of apple cultivation and grafting were practised.

In medieval times, new varieties began to emerge: the Old English Pearmain was recorded in 1204 and the Costard apple emerged as the main culinary apple. Another dark age passed until the sixteenth century, when the science of horticulture began to evolve and be widely practised. Apple varieties still in cultivation, such as the Devonshire Quarrenden and Pitmaston Pineapple, were created as apple breeding became more widespread during the seventeenth century.

The late eighteenth and nineteenth centuries were the golden age of apple growing and breeding in Britain. Keen amateur growers had the expertise to recognise chance seedlings with potential, such as Blenheim Orange or Bramley's Seedling. Richard Cox and Thomas Laxton adopted a more scientific

Left: Crab apples are an attractive feature in the garden.

approach to breeding apples. Hundreds of new varieties were created during the Victorian era, culminating in the Great Apple and Pear Show organised by the Royal Horticultural Society (RHS) in 1883. New rootstocks began to be developed and trees were trained in all kinds of fancy shapes.

During the twentieth century, apple growing became an increasingly scientific affair. Breeding and rootstock development moved from nurseries to research stations, such as East Malling, Long Ashton and the John Innes Institute. Now, in the twenty-first century, we are faced with the challenges of genetic modification and climate change. The romance of previous times has disappeared, but there is still plenty of enjoyment to be had from growing our own apples.

Cultivation of apples

Apple trees are the easiest fruit trees to grow. They will tolerate a wide range of soil conditions, climate and aspects. It is possible to grow apple trees almost everywhere in the British Isles, because they are less demanding of sunny, sheltered sites than other fruit trees. They are, however, susceptible to a wide range of pests and diseases that can cause serious harm to both the tree and the fruit, so it is important to choose disease-resistant varieties and inspect your trees regularly to catch any problems at an early stage.

For full details of pest, disease and other apple tree problems, and how to deal with them, see Chapter 9 (pages 145-50). See Chapter 2 (pages 31-33) for information on rootstocks.

Conditions
The ideal conditions for apples are a sheltered site, south- or west-facing, with a deep, fertile,

well-drained soil. The ideal soil pH is between 6.3 and 6.8. However, apples are not fussy trees; they are tolerant of a wide range of conditions without a significant decline in cropping. It is unlikely that you will have much choice in where to grow your trees, so the important thing is to make the most of your site, following the advice given in Chapter 1.

Feeding and watering
If your soil is poor or if your trees are not growing well, they can be fed in the spring, just before growth starts. A general-purpose fertiliser, such as chicken manure pellets, or a proprietary organic fertiliser can be useful, but beware of feeding too heavily or with too much nitrogen. This can lead to soft, sappy growth that is more prone to certain pests and diseases. As an alternative, top-dressing with manure or garden compost is a good practice. Potassium, responsible for the development of both flowers and fruit, is an important nutrient for apple trees in particular. Rock potash and wood ash are valuable sources of potassium. Some cultivars are described as potash-demanding, meaning that they need higher levels of potassium in order to crop well.

It is unlikely that you will need to water apple trees, with the exception of young trees in dry conditions in the summer after planting, or on very free-draining soil.

Pollination
Apple trees are generally not self-fertile, so you will need to choose varieties that will pollinate each other (see Chapter 3). Apple varieties are usually listed with a number or letter that indicates the flowering group (also known as the pollination group). This indicates the time that the particular variety is in flower. To ensure successful pollination, two

Crab apple blossom is not only beautiful but is also a valuable source of pollen to pollinate apple trees.

separate varieties must be flowering at the same time. This is achieved by planting a variety with the same number or letter, or an adjacent number or letter. For example, Lord Lambourne, in pollination group C, can be pollinated by apples such as Christmas Pearmain, in group B; Scotch Bridget, in group C; or Ashmead's Kernel, in group D.

Some apples are triploids, meaning that they have no viable pollen of their own (see Chapter 3, page 40). This means that two other apple varieties are needed – to pollinate the triploid, and to pollinate each other.

Planting a crab apple that flowers over a long period (as most do) can be a valuable aid to successful pollination.

Fruit thinning

It is preferable to thin heavy crops of apples. This will produce larger fruits of better quality. It also minimises the risk of biennial cropping and branches breaking from the strain of heavy crops. Thinning is best carried out in mid-July, once the June Drop (see page 41) has taken place.

Dessert apples can be thinned to leave fruits 10-15cm (4-6") apart, with one to two fruits per cluster. Cooking apples, because of their larger size, should be thinned to leave fruits 15-20cm (6-8") apart, with just one fruit per cluster.

Where a cluster of fruits has developed, there will often be a slightly misshapen fruit in the centre of the cluster; this is known as the king fruit and should be removed. Also thin out any blemished or small fruits, leaving the large healthy fruits to grow on. Thinning can be carried out with scissors or fingers and thumb.

Young trees should not be allowed to bear a heavy crop, because the tree's energy will be diverted from producing strong growth towards producing fruit. In extreme cases this can lead to the tree becoming stunted. It is best to remove all fruit in the first two years.

Apple varieties

Choosing apple varieties can be a bewildering task. There are over 2,000 varieties still grown in Britain, so narrowing it down to the varieties that are right for you can be time-consuming. However, it is worth taking the time at this stage, because the choice of variety is crucial to later success. It is tempting to pick a variety that you buy from the supermarket, thinking that it will grow well in your garden, but common supermarket apples do not necessarily make good garden apples. Gala, for example, is very susceptible to scab, while Braeburn often fails to ripen properly in an English summer, except in the most favoured locations.

You can use the list of questions on page 49 to help you choose which varieties best suit your needs. Remember that you have a choice of harvest time as well as season of use. This can be important for cider or juice apples, when it is easiest to carry out all the juicing and harvesting at one time. Early apples are in season from the end of July, but will keep for only a few weeks. There are many varieties for eating from September through to November, but this is when everyone has a glut; would it be better to choose varieties that are suitable for keeping? Given suitable conditions, some varieties can be kept until April or even May.

Although apples can be divided into those used for eating fresh, cooking or cider, there are also many dual-purpose apples. Bramley's Seedling, for example, can be used for cooking and for producing a sharp juice. Tom Putt, an apple well known in the West Country, can be used for eating, cooking and cider. Some cooking apples become sweeter during storage, so can be eaten as a dessert apple after Christmas.

Remember, also, to choose varieties suitable for the climate where you live. Particularly in the wetter parts of Britain, you will need to choose varieties with resistance to the fungal

SPUR-BEARERS AND TIP-BEARERS

Most (about 75 per cent) of apple trees are spur-bearers: they produce most of their fruit on knobbly growths – spurs – that form on two-year-old or older wood. With practice this type of tree can be recognised by the presence of the knobbly spurs, which are easily spotted in winter.

Tip-bearers, on the other hand, produce the majority of their fruit from buds on the ends of shoots that were produced in the previous year. Grenadier and Beauty of Bath are examples of tip-bearers. See Diagrams 28 and 30 on pages 188 and 189 for an illustration of the distinction.

A quick internet search or look in a reference book will tell you whether a given variety is a tip-bearer or a spur-bearer. Some varieties are partial tip-bearers, which are somewhere in between – they form most of their fruit like tip-bearers, but produce a significant amount on spurs. Bramley's Seedling and Worcester Pearmain are common examples of partial tip-bearers.

In the charts in this chapter, all varieties are spur-bearers unless identified as tip-bearers.

diseases scab and canker. In the drier parts of England, resistance to mildew is more important. Some varieties need a warm summer to ripen properly, so are not suitable for growing in the north of the British Isles. Use Appendices 2.1-2.4 in this book to help you to narrow down your choice. An online search tool such as that available at www.keepers-nursery.co.uk is now the most efficient way to build in all the criteria involved in selecting varieties.

Dessert apples

There is a vast choice of dessert apple varieties, including apples that keep well into the following year. Where possible, taste the varieties you are interested in before buying them. If they are not available in the shops, you might find that your local nursery has an open day where you can sample the taste of different varieties. Tasting is also possible at some Apple Days.

Recommended varieties

In the chart overleaf are some favourite varieties that you might wish to choose from. Of the thousands of eating apple varieties, there are some that are grown time and again, either because they taste so good or because they are good all-rounders. Some varieties that would normally be included are missing from this list because they are difficult to grow. Cox's Orange Pippin is the prime example of this – while it is one of the best-tasting apples, it is very susceptible to scab, canker and mildew, so difficult to grow successfully without spraying regularly. Other varieties that are susceptible to certain diseases are included because they are suited to growing in certain areas of the UK. James Grieve, for example, is included even though it is slightly susceptible to scab and canker. This slight susceptibility means that it is more suited to the drier eastern areas of the country, rather than the wetter western areas

THE BLOODY PLOUGHMAN APPLE

The Bloody Ploughman is a deep red dessert apple that hails from the Carse of Gowrie in Scotland. Rumour has it that it was named after a ploughman who was caught stealing apples on the Megginch estate. He was shot for his deeds. His widow threw the apples on to the compost heap, where one of them sprouted and grew into the apple tree we know today. A more colourful version of the story has it that the tree sprouted on top of the grave of the ploughman. Just to add to the story, the flesh of the apples is red!

The Bloody Ploughman apple.

where such fungal diseases thrive. It is also a good pollinator and a fine variety for juice production, for which scab is less important than on dessert apples.

There is no such thing as the perfect apple: you will need to compromise somewhere along the line. My suggestion is that you choose disease-resistant cultivars wherever possible, letting the compromise fall on another area of the tree's qualities. Sunset, for example, is a good substitute for Cox's Orange Pippin; although the apples are small and don't carry quite the depth of flavour of a Cox, a healthy Sunset tree is preferable to a disease-ridden Cox.

Varieties are listed in order of season of use. See page 198 for details of how to store late- and mid-season apples. All varieties are spur-bearers, except those listed as tip-bearers (see box on page 168).

Recommended dessert apple varieties

Variety	Characteristics of the fruit	Characteristics of the tree	Flowering group	Picking date	Season of use	Pest & disease resistance
BEAUTY OF BATH	An early apple with a fruity, sharp-sweet taste. Fruit may drop before fully ripe.	Spreading, vigorous tree, heavy cropper. Sulphur-shy, potash-demanding, tip-bearer. Suitable for northern Britain.	C	Early August	August	Resistant to scab, slightly susceptible to canker.
DISCOVERY	Keeps well for an early apple. Distinctive flavour, crisp and juicy. Good for juicing.	Moderately vigorous, slow to bear, heavy cropper. Partial tip-bearer. Frost-resistant blossom. Suitable for northern Britain.	C	Mid–late August	August–September	Resistant to scab and mildew.
DEVONSHIRE QUARRENDEN	Dark red, sharp-sweet early apple with a strawberry, winey taste.	Initially upright, later spreading, low vigour, moderate cropper. Often biennial.	B	Late August	Late August–early September	Slightly susceptible to scab.

Variety	Characteristics of the fruit	Characteristics of the tree	Flowering group	Picking date	Season of use	Pest & disease resistance
TYDEMAN'S EARLY WORCESTER	Sweet with strawberry flavour.	Spreading, almost weeping, moderate vigour, good cropper. Partial tip-bearer. Suitable for northern Britain.	D	Late August–early September	Late August–September	Resistant to scab and mildew, susceptible to fireblight.
SCRUMPTIOUS	A high-quality sweet early apple with a strawberry undertone.	Moderate vigour, upright becoming spreading. Heavy cropper, suitable for wall training.	D	September	September	Resistant to scab and canker.
ELLISON'S ORANGE	Intense aromatic flavour, similar to Cox's Orange Pippin, but with slight aniseed taste. Juicy.	Moderate vigour, heavy cropper, attractive frost-resistant blossom. Slightly biennial. Suitable for northern Britain.	D	Mid–late September	September –October	Slightly susceptible to canker. Very resistant to scab and mildew.
JAMES GRIEVE	A sharp, juicy, almost savoury apple. Also a cooker early in the season. Good for juicing.	Spreading, moderate vigour, heavy cropper. Partial tip-bearer. Suitable for northern Britain.	D	Early September	September –October	Slightly susceptible to scab and canker. Resistant to mildew.

(Cont.)

Sulphur-shy: These varieties suffer from sulphur sprays, used to combat fungal diseases.
Potash-demanding: These varieties need higher levels of potassium to produce worthwhile crops.

Variety	Characteristics of the fruit	Characteristics of the tree	Flowering group	Picking date	Season of use	Pest & disease resistance
WORCESTER PEARMAIN	Sweet, intense strawberry flavour.	Moderate vigour, upright becoming spreading, slow to bear, hardy, heavy cropper. Partial tip-bearer. Frost-resistant blossom.	D	Early–mid September	September –October	Susceptible to scab and canker, resistant to mildew.
LIMELIGHT	A new variety with a crisp, refreshing, sharp-sweet flavour. Good for juicing.	Compact tree, upright becoming spreading. Heavy cropper.	D	Mid–late September	September –November	Resistant to scab and canker.
CHARLES ROSS	Crisp and juicy with sweet, aromatic flavour. Also used for cooking and juice.	Moderate vigour, spreading, hardy. Good for chalk soils. Sulphur-shy. Frost-resistant blossom. Suitable for northern Britain.	C	Mid-September	Mid-September –November	Resistant to scab, susceptible to canker and capsid bug.
COX'S POMONA	Brisk, sharp, delicate flavour. Thin skin, susceptible to bruising. Also used for cooking.	Upright becoming spreading, moderate vigour, heavy cropping. Suitable for northern Britain.	D	Mid–late September	September –December	Some resistance to scab and canker.

(Cont.)

Variety	Characteristics of the fruit	Characteristics of the tree	Flowering group	Picking date	Season of use	Pest & disease resistance
LORD LAMBOURNE	Crisp, juicy flesh, sweet with balancing acidity. Good for juice.	Compact tree, good cropper. Partial tip-bearer.	C	Mid–late September	Late September –December	Susceptible to fireblight.
BLENHEIM ORANGE	A classic English apple with a dry, nutty flavour. Also cooks to a stiff purée.	Vigorous tree, upright becoming spreading. Slow to bear, heavy cropper. Triploid, biennial tendency, partial tip-bearer. Frost-resistant blossom. Suitable for northern Britain.	D	Late September –early October	October–December	Slightly susceptible to scab and canker. Resistant to mildew.
EGREMONT RUSSET	A firm, crisp, dry apple with a rich, nutty flavour.	Compact tree, heavily spurred, upright. Good for wall training and pot culture. Slight biennial tendency. Frost-resistant blossom. Suitable for northern Britain.	B	Late September –early October	October–December	Slightly resistant to canker, resistant to mildew, very resistant to scab.
FALSTAFF (and RED FALSTAFF, pictured)	A refreshing, crisp, juicy dessert apple. Good for making juice.	Moderately vigorous tree, heavy cropping. Good pollinator. Good for wall training. Frost-resistant blossom. Suitable for northern Britain.	C	Early October	October–December	Frost-resistant. Fairly resistant to scab and canker.

(Cont.)

Variety	Characteristics of the fruit	Characteristics of the tree	Flowering group	Picking date	Season of use	Pest & disease resistance
PITMASTON PINEAPPLE	An old variety with crisp and nutty, small, sweet yellow apples.	Moderate vigour, upright. Heavy cropper, biennial cropper. Suitable for areas of high rainfall.	D	Early October	October–December	Resistant to scab and canker.
RAJKA	A new variety from the Czech Republic, sweet and juicy with some acidity and a hint of strawberry.	Moderate vigour, upright becoming spreading. Heavy cropper, but needs a warm summer to ripen well. Suitable for areas of high rainfall.	D	Mid-October	October–December	Fairly resistant to scab, canker and mildew.
SUNSET	Crisp and juicy, intense aromatic flavour, similar to Cox's Orange Pippin.	Compact, free-spurring. Good for wall training and pot culture. Heavy cropper. Frost-resistant blossom. Suitable for northern Britain and areas of high rainfall.	C	Late September	October–December	Resistant to scab, slightly susceptible to canker.
HEREFORDSHIRE RUSSET	A promising new russet variety with a high-quality aromatic taste.	Upright becoming spreading, moderate vigour. Heavy cropper. Suitable for areas of high rainfall.	C	Late September	October–January	Fairly resistant to scab and canker.

(Cont.)

Variety	Characteristics of the fruit	Characteristics of the tree	Flowering group	Picking date	Season of use	Pest & disease resistance
FIESTA (syn. RED PIPPIN)	A crisp, juicy apple that keeps well.	Spreading, compact tree, heavy cropper. Suitable for wall training and pot culture.	D	Mid–late September	October–February	Resistant to scab and mildew.
ORLEANS REINETTE	Rich orange, nutty flavour. Also used for cooking.	Upright becoming spreading, bears young, irregular cropping. Biennial tendency.	E	Mid-October	November–January	Resistant to scab, mildew and canker. Susceptible to fireblight.
ADAM'S PEARMAIN	Excellent nutty, aromatic flavour.	Compact, spreading tree. Good cropper. Attractive pink frost-resistant blossom. Partial tip-bearer, often biennial. Suitable for pot culture.	C	Mid-October	November–March	Resistant to scab, slightly susceptible to canker.
ROSEMARY RUSSET	Sweet-sour, excellent acid-drop flavour. Juicy.	Moderate vigour, upright, hardy. A good apple for difficult conditions. Attractive blossom. Moderate cropper. Suitable for areas of high rainfall.	C	Early–mid-October	November–March	Resistant to scab, canker and mildew.

(Cont.)

Variety	Characteristics of the fruit	Characteristics of the tree	Flowering group	Picking date	Season of use	Pest & disease resistance
TOPAZ	A new variety from the Czech Republic with a good, sharp flavour.	Moderate vigour, upright becoming spreading. Heavy cropper. Suitable for areas of high rainfall.	D	Mid-October	November –March	Resistant to scab, fairly resistant to canker.
ASHMEAD'S KERNEL	Juicy, refreshing, excellent acid-drop flavour. Good keeper.	Moderate vigour, upright, erratic cropper. Suitable for northern Britain and areas of high rainfall.	D	Early–mid October	December –February	Resistant to scab, canker and mildew. Susceptible to bitter pit.
WINSTON	Sweet-sharp, aromatic, nutty. Skin tough.	Moderate vigour, upright, bears young, good cropper. Tendency to produce lots of small fruit. An apple with few problems, good for difficult locations. May not ripen fully in cold districts in poor summers. Partial tip-bearer. Frost-resistant blossom. Suitable for northern Britain and areas of high rainfall.	D	Mid–late October	December –April	Very resistant to scab, canker and mildew.

Cooking apples

When choosing cooking apple varieties, factors such as disease resistance and keeping qualities still come into play, but the cooking quality is a new factor that needs to be considered. The ubiquitous Bramley's Seedling is well known for cooking to a fluffy purée, but many cooking apples keep their shape. In fact, Britain is one of the few places in the world where apples are grown and used specifically for cooking. Most countries use dessert apples for cooking, as in the classic tarte aux pommes from France.

Recommended varieties

Most of the following varieties need plenty of sugar to sweeten them, while some, such as Annie Elizabeth, are quite sweet already. Charles Ross, Cox's Pomona and James Grieve, in the recommended dessert apple varieties chart, are also good cooking apples. Varieties are listed in order of season of use.

Recommended cooking apple varieties							
Variety	Characteristics of the fruit	Characteristics of the tree	Flowering group	Picking date	Season of use	Pest & disease resistance
GRENADIER	A sharp, early cooking apple that cooks to a purée.	Moderate vigour, upright becoming spreading. Potash-demanding. Heavy cropper. Good pollinator. Suitable for areas of high rainfall.	B C D	Mid-August	Mid-August–September	Very resistant to scab and canker. Resistant to mildew. Susceptible to capsid bug.
KESWICK CODLIN	Old-fashioned fruit with a good flavour. Cooks to a juicy purée that needs little sugar. Used for jelly making.	Moderately vigorous tree. Heavy cropper. Biennial tendency.	B	Early–mid-August	Mid-August–September	Some resistance to scab and canker.
REVEREND W. WILKS	Cooks to a light, sweet purée.	Free-spurring tree of low vigour. Suitable for pot culture and wall training. Good cropper. Biennial tendency. Suitable for northern Britain and areas of high rainfall.	B	Late August–early September	Late August–November	Resistant to scab, mildew and canker.

(Cont.)

Variety	Characteristics of the fruit	Characteristics of the tree	Flowering group	Picking date	Season of use	Pest & disease resistance
PEASGOOD'S NONSUCH	Very large apple that cooks to a sweet, delicate purée. Good for baked apples.	Moderately vigorous, spreading tree. Good cropper. Frost-resistant blossom.	C	Mid-September	September –December	Some resistance to scab. Susceptible to canker.
STIRLING CASTLE	Cooks to a sharp purée with a good fruity flavour.	Weak, spreading tree. Suitable for northern Britain.	C	Mid-September	September –December	Very resistant to scab. Slightly susceptible to mildew.
LORD DERBY	Sharp, strong-flavoured apple that keeps some of its shape when cooked.	Vigorous tree. Good cropper. Potash-demanding. Frost-resistant blossom. Suitable for northern Britain and areas of high rainfall.	D	Late September	October – December	Resistant to scab, canker and mildew.
GOLDEN NOBLE	Perhaps the best-flavoured of all cooking apples. It has a strong fruity flavour and keeps some of its shape when cooked.	Moderately vigorous tree, upright becoming spreading. Good cropper. Partial tip-bearer. Frost-resistant blossom. Suitable for areas of high rainfall.	E	Early October	October– February	Resistant to scab, mildew and canker. Susceptible to fireblight.

(Cont.)

Variety	Characteristics of the fruit	Characteristics of the tree	Flowering group	Picking date	Season of use	Pest & disease resistance
BRAMLEY'S SEEDLING	Well-known apple that cooks to a sharp, strongly flavoured purée. Also used for juicing.	Very vigorous spreading tree. Good cropper. Triploid. Partial tip-bearer. Sometimes biennial. Frost-resistant blossom. Suitable for northern Britain.	C	Early October	November –March	Slight suscep-tibility to scab and canker. Resistant to mildew. Prone to bitter pit.
LANE'S PRINCE ALBERT	Cooks to a sharp purée of good flavour. Also used for juicing.	Weak, twiggy, spreading tree. Good cropper. Sulphur-shy. Suitable for northern Britain and areas of high rainfall.	C D E	Mid-October	November –March	Very resistant to scab. Resistant to canker. Susceptible to mildew.
NEWTON WONDER	Cooks to a juicy purée of good flavour.	Very vigorous, spreading tree. Sulphur-shy. Potash-demanding. Heavy cropper. Biennial tendency. Frost-resistant blossom. Suitable for northern Britain and areas of high rainfall.	D	Mid-October	November –March	Resistant to scab. Very resistant to canker. Slightly susceptible to mildew. Susceptible to bitter pit.
ANNIE ELIZABETH	A sweet, light-flavoured apple that keeps its shape when cooked.	Upright tree of moderate vigour. Can drop fruit before it is ripe. Good cropper. Frost-resistant blossom. Suitable for northern Britain and areas of high rainfall.	E	Early–mid-October	November –April	Resistant to scab, mildew and canker.

(Cont.)

Cider apples

Choosing varieties of apple for the production of cider is a completely different matter from choosing dessert and culinary varieties. The season of use is important, as all the trees in an orchard can be juiced together if they are all ready at the same time. More important, however, is the type of cider apple. With the exception of single-variety (or 'vintage') cider, most cider is made from a combination of different types of cider apple, the main types being sweets, bittersweets, sharps and bittersharps. The amount of tannin and the degree of acidity largely determine the type of cider apple.

Sweet cider apples have a high sugar level. The sugars encourage the process of fermentation and balance the acidity of the bitter apples.

Bittersweet cider apples are rich in both sugars and tannin. The tannins are responsible for the astringent taste of the apples and the rounded flavour and body of the cider.

Sharps bring acidity to cider. Cooking apples such as Bramley's Seedling can be used, but cider apple varieties such as Brown's Apple are more suitable.

Bittersharps are high in acidity and tannins. They are often used for making single-variety ciders – Kingston Black being a prime example.

There are no fixed proportions of the different groups to use in making cider. There are many different types of cider, and experimenting to make your own blend can be half the fun. It is worth noting that many cider apples have a biennial tendency (see Chapter 3, page 41).

Recommended varieties

Some of the more common cider varieties are listed below, but it is well worth trying your own local cider varieties, especially if you live in an area known for its cider making. There are wonderful names to tempt you as well: Buttery d'Or from Dorset, Slack ma Girdle from Devon, Greasy Jack from Oxfordshire and Ten Commandments from Herefordshire. Varieties are listed in order of season of use.

Recommended cider apple varieties

Variety	Characteristics of the fruit	Characteristics of the tree	Flowering group	Picking date	Season of use	Pest & disease resistance*
ASHTON BITTER 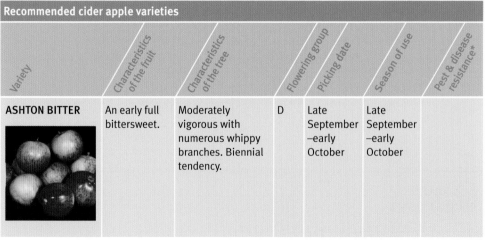	An early full bittersweet.	Moderately vigorous with numerous whippy branches. Biennial tendency.	D	Late September –early October	Late September –early October	

(Cont.)

Variety	Characteristics of the fruit	Characteristics of the tree	Flowering group	Picking date	Season of use	Pest & disease resistance*
ELLIS BITTER	An early bittersweet.	Vigorous tree, upright becoming spreading. Partial tip-bearer. Heavy cropper with slight biennial tendency.	F	Late September –early October	Late September –early October	Susceptible to scab. Resistant to mildew.
MAJOR	An early bittersweet of excellent quality.	A vigorous spreading tree. Heavy cropper. Biennial tendency.	F	Late September –early October	Late September –early October	Slightly susceptible to scab. Susceptible to canker.
SOMERSET REDSTREAK	An early mild bittersweet, best blended, but can be used to make a vintage cider.	Upright tree of moderate vigour. Biennial tendency. Heavy cropper, which can cause broken branches.	D	End September –mid-October	End September –mid-October	Resistant to scab, slightly susceptible to mildew and brown rot.
FREDERICK	A mid-season sharp of high quality.	Moderately vigorous with weeping habit. Moderate cropper.	D	Mid-October	Mid-October	
BROWN'S APPLE	Full sharp.	Vigorous spreading tree. Biennial. Heavy cropper.	E	Mid-October –early November	Mid-October –early November	Slightly susceptible to scab, mildew and canker.

(Cont.)

Variety	Characteristics of the fruit	Characteristics of the tree	Flowering group	Picking date	Season of use	Pest & disease resistance*
HARRY MASTERS JERSEY	Medium-full bittersweet of vintage quality.	Low vigour. Good cropper. Often biennial. Tip-bearer.	D	Mid-October –early November	Mid-October –early November	
KINGSTON BLACK	A mild bittersharp of distinctive vintage quality.	Moderately vigorous with spreading growth. Slow to bear, moderate cropper.	D	Mid-October –early November	Mid-October –early November	Susceptible to scab, very susceptible to canker.
SWEET COPPIN	Sweet of vintage quality. Also used for juice.	Spreading tree of moderate vigour. Sulphur-shy. Biennial tendency. Heavy cropper.	D	Late October –early November	Mid-October –early November	Susceptible to mildew.
DABINETT	Full bittersweet of vintage quality.	Spreading tree of low vigour. Potash-demanding. Sulphur-shy. Heavy and regular cropper.	D	Mid-October– November	Mid-October– November	Slightly susceptible to scab and mildew.
STOKE RED	Good-quality late bittersharp.	Spreading tree of moderate vigour. Biennial. Heavy cropper.	G	Late October	Late October	Very resistant to scab. Susceptible to fireblight.

(Cont.)

Variety	Characteristics of the fruit	Characteristics of the tree	Flowering group	Picking date	Season of use	Pest & disease resistance*
YARLINGTON MILL	Medium bittersweet.	An upright tree of moderate vigour. Heavy cropper. Biennial.	D	Late October –mid-November	Late October –mid-November	Susceptible to scab and fireblight. Resistant to mildew and canker.
CRIMSON KING	Late medium sharp of vintage quality. Also used for cooking.	Vigorous spreading tree. Suitable for areas of high rainfall.	C	Mid-November	Mid-November	Resistant to scab, canker and mildew.

* Where no details are given on pest and disease resistance, this is because information is not readily available for these varieties. This is particularly the case for the less common varieties.

Pruning apple trees

Pruning apple trees is often thought of as a mysterious skill that only a few knowledge-able people possess; a cause of bafflement for the novice. Some people stand in front of their apple tree holding a pair of secateurs, scared to make a cut in case it proves fatal. At the other extreme are those who wield a saw to cut off large swathes of the tree. The former is far preferable to the latter, but of course the right approach is somewhere in between. If you only follow the simple system of regulated pruning described in Chapter 8 (page 113), you will not go far wrong. There are refinements to this system of pruning that will help you to get the most out of your apple trees, and these are described in the following pages.

Many people think that pruning is some-thing that happens when a tree is mature, but formative pruning is needed to create a healthy framework of branches while the tree is still young. There are many types of formative pruning that can be used success-fully on apple trees. In order to keep things simple, only the tree forms that are most commonly used in gardens and small orchards are described in detail here. These are the **bush**, **standard**, **cordon**, **espalier** and **stepover**. In addition, apple trees can be trained as spindlebushes and pyramids. The techniques for training an apple pyramid are the same as those for a pear pyramid (see Chapter 11, page 218). Spindlebushes are not covered in detail here because this is a form that is mostly used in commercial orchards.

TIMING OF PRUNING

Apple trees are normally pruned when they are dormant, from December through to the beginning of March. Pruning at this time encourages growth. However, there are some circumstances when pruning in the summer, which doesn't encourage growth, is more appropriate:

- Restricted forms of tree, such as cordons and espaliers, are normally pruned in August (see pages 193-7).
- Trees that have been pruned too hard will throw up a number of vigorous shoots as a result. These should be thinned out in the summer (see Chapter 9, page 142)
- Pruning can also be carried out in the summer to remove shoots that are shading ripening apples and causing congestion, preventing a heathy flow of air through the crown of the tree. Only small amounts of growth need to be removed in this case.

Formative pruning

Formative pruning is the process of building up a framework of branches that will serve the tree for the rest of its life. The pruning required will depend on the form of apple tree that is being grown (see Chapter 8, pages 109-12). However, the early stages will be similar for most forms. This early pruning is likely to include the removal of some laterals and the pruning of the central leader. Where laterals are to be removed below the height of the first branches, this is best done over two years in order to help thicken the trunk (see Diagram 27, pages 185-6). See also formative pruning techniques, page 108.

One of the aims of formative pruning is the creation of a number of well-spaced laterals at a wide angle to the trunk. Branches with a narrow angle to the trunk are liable to split from the trunk later in the tree's life, particularly when they bear a heavy crop of apples. When the leader is pruned, the tendency is for the tree to produce a number of upright shoots known as competing leaders. The process of nicking, on apples and pears, helps to counteract this tendency.

Nicking (see Chapter 8, page 106) just below the two or three top buds permits only weak growth from these buds. The buds below these will grow on strongly at the desired wide angles. Late spring is the best time to carry out this practice. An alternative to nicking is to wait a year, until the tree has naturally formed branches with wide angles, before removing the leader. This is simpler, but also wasteful of the tree's energy.

An apple tree trained as a bush. The variety is Sunset.

Formative pruning of an apple bush

The bush is the most common form of apple tree: it is easy to grow and maintain and suitable for a variety of dwarfing and semi-dwarfing rootstocks. The aim is to produce a goblet-shaped tree on top of a clear trunk. The height of the first branches will be 60-90cm (2-3'); lower on more dwarfing rootstocks and up to 1.2m (4') on an MM106 rootstock.

In the first year (starting with a maiden, or one-year-old tree), prune the leader around 15cm (6") above the height you want the first branches to emerge (assuming the leader has reached the required height – if not let it grow on and wait until next year). Use the technique of nicking to ensure the formation of wide-angled branches.

In the second year, a number of laterals will have formed. Those that are emerging where you want a clear trunk can be cut back to around three buds. These will be cut off completely the following year. Above this, look for three to five wide-angled branches spaced evenly around the tree. These laterals can be shortened by about half of the previous season's growth to an outward-facing bud (or an upward-facing bud if the lateral is horizontal). The process of cutting to outward-facing buds helps to create a spreading tree with a clear centre.

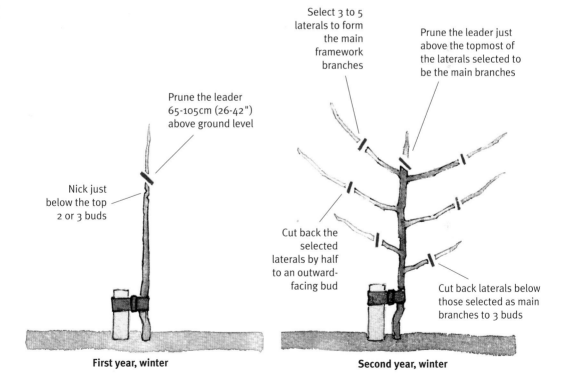

Select 3 to 5 laterals to form the main framework branches

Prune the leader just above the topmost of the laterals selected to be the main branches

Prune the leader 65-105cm (26-42") above ground level

Nick just below the top 2 or 3 buds

Cut back the selected laterals by half to an outward-facing bud

Cut back laterals below those selected as main branches to 3 buds

First year, winter

Second year, winter

Diagram 27 (1) Formative pruning of an apple bush.

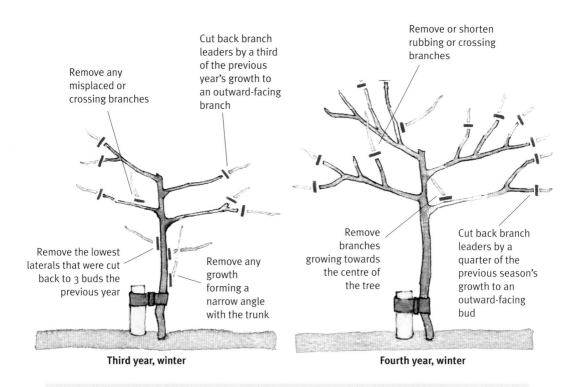

Remove any misplaced or crossing branches

Cut back branch leaders by a third of the previous year's growth to an outward-facing branch

Remove the lowest laterals that were cut back to 3 buds the previous year

Remove any growth forming a narrow angle with the trunk

Third year, winter

Remove or shorten rubbing or crossing branches

Remove branches growing towards the centre of the tree

Cut back branch leaders by a quarter of the previous season's growth to an outward-facing bud

Fourth year, winter

Diagram 27 (2) Formative pruning of an apple bush.

In the third year, sublaterals (small side branches) will be growing from the laterals selected as the main branches. These and the new growth of the main branches can be shortened by around a third of the previous year's growth. As time goes on, this process of shortening the extension growth (or tip pruning) continues in order to encourage the growth to fill out, but is done more lightly each year: after the third year, only a quarter of the previous season's growth is removed. More vigorous growth is pruned less hard, because pruning stimulates growth.

Misplaced branches, particularly those growing inwards to the centre of the tree, can

be removed completely. Eventually, the tree, if viewed from above, should resemble a bicycle wheel, with the hub (trunk) in the middle and spokes (branches) radiating out in an even manner. Any branches that grow in a way that interferes with this pattern are candidates for removal.

Some varieties are very upright in their growth habit, particularly when young. With such trees it can be difficult to establish much horizontal growth through pruning alone, so tying branches down can be effective. The technique is simple: tie string from the branch to a heavy stone on the ground, using the tension of the string to pull the branch to a more horizontal angle. This needs to be done while the branches are still young, so that they retain enough flexibility to bend. The string can be gradually tightened until the branch adopts a more horizontal angle. Remember, however, that most varieties will adopt a more spreading habit with age, particularly under the influence of heavy crops, so it is best not to overdo this practice.

Pruning an established apple bush

As the tree becomes more established, pruning moves from formative pruning towards pruning that keeps the tree growing satisfactorily while also encouraging healthy fruit production. To this end, it is necessary to know whether the variety is a tip-bearer or a spur-bearer (see page 168).

When pruning an established **spur-bearer**, the method of regulated pruning described in Chapter 8 (page 113) is the basic approach. In addition, spur-pruning will produce better results. This is the practice of encouraging sublaterals to become fruit-producing spurs and then keeping them in good condition.

Diagram 28 overleaf shows a typical lateral on a spur-bearer. The older wood to the right already has spurs formed on it, while the younger wood to the left has sublaterals growing out of it. The weakest sublaterals are unlikely to make fruiting spurs and should be removed right to the base. Likewise, the most vigorous shoots are probably too vigorous to become fruiting spurs and should also be removed. The shoots that are between these two in size should be reduced in length to four or five buds. This encourages them to form fruit buds during the summer following pruning. These fruit buds will then bear fruit one year later.

A young bush apple tree, before and after pruning.

A young branch on an apple tree. To the right is new wood, clothed in leaf buds. To the left is two-year-old wood, with the first fruiting spur formed.

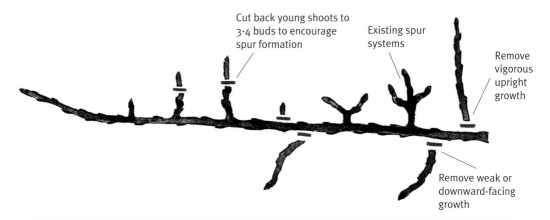

Cut back young shoots to 3-4 buds to encourage spur formation

Existing spur systems

Remove vigorous upright growth

Remove weak or downward-facing growth

Diagram 28 Pruning a lateral branch on a spur-bearing apple tree.

After a few years of bearing fruit, spurs will become elongated and crowded, bearing smaller fruits. At this stage, it is necessary to carry out spur thinning (see Diagram 29) to maintain the production of good-quality fruits.

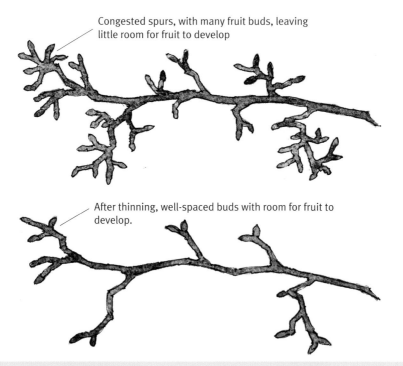

Congested spurs, with many fruit buds, leaving little room for fruit to develop

After thinning, well-spaced buds with room for fruit to develop.

Diagram 29 Spur thinning on an apple tree.

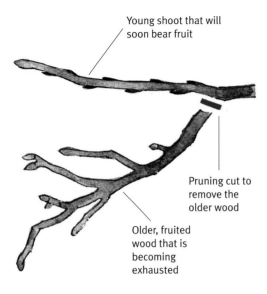

Young shoot that will soon bear fruit

Pruning cut to remove the older wood

Older, fruited wood that is becoming exhausted

Diagram 30 Pruning a tip-bearer.

Formative pruning of a standard or half standard apple tree

The formative pruning of a standard or half standard tree is initially that of developing a clear trunk to the required height, followed by the formation of a sound framework of branches in the pattern required. A half standard has a clear trunk of around 1.5-1.7m (5'-5'8"), while a standard has a clear trunk of 1.8m (6'). Where grazing is carried out under the trees, the height of the first branches will depend on the type of animal that is grazing and the height of the guard. It is vital that the lowest branches are kept well clear of the top of the guard, in order to prevent damage to the tree caused by rubbing on it. Traditionally, half standards were grown where sheep grazed; full standards in orchards grazed by cattle.

The pruning of an established **tip-bearer** follows a different pattern (see Diagram 30). Most fruits form on the ends of smaller branches. A system known as 'renewal pruning' is followed, where wood that has fruited for a few years and is becoming exhausted is cut back to a replacement shoot. Some branch leaders are tip-pruned, partly to avoid heavy crops pulling down long branches, but also to produce more shoots that will fruit in time.

In addition, the principles of regulated pruning (see page 113) are followed – removing dead, diseased and damaged wood, keeping the middle of the tree clear, removing misplaced and rubbing branches and pruning to encourage outward-facing growth.

Partial tip-bearers are best pruned using a combination of the two methods: the spurs can be treated as for a spur-bearer, but otherwise prune the tree as you would a tip-bearer.

Mature standard apple trees, pruned to allow grazing underneath.

It is important to clear the trunk in stages. The gradual removal of laterals (side shoots) helps the trunk to thicken. Diagram 31 shows how the trunk is divided into three sections. In the first year, the laterals are removed completely from the bottom third of the trunk, shortened in the middle third and allowed to grow on the top third. If the tree has only a few stubby laterals when planted, or even none at all, the pruning shown as year 1 can be delayed until the following year.

During years 2 and 3, the process of clearing the trunk continues until laterals are growing at or above the height required.

Once this height is reached, there is a choice of types of standard (or half standard). The leader can be allowed to grow on without pruning. This will produce a central-leader standard (see Diagram 32). Alternatively, the leader can be pruned out to produce an open-centred (or branch-headed) standard (see Diagram 33, page 192). Each variety will have a different habit; some will keep their leader for a long time, while others will lose their dominant leader fairly quickly. It is important to be guided by the habit of the tree. If you try to impose a central leader form on a tree that has a habit of forking, you will be fighting a losing battle. If you are

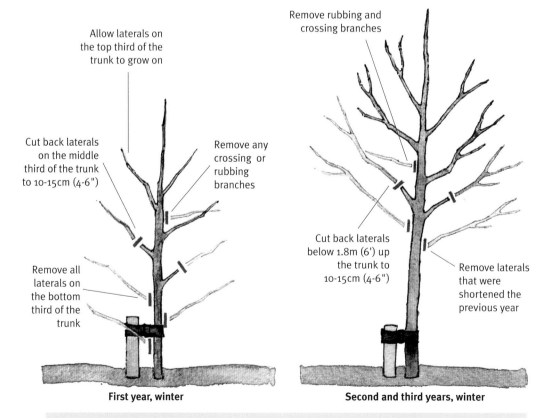

Allow laterals on the top third of the trunk to grow on

Cut back laterals on the middle third of the trunk to 10-15cm (4-6")

Remove any crossing or rubbing branches

Remove all laterals on the bottom third of the trunk

First year, winter

Remove rubbing and crossing branches

Cut back laterals below 1.8m (6') up the trunk to 10-15cm (4-6")

Remove laterals that were shortened the previous year

Second and third years, winter

Diagram 31 Pruning a standard or half standard apple tree.

growing standards on a windy site, it is help-ful to keep the tree compact and strong rather than letting it get too tall. This can be achieved by pruning a little harder than normal and by removing the leader, training in new growth to form a replacement leader.

When the leader is pruned, use the tech-nique of nicking (see Chapter 8, page 106) to ensure the production of wide-angled branches. If a replacement leader is required, the strongest and most upright shoot can be retained to form the new leader. Alterna-tively, the leader can be removed one year later, once it is clear where strong laterals are forming (as in Diagram 33 overleaf). Some-

times a shoot of similar size to the leader will form next it. This is known as a competing leader. Any competing leaders should be removed at an early stage (see photos on page 109) .

In years 2 to 3, the process of forming the framework branches begins. This is the same process as described on pages 185-6 for a bush tree. In effect, what you are doing is growing a vigorous bush on top of a clear trunk. Even if you are growing a standard

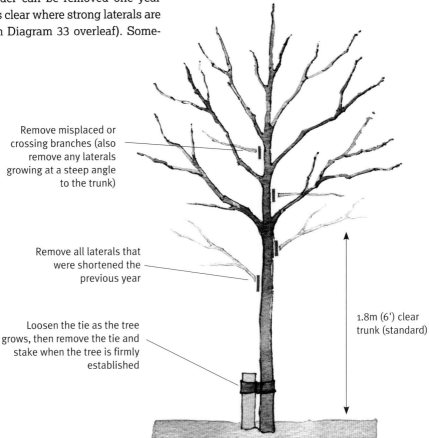

Remove misplaced or crossing branches (also remove any laterals growing at a steep angle to the trunk)

Remove all laterals that were shortened the previous year

Loosen the tie as the tree grows, then remove the tie and stake when the tree is firmly established

1.8m (6') clear trunk (standard)

Diagram 32 Forming a central-leader standard.

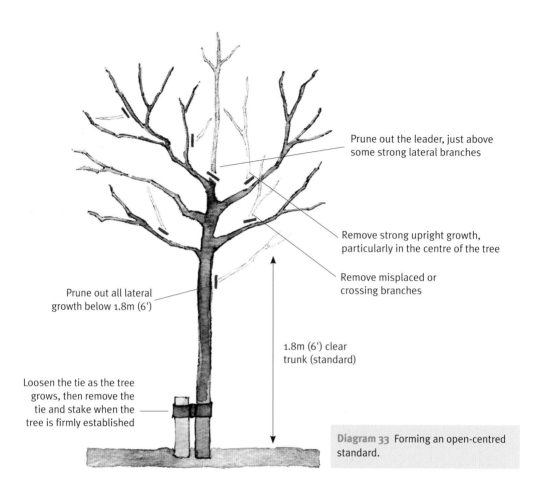

Prune out the leader, just above some strong lateral branches

Remove strong upright growth, particularly in the centre of the tree

Remove misplaced or crossing branches

Prune out all lateral growth below 1.8m (6')

1.8m (6') clear trunk (standard)

Loosen the tie as the tree grows, then remove the tie and stake when the tree is firmly established

Diagram 33 Forming an open-centred standard.

with a central leader retained, the process is similar. When selecting branches to keep, remember that these major limbs will develop side branches that can become quite large over time. Don't be tempted to keep too many branches that will eventually conflict with each other. Allow plenty of space (and hence light) for branches to develop.

Pruning an established standard or half standard apple tree

This is essentially a question of following the principles of regulated pruning described in Chapter 8, page 113. A standard apple tree, grown on an M25 rootstock, will form a large tree, up to 10m (33') in height and spread. It is no use pruning hard to reduce the size of the tree, as this will make the tree grow more vigorously. Because of the large size of standard trees, it is important to prune so as to allow a good air circulation through the tree; this helps to avoid the build-up of fungal diseases such as scab and canker.

The size of standard and half standard trees means that the techniques of pruning suited to spur- and tip-bearers are too fiddly to implement on such a large scale. Instead, branches that are becoming exhausted can be cut back to younger growth further down the branch, which will replace the exhausted growth (renewal pruning – see page 189). See Diagram 30, page 189.

See also the techniques in Chapter 17, page 314, for dealing with a neglected tree.

Formative pruning of a cordon apple tree

A cordon is a restricted form of apple tree that is planted an angle of about 45 degrees. It is maintained as a single stem form with a system of spurs encouraged and maintained along the length of the trunk. This form of training is suited to spur-bearing varieties grown on the more dwarfing rootstocks.

Initially, a maiden or feathered maiden is planted at a 45-degree angle, with the trunk securely tied to a bamboo cane, which in turn is tied to the support wires. Any laterals growing at planting time (winter) can be reduced in length to about four buds.

After planting, the pruning of the laterals, and later the spur systems, is carried out in late summer. In southern England, the beginning of August is usually the right time. Further north, in wet areas, or in a wet summer, the pruning can be delayed until later in August, or even into September. The aim is to avoid excessive young growth from pruning cuts. Experience will determine the best time in your region.

In the summer after planting, any sublaterals (side shoots) growing from the existing laterals (i.e. those pruned after planting) can be shortened to one leaf. Any newly formed laterals can be cut back to three or four leaves above the basal cluster (see Diagram 34 overleaf).

Apple trees trained as cordons.

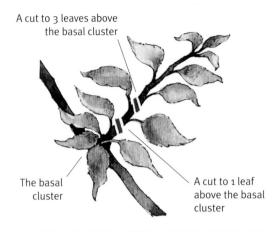

A cut to 3 leaves above the basal cluster

The basal cluster

A cut to 1 leaf above the basal cluster

Diagram 34 Pruning a lateral on a cordon apple tree.

The aim of this pruning is to form a system of spurs that will bear fruit. Any blossom forming in the first year should be removed.

If an area of the trunk remains bare, without laterals, the technique of notching (see page 106) can be used to encourage laterals to form. This is best done in late spring.

Pruning an established cordon apple tree

The process of pruning the laterals, described above, is continued over the following years. By this time, a healthy system of spurs will have built up. Eventually, these spurs will become congested, producing large quantities of small fruit. The spurs can now be thinned during the winter months, reducing the number of fruit buds on each system (see Diagram 29, page 188).

Once the central leader has reached the top of the support wires, it can be cut back or cut to a weaker shoot in order to inhibit further growth. This is carried out in May.

Formative pruning of an espalier apple tree

An espalier is a tree with a central leader and tiers of horizontal branches. Two to four tiers are most common. Although espaliers are grown on the more dwarfing rootstocks, more tiers can be fitted in by using a more vigorous rootstock. The most vigorous rootstock normally used is MM106.

As with a cordon, a compact spur-bearing variety should be chosen. It is possible to buy trees from some nurseries that have undergone the first stages of pruning into an espalier. They have the advantage of coming into fruiting earlier. However, they are expensive and you will miss out on the satisfaction of training the tree from the beginning.

The first task is to put the support wires in place. They should be held in place by vine eyes, so that they are 10-12.5cm (4-5") away from the wall, to allow good air circulation. The horizontal wires should be 40-50cm

An apple tree trained as an espalier.

(1'4"-1'8") apart. Straining bolts can be used to keep the wires taut. Alternatively, the wires can be strained between strong posts if an espalier tree is grown in the open.

Assuming that you are planting a maiden, after planting cut the leader to a strong bud just above the lowest support wire (around 40-50cm [1'4"-1'8"]). This bud will be trained in to form the new leader. The growth from the next two buds down (one on each side of the trunk) will form the first horizontal tiers, or arms.

Initially, the two arms are allowed to grow at around 45 degrees, supported by bamboo canes. By the end of the summer, these arms are brought down towards the horizontal and tied to the support wires. If one arm is weaker than the other, it can be left in a more vertical position to encourage greater vigour. Moving the arms up and down like this, in the first year of their growth, while they are still flexible, is a way of manipulating the growth to form a balanced tree. The leader is allowed to grow upright, also supported by a cane.

The process of forming new tiers is repeated each year until the desired height is reached. Any growth apart from the leader and the arms should be cut hard back during the summer. This growth can be used as a

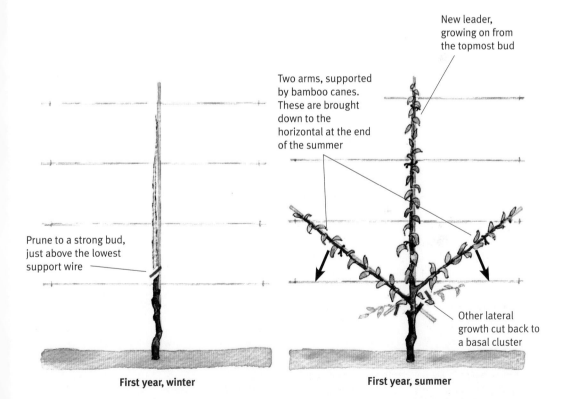

New leader, growing on from the topmost bud

Two arms, supported by bamboo canes. These are brought down to the horizontal at the end of the summer

Prune to a strong bud, just above the lowest support wire

Other lateral growth cut back to a basal cluster

First year, winter

First year, summer

Diagram 35 Pruning an apple espalier.

replacement should any serious problem arise with one of the developing arms. Once it is clear that it is not needed, it can be removed completely during the winter. It is preferable to cut the leader to buds on alternate sides each year to help maintain a balanced-looking tree. If one tier is still weaker than the other, it can be tip-pruned to encourage more vigour.

Pruning an established espalier apple tree

Once the leaders and arms have reached the extent of their required growth, they are cut back during the summer in order to restrict further growth. This process is continued as needed during the life of the tree. As with cordons (see page 194), most pruning of an established espalier is carried out during August. The aim is to prune the tree just as the growth is slowing down, so that little regrowth appears after pruning. If regrowth

does appear, it can be cut back during the autumn.

Once the arms are established, cut back the laterals emerging from them to three or four leaves above the basal cluster. Shoots that grow out from the laterals can be cut back hard, to one or two leaves. Over time, a system of fruiting spurs will develop as a result of this summer pruning.

Any vigorous growth, either from the arms (usually the top tier) or from the trunk, should be removed completely, although it can be helpful to leave two shoots at the top of the tree to take up some of the vigour. These can be pruned off the following spring. Eventually, the fruiting spurs will become congested and need spur thinning (see Diagram 29, page 188). This is carried out during the winter. Cropping can be heavy, in which case fruit thinning is recommended, in order

Espalier apple trees can be used as a boundary between different areas of the garden.

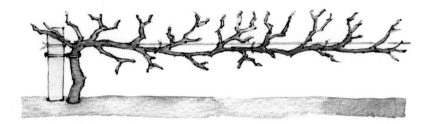

Diagram 36 A stepover apple tree.

to produce good-quality fruit and not to exhaust the tree, which can encourage biennial cropping.

Pruning a stepover apple tree

A stepover apple tree is a single trunk bent over to form a horizontal arm, supported by a single wire. Stepovers are often used as productive boundaries, perhaps surrounding a vegetable border or potager. A compact, spur-bearing variety is needed, grown on one of the more dwarfing rootstocks. It is necessary to plant a maiden because the leader is gradually tied down during the first year of growth, slowly becoming more horizontal. Otherwise, the principles of pruning are the same as for pruning one branch of an espalier, with the laterals being shortened during August.

An alternative is to train an espalier with just one tier, producing two arms, rather than the one arm of a stepover.

Harvesting apples

If you have read through Chapter 9 (Problems of fruit trees), it is easy to despair of ever having apples that escape the ravages of pests and diseases, but the time will come when your crop of apples is ready for har-

vesting. Having nurtured your crop through to this point, it is worth taking care now in order to enjoy your fruits at their best.

Harvesting your crop at the correct readiness is most important. If you know the name of the variety, it will be possible to identify a picking date from books (for example, using the tables in this book) or the internet – but this is only a guide: the ripening of the fruit will vary from season to season and in different areas.

There will be several clues to show you that your apples are nearly ripe. One is that you might notice windfalls appearing under the tree. Also, many apples will start to become brighter in colour as the picking date approaches. The biggest clue, however, is that when you attempt to pick an apple, it parts easily from the stem if twisted gently. Not all the apples on a tree will be ready at the same time; those in the sunniest positions will ripen first. If you find that you have to pull hard when picking, or that you are breaking twigs, come back in a few days' time. Once the apples are ready, make sure that you treat them gently, while picking and afterwards. Fruit that is bruised at this stage will not keep for long.

A long-handled picker can be used for picking apples high in the tree.

Crimson Bramley apples in March. After being kept in a garden shed over winter, the green has turned to yellow and the red become deeper.

It can be difficult to harvest apples from the top of taller trees. Fruit-picking tools can be helpful for these hard-to-reach fruits. They can be bought fairly cheaply, either as a complete tool or as a head that fits on to a pole in combination with other tools. When picking plums, try to harvest so that the stalk remains with the fruit.

Storing and using apples

While many apples can be eaten straight from the tree, others will taste very sharp when picked but will sweeten and develop their true flavour in storage. Early apples, ready in August and September, can be eaten immediately, or kept for just a few weeks, after which they will go soft and mealy. Mid-season apples are picked in October and will keep for a month or two. Usually they will keep sufficiently well in a cool place, but they will keep a little longer if kept in ideal conditions. A plastic bag in the fridge is a simple way to keep a small number of apples in good condition.

Late-season, or keeping, apples are also picked in October, but will not be ready to eat until their full sweetness and flavour has developed in storage. These varieties can be very useful to grow, for they will provide you with apples during the winter, when home-grown apples are scarce. If you are careful, you can keep some until April.

Keeping apples is easy, provided that a few simple guidelines are followed:

- Start off with good-quality fruit from a suitable variety. Put any blemished or bruised apples to one side for early eating.
- Inspect your apples regularly. It is easy for rots to spread in storage, so remove

any infected apples as soon as they are spotted.

- Keep in a cool, frost-free place. These days, this is likely to be a shed or garage. Some humidity and ventilation will lengthen the keeping time. The ideal temperature is 3-5°C (37-41°F), but it is likely that most outbuildings will be somewhat warmer for some of the time.
- Use suitable containers. In the past, purpose-built wooden trays were used. These are now few and far between and have been superseded by modern materials. It is possible to use cardboard apple boxes from a greengrocer, together with the trays that form layers, but the humble plastic bag is the most effective container that controls the humidity effectively and keeps the fruits isolated so that rot doesn't spread too far.

An apple rack, specially designed for storing apples.

Keeping apples in plastic bags

The ideal bag is clear, to allow for easy inspection, and large enough to contain four or five apples. Place the apples carefully in the bag and fold over the end, but don't seal it completely. Make three holes with the end of a pencil; this will allow the correct balance of humidity and air circulation. Place the bag in the dark in a suitable outbuilding. Inspect regularly, removing any apples that are in less than perfect condition.

Juicing

This is one of many ways of making use of a glut of apples. Almost any apples can be juiced, but some will give better results than others. Those with a high juice content and robust flavour tend to be best. Some apples will make a fine juice on their own, while blends of different varieties can give excellent results.

Blends are usually a mixture of different types of apples, such as full sharps (e.g. Bramley's Seedling or Brown's Apple), together with medium sharps (e.g. Falstaff, Lord Lambourne or James Grieve) and sweets (e.g. Northwood or Sweet Coppin). Full sharps are usually cooking or cider apples, with a particularly sharp taste, while medium sharps are somewhat sweeter, with less acidity. Sweets, as their name implies, are sweet apples, although they can be sweet cider apples as well as dessert apples.

See Appendix 2.6 for details of varieties suitable for juicing, and a description of the juice they make.

Commercial blends are often around 10-15 per cent full sharps, 75 per cent medium sharps and 10-15 per cent sweets, or 70-80 per cent full sharps and 20-30 per cent sweets.

You can experiment with making up your own blends from the different trees in your garden or orchard, or get together with your neighbours, or even the whole street or village where you live. Grouping together with other people can bring down the cost of hiring or buying equipment. Presses can be bought from Vigo (See Resources) or rented from some orchard groups. It is worth using decent-sized equipment to make the process more efficient – it can take forever to make a bottle of juice using the smallest presses, whereas the juice can flow from a large press like a small waterfall.

Adding 5g of ascorbic acid (Vitamin C) per 10 litres of juice (1/5 ounce per 17.5 pints) will help to prevent the apple juice from turning brown through oxidisation and also bring out the flavour of the juice.

Apple juice stored in the fridge will last only three or four days, while juice that is frozen or pasteurised will last a long time. Apple juice for freezing should be placed into plastic bottles that are not quite full to the top. Glass bottles can be used for pasteurising: this can be done in a home-made way using large containers to heat the bottles of juice, or by using a purpose-built pasteuriser that can handle large quantities of bottles at one time. Good hygiene standards and heating the juice to the correct temperature are vital to achieve effective preservation. The water surrounding the bottles should be heated to 77°C (170°F) for 30 minutes – this will kill

Making apple juice on a traditional-style apple press.

the yeasts that would otherwise start the process of fermentation.

Making cider

Cider making is an art that has developed over the centuries, giving rise to a variety of drinks from rough farmyard scrumpy through to the refined ciders that are popular today.

Unfortunately, making cider is not a way to preserve most dessert and cooking apples. The production of good cider relies on the use of cider apple varieties containing high levels of tannin (see page 180). It is beyond the scope of this book to provide a detailed description of the methods for making cider, but there are a number of books available on the subject; see the Resources section for books and websites on cider making.

Apples and crab apples can also be made into very acceptable wine.

Drying

Drying apples is a method of preserving them that dates from the times when freezers were unknown. Although seldom used today, drying apples gives them a completely different taste and texture from freezing. Cored slices of apples about 5mm (1/8") thick can be dried in a low oven, or even over a house radiator. As soon as the slices are cut, they should be dipped into solution of 100ml (3.5fl oz) of lemon juice, 200ml (7fl oz) water and a teaspoon of sugar; this prevents the apples from turning brown. Lightly salted water can be used as an alternative.

If using an oven, the slices of apples can be threaded on to bamboo canes or skewers cut to fit the width of the oven. Set the oven to its lowest temperature, somewhere around 110°C (225°F) or Gas Mark 1/4. Leave the oven door slightly ajar and 'cook' for about 8 hours. Cool for at least 12 hours in a dry place before the rings are packed into a dry jar or similar container. Purpose-made drying boxes or dehydrators are also available for drying fruit.

Bottling

Another 'old-fashioned' method, the process of bottling involves packing slices of apple into bottling jars, covering them with syrup and then sterilising and sealing the jars to prevent the entry of bacteria. There are various methods of bottling apples (see the Resources section for a couple of relevant books). Although bottling apples is quite feasible, it is better suited to softer fruit, such as peaches and cherries, which usually arrive in smaller quantities.

Preserves and chutneys

There are many ways of using apples in preserves and chutneys. This is essentially using sugar or vinegar to preserve the fruit and other ingredients. Apples are a good base for chutneys, and their high pectin content plays a useful role in helping preserves to set. Apples can also be used in sauces, relishes, jams and jellies. Crab apple jelly is a highly prized preserve, and a good use of a fruit that is often left unused.

Freezing

The advent of home freezing has made the preservation of gluts of fruit such a simple task, suitable for modern lifestyles, when many of us seem to have so little time. Apples are most commonly frozen after being cooked into a purée, but they can also be frozen as slices, either after blanching for 1-2 minutes, or after being dipped into a solution to prevent discolouration, as for drying.

Chapter 11

Pears

"There are only ten minutes in the life of a pear when it is perfect to eat."
Ralph Waldo Emerson

Pears are a wonderful fruit when they are at their best: 'juicy', 'melting' and 'buttery' are all words that have been used to capture the unique flavour of this fruit. There are also subtle undertones to the flavour, from the rosewater taste of Joséphine de Malines to the musky flavour of Jargonelle.

However, throughout the British Isles there are back gardens with stunted Conference trees, producing a few scabby pears each year. You can do much better than this – growing pears well requires a little skill and knowledge, but it is not difficult. If you follow a few simple rules and treat your pears kindly, you will be rewarded with large crops of delicious fruit. In addition, you will enjoy picturesque blossom in the springtime and even good autumn colour on some varieties.

The history of pear growing in Britain

It is thought likely that pears originated from the Caucasus – a mountainous region that includes parts of Iran, Turkey and Georgia.

The European cultivation of pears seems to have been furthered by the Romans, who probably brought pears to Britain. Pliny's *Natural History* records 36 varieties of pear known at this time; it is likely that they were all used for cooking. Black Worcester is a cooking pear, still grown today, that is thought to originate from Roman times.

After the Romans left Britain, pear cultivation was continued in monasteries through the Dark Ages. Although occasional records of English cultivation crop up, pear growing seems to have been much more popular in Belgium and France. It is thought that perry pears arrived from France at the time of the Norman Conquest.

Richard Harris, fruiterer to Henry VIII, introduced continental varieties of pear to the royal orchards in Kent. During the eighteenth century, modern pear breeding started in Belgium. The hard, gritty pears of previous centuries were left behind as new varieties were developed with a soft, buttery texture. The first modern varieties, which are still

Left: Pear trees can be decorative in a garden, as well as providing tasty fruit.

Pear blossom is a beautiful addition to the garden in spring.

grown today, such as Doyenné d'Été and Glou Morceau, were raised in Mons at this time.

Many of the varieties in cultivation today were developed on the continent in the nineteenth century. Doyenné du Comice, Joséphine de Malines and Nouveau Poiteau all date from this period. This early development in Belgium and France was helped by the temperate climate that is ideally suited to growing pears; it was only during the nineteenth century that British pear breeding began to catch up. The prolific fruit nursery Rivers of Sawbridgeworth raised a number of cultivars including Conference, the most popular pear in British gardens.

Amazingly, the most widely grown pear today came from a chance seedling found in a garden in Berkshire. Williams' Bon Chrétien (also known as Bartlett) has been grown all around the world, and is particularly suitable for canning.

Modern breeding programmes have continued in Britain, notably at Long Ashton Research Station, the John Innes Research Institute and East Malling Research. Concorde, released in 1984, is proving to be the most promising of the recent cultivars.

Cultivation of pears

Pears need a warm, sheltered site to give of their best. For this reason, they are most suited to the southern half of the British Isles. Further north, they can be trained against a south-facing wall, or varieties suited to a cooler climate can be chosen (see Appendix 3.2).

Pears are susceptible to canker, scab and fireblight – serious diseases that can affect both the tree and the fruit. Choosing varieties resistant to these diseases (see Appendices 3.3 and 3.4) will help you raise healthy trees. Regular inspection of your trees will enable you to catch pests and diseases early, while they are still easy to control.

For details of pest, disease and other problems with pear trees, and how to deal with them, see Chapter 9 (pages 150-3). See Chapter 2 (page 33) for information on rootstocks.

Conditions

Pears will grow happily in a variety of soils, preferring a deep, well-drained but moisture-retentive soil, with a pH of 6-7. They have more need of moisture retention than apples, so a clay loam is ideal.

They suffer when the soil is thin or dry, particularly over chalk. For light or dry soil, it is helpful to retain the moisture content and improve nutrient levels by mulching with compost or manure. Pears flower during April, so can be prone to damage by late frosts in colder areas or in frost pockets.

Pears benefit from a warm, sunny and sheltered position; some cultivars will only ripen with the added protection of wall training. Likewise, wall training can help pear cultivation to succeed where inclement conditions such as exposure, poor climate or altitude would otherwise prevent it. Growing pears on a slope facing towards the south or west also helps to maximise the available sunlight and warmth. For northern areas, or where conditions are less than favourable, there are cultivars to choose that are more suitable than some of the more delicate French varieties – for example, Hessle, a hardy Yorkshire pear.

Feeding and watering

Pears need a good level of soil moisture to grow well. Incorporating bulky organic material at planting time or mulching with compost or manure will help to retain moisture. Even so, watering may be necessary, particularly for young trees or on free-draining soils. Wall-trained trees should be checked regularly during the summer because the soil at the base of a wall can dry out quickly.

Pears benefit from feeding, preferably during the late winter. A general-purpose fertiliser such as pelleted chicken manure will improve both growth and fruiting. A foliar feed of liquid seaweed applied during the growing season will also help to ensure strong shoot growth.

Pollination

Choosing pear cultivars that will pollinate each other successfully is not a simple matter. Firstly, it should be assumed that all cultivars are self-incompatible, i.e. they need a tree of another variety to pollinate them. The only genuine exception is Improved Fertility, which is self-fertile. Conference is not actually self-fertile, but it will produce some (misshapen) fruits if planted on its own.

Also, many pear cultivars are triploids (see Chapter 3, page 40). This means that they do not have viable pollen of their own; they therefore need another variety to pollinate them and are not capable of acting as pollinators to other varieties – so a third tree is needed to pollinate the second variety in turn. Catillac, Jargonelle, Merton Pride, Pitmaston Duchess, Uvedale's St Germain and Vicar of Winkfield are some common triploid varieties.

Bearing the above in mind, you will need to choose two or more cultivars that flower at the same time. There is, however, another complication, which is that there are two incompatibility groups: the varieties within these groups will not pollinate each other. The groups are:

1. Beurré d'Amanlis, Conference (although Beurré d'Amanlis will pollinate Conference. So, in effect, this incompatibility 'group' just means that Conference won't pollinate Beurré d'Amanlis.)

2. Fondante d'Automne, Laxton's Progress, Laxton's Superb, Louise Bonne of Jersey, Précoce de Trévoux, Seckle, Williams' Bon Chrétien.

If in doubt, the easiest method is to use the search facility on a fruit tree website, for example www.keepers-nursery.co.uk. This will show all the suitable pollinators for any variety, removing any of the complications that can confuse the novice.

Fruit thinning

Pears benefit from thinning of heavy crops. This will produce larger fruits of better quality, and also minimises the risk of branches breaking from the strain of large crops. Thinning is best carried out in mid-July, once the June Drop (see page 41) has taken place.

Fruits are best thinned to leave one fruit every 10-15cm (4-6"), or one to two fruits per cluster. Vigorous trees with healthy growth are able to support a higher density of fruit.

Young trees should not be allowed to bear a heavy crop until they are well established. This can lead to the tree becoming stunted because it is putting its energy into fruit production instead of growing vigorously.

Pear varieties

The number of pear cultivars widely available in Britain is not large, but paying careful attention to the choice of varieties will pay dividends later on. Most of the questions in the box on page 49, to help you choose suitable varieties, apply to pears.

Firstly, think how you intend to use your pears. Although the large majority of pears are for dessert use, there are also varieties for cooking and perry that can easily be overlooked.

Secondly, take a good look at the conditions you have available for growing pears. Do you have a warm, sheltered location that will allow you to grow a wide range of varieties, or will you need to select more robust varieties to ensure success?

As with apples, climate can play a vital role in whether your pears will succeed or fail. Pears are susceptible to scab and canker, fungal diseases that are more common in the wetter western areas of Britain, so choosing varieties resistant to these diseases can be vital. As you move further north, the choice of varieties that will succeed reduces. Late-flowering varieties, or those with frost-resistant flowers, will be more likely to crop well. Fireblight is now a common problem across large parts of southern England. If global warming produces warmer, more humid summers, the problem may well get worse, so resistance to fireblight could be an important factor (see Appendix 3.4 for resistant varieties).

Most pears will not keep for long, so there is actually more than a grain of truth in Ralph Waldo Emerson's quotation at the beginning of this chapter. There are, though, a few varieties that will keep for a while. As a result, these are well worth considering to avoid a glut of pears in the early autumn.

Most varieties of pear are spur-bearing. In the charts in this chapter, all varieties are spur-bearing unless identified as tip-bearing. (See box on page 168 for an explanation of the difference – this is the same for pears as for apples.)

Dessert pears

Taste and texture come into play when choosing dessert varieties. There are two main types of dessert fruit: the soft, buttery textured pears, often of continental origin; and the harder types, typified by Conference. This is purely a matter of taste, as cultivars of both types will grow well in the British climate.

Recommended varieties

The varieties listed here are chosen for their all-round growth and fruiting potential, disease resistance and taste. There is little information available about disease resistance for some of the less well-known varie-

ties. Some popular varieties have been left out because of their susceptibility to disease. Conference is a prime example, because it is susceptible to canker, mildew and scab – there are other varieties that will perform better. Concorde is a similar type of pear that is less prone to disease. Doyenné du Comice (often referred to as just Comice) is another example: it is an excellent pear, but susceptible to scab, mildew and fireblight. As with all fruit, there is no perfect variety – you will need to judge what compromise is best to make, depending on your requirements and conditions.

Varieties are listed in order of season of use.

Recommended dessert pear varieties

Variety	Characteristics of the fruit	Characteristics of the tree	Flowering group	Picking date	Season of use	Pest & disease resistance*
JARGONELLE	A very early pear that is tender and juicy.	Moderately vigorous tree with a spreading habit. Tip-bearer. Triploid. Suitable for northern Britain and areas with late frosts.	C	Early–mid-August	August	Resistant to scab.
BETH	A reliable early pear with good flavour.	Compact, upright spur-bearer, heavy cropper.	D	Late August–early September	Late August–September	

(Cont.)

Variety	Characteristics of the fruit	Characteristics of the tree	Flowering group	Picking date	Season of use	Pest & disease resistance*
GORHAM	A sweet, juicy pear with a musky flavour.	Moderate vigour, upright. Cropping moderate to good. Suitable for northern Britain	E	Early–mid-September	Mid–late September	Resistant to scab, mildew and fireblight.
MERTON PRIDE	A good-quality, juicy dessert pear with creamy, melting flesh.	Vigorous, spreading tree, a good cropper that spurs freely. Triploid. Intolerant of chalk soils.	D	Early–mid-September	Mid–late September	
WILLIAMS' BON CHRÉTIEN	A first-class pear with melting, juicy flesh.	Moderately vigorous, spreading tree, intolerant of chalk soils. Suitable for northern Britain and areas with late frosts.	D	Early September	Mid–late September	Susceptible to scab, mildew and fireblight. The sport known as Glow Red Williams has some resistance to scab.
FONDANTE D'AUTOMNE	Excellent, melting, juicy pear with musky flavour.	Spreading tree with low vigour. Bears young. Reliable cropper. Red leaves in autumn.	D	September	Mid-September –October	Resistant to scab and canker.

(Cont.)

Variety	Characteristics of the fruit	Characteristics of the tree	Flowering group	Picking date	Season of use	Pest & disease resistance*
ONWARD	Excellent-quality fruit with a sweet yet acid flavour.	Tree of moderate vigour, upright becoming spreading. Spurs freely. Good, reliable cropping. Intolerant of chalk. Suitable for northern Britain and areas with late frosts.	E	Mid–late September	Late September –mid-October	Some resistance to scab.
HESSLE	Not a first-class pear, but good for cooler areas. Juicy flesh, lacking a distinct flavour. Suitable for northern Britain.	Vigorous, upright tree, becoming spreading with age. Heavy cropper.	D	Early–mid-September	Late September –October	Resistant to scab, canker and mildew.
BEURRÉ HARDY	Tender, juicy flesh with a rosewater flavour.	Vigorous, upright tree. Slow to bear. Regular cropper. Good autumn colour. Prefers a warm location. Intolerant of chalk soils. Poor pollinator. Suitable for areas with late frosts.	D	Late September –mid-October	October	Resistant to scab. Susceptible to mildew and fireblight.
LOUISE BONNE OF JERSEY	A lovely red-skinned pear with an unusual sweet/acid flavour.	Moderately vigorous tree, upright then spreading. Regular and good cropper, intolerant of chalk soils. Partial tip-bearer. Suitable for northern Britain.	C	Mid–late September	October–November	Very resistant to scab.

(Cont.)

Variety name	Characteristics of the fruit	Characteristics of the tree	Flowering group	Picking date	Season of use	Pest & disease resistance*
CONCORDE	A juicy pear with sweet, smooth flesh.	Compact, upright tree that spurs freely, excellent for wall culture. Heavy cropper.	E	Mid–end September	October– December	Resistant to scab and partially resistant to canker.
NOUVEAU POITEAU	A juicy pear with a rich flavour.	Moderately vigorous. A reliable, heavy cropper. Suitable for areas with late frosts.	E	Early–mid-October	November	Resistant to scab and canker.
JOSÉPHINE DE MALINES	A small winter pear with fine, aromatic flavour.	Weak tree needing a warm location. Heavy cropper. Tip-bearer, so not suitable for wall culture. Intolerant of chalk.	D	Late October	January– February	Resistant to scab.

* Where no details are given on pest and disease resistance, this is because information is not readily available for these varieties. This is particularly the case for the less common varieties.

Cooking pears

All pears can be cooked – it is true that some are more suitable than others, but if you use any dessert variety of pear you will not be disappointed. However, there are also distinct varieties of cooking pears that differ markedly from dessert pears. Sometimes known as warden pears, they tend to be large, hard and often gritty. They need to be stored in frost-free conditions, ripening slowly until their season of use, between December and May. They can be stewed or baked, taking about two hours to soften sufficiently.

Recommended varieties

There is a limited choice of varieties, so all the most commonly available ones are listed in the chart here. They are in order of season of use.

Recommended cooking pear varieties

Variety name	Characteristics of the fruit	Characteristics of the tree	Flowering group	Picking date	Season of use	Pest & disease resistance*
BELLISSIME D'HIVER	An excellent culinary pear, the flesh turning pink on cooking.	Vigorous, upright tree, well spurred. Reliable cropper.	C	October	Late November –April	
VICAR OF WINKFIELD	A cooking pear with good flavour when ripened well, which can be difficult. Also used as a winter dessert pear.	Attractive, spreading tree. Triploid. Fruit may sometimes drop early, making storage problematic.	C	Late September –October	December –February	
UVEDALE'S ST GERMAIN	A second-class cooking pear with gritty flesh.	Vigorous, heavy-cropping tree. Triploid.	C	Late October	December –March	
BLACK WORCESTER	A very old variety with slightly gritty, yellow flesh.	Moderately vigorous, spreading tree with attractive autumn colours. Reliable and heavy cropper. Suitable for northern Britain.	C	October	December –April	
CATILLAC	One of the best-flavoured culinary pears, the flesh turning pink on cooking.	Vigorous and spreading tree, heavy cropping and reliable. Triploid. Intolerant of chalk. Suitable for northern Britain.	D	Mid–late October	January– May	Very resistant to scab.

* Where no details are given on pest and disease resistance, this is because information is not readily available for these varieties. This is particularly the case for the less common varieties.

Perry pears

Perry is pear's equivalent of cider – a fermented drink, which can be of excellent quality, made from a specific type of pear known as perry pears. These are astringent and suitable only for perry production.

Perry pears have been cultivated in France for over a thousand years; they are thought to have arrived in Britain with the Normans in the eleventh century. In England, perry pears have largely been grown in Gloucestershire, Herefordshire and Worcestershire, particularly on the heavier clay soils, where pears will prosper. As with cider, perry has gone in and out of fashion over the years. It is currently undergoing a revival, both as a cheap popular drink and as a fine drink to be compared with wine. As a result, perry pear trees are being planted again.

Traditionally, perry pears were planted on pear rootstocks, producing large trees that could live for two to three hundred years. Because of their large size and slowness to bear, they were often intercropped, either with cereals in a farm situation, or with other fruit trees on more dwarfing rootstocks. Nowadays, perry pear trees are often planted on Pyrodwarf rootstocks in order to give a quicker and more accessible crop that also has some resistance to fireblight.

Most perry pear varieties do not need blending to make perry; a superior result is often obtained by using a single variety. Many of the varieties currently grown date from seventeenth and eighteenth centuries, but have survived the test of time because they are resistant to scab and canker. Fireblight, however, can be a serious problem, particularly because the size of the mature trees

A perry pear tree.

makes pruning out diseased wood difficult. Late-flowering varieties are most at risk of contracting fireblight.

Recommended varieties

Varieties are listed in order of picking date. The 'milling period' refers to the time after harvesting in which the fruit must be processed – this period of time can be very short for some of the early varieties. Flowering times for perry pears are described as early, mid or late, because of the lack of precise information available for these pears. Another variety that flowers at the same time is needed to ensure pollination.

Recommended perry pear varieties

Variety	Characteristics of the fruit	Characteristics of the tree	Flowering time	Picking date	Milling period	Pest & disease resistance*
THORN	Produces medium-acid, low-tannin perry of average-to-good quality.	Moderately vigorous tree, upright and compact. Heavy cropping.	Mid	End September	1 week	Resistant to scab.
BLAKENEY RED	Medium-acid, medium-tannin perry of fairly good quality.	Medium-to-large tree, upright becoming spreading. Very heavy and reliable cropper. Also used for cooking.	Mid	Late September–early October	1 week	
JUDGE AMPHLETT	Vintage-quality, medium-acid, low-tannin perry.	Moderately vigorous tree with twiggy growth. Regular, heavy cropper.	Early	Late September–early October	1 week	Very resistant to scab.
HENDRE HUFFCAP	Good-quality perry with low-to-medium acid and low tannin.	Tall, upright tree, prone to breaking limbs due to heavy crops. Regular cropper.	Mid	Early October	2 weeks	Resistant to scab.
WINNAL'S LONGDON	Good-quality perry, medium-to-high acidity, low tannin.	Large, vigorous tree, heavy cropping.	Mid	Early October	1 week	Very resistant to scab.

(Cont.)

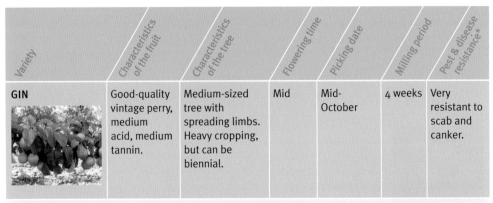

Variety	Characteristics of the fruit	Characteristics of the tree	Flowering time	Picking date	Milling period	Pest & disease resistance*
GIN	Good-quality vintage perry, medium acid, medium tannin.	Medium-sized tree with spreading limbs. Heavy cropping, but can be biennial.	Mid	Mid-October	4 weeks	Very resistant to scab and canker.

* Where no details are given on pest and disease resistance, this is because information is not readily available for these varieties. This is particularly the case for the less common varieties.

Asian pears

Asian (or nashi) pears are derived from different *Pyrus* species from European pears, but they share some of the same characteristics, so Asian pears can be pollinated by European pears. The fruits, however, are quite different, looking more like an apple than a pear. They also ripen on the tree, unlike European pears. The fruit has a delicate flavour and gritty but juicy flesh.

Asian pears require warm summers to ripen properly. At present they can be grown successfully in southern England in most summers, but as global warming increases it is likely that their cultivation will become more widespread further north.

The cultivation of Asian pears is similar to that of European pears, although the Asian varieties are not generally compatible with quince rootstocks. As a result, they are usually available on Pyrodwarf and wild pear rootstocks. Asian pears suffer from the same pests and diseases as European pears.

The fruits change colour as they ripen, from a russet brown to a golden yellow. It is best to avoid picking these pears after heavy rain, when the sweetness declines. Fruits are generally rather delicate, bruising easily and keeping for just a few weeks.

Asian (or nashi) pears.

Recommended varieties

Only some varieties of Asian pear perform well in the British climate. Trials are still progressing to ascertain which are the most suitable varieties. The following varieties look likely to perform well here.

Varieties are listed in order of season of use.

Recommended Asian pear varieties							
Variety name	Characteristics of the fruit	Characteristics of the tree	Flowering group	Picking date	Season of use	Pest & disease resistance
SHINSUI	Russet-coloured fruit, with juicy and fairly smooth flesh of good flavour.	Vigorous tree with few branches. Light cropper, needs little pruning.	C	Late July–late August	Late July–late August	Susceptible to scab, with slight susceptibility to mildew and fireblight.
SHINSEIKI	Greenish-yellow fruit with coarse, juicy flesh of average flavour.	Moderately vigorous, spreading tree. Heavy cropper.	C	Mid-August–early September	Mid-August–early September	Susceptible to scab, mildew and fireblight.
NIJISSEIKI (syn. TWENTIETH CENTURY)	Small yellow fruit with crisp, juicy flesh of good flavour.	Weak-growing tree. Fruit can need thinning because of heavy crops.	C	Mid-September–late October	Mid-September–mid-October	Susceptible to mildew, scab and canker.

Pruning pear trees

Pear-tree pruning is very similar to apple-tree pruning. Most pears, being spur-bearing (see Chapter 10, page 224), also fruit on two-year-old or older wood. The few tip-bearing pears produce their fruit from fruit buds at the end of shoots formed during the previous summer.

The main difference between apples and pears is that pear growth tends to be more upright, with a few exceptions. For this reason, encouraging the tree to grow laterally, by pruning to an outward-facing bud or shoot, is particularly important for pears, especially during formative pruning.

TIMING OF PRUNING

Pear trees are usually pruned when they are dormant: from December, when all the leaves have fallen, until the end of February, or into March in colder winters or areas. Pruning during the winter encourages growth, but there are some circumstances when pruning in the summer, which doesn't encourage growth, is more appropriate:

Restricted forms of tree, such as cordons and espaliers, are normally pruned in early August (see Chapter 10, pages 193-7).

Trees that have been pruned too hard will throw up a number of vigorous shoots as a result. These should be thinned out in the summer (see Chapter 9, page 142)

Pruning can also be carried out in the summer to remove shoots that are shading ripening pears and causing congestion, preventing a heathy flow of air through the crown of the tree. Only small amounts of growth need to be removed in this case.

Regulated pruning (see Chapter 8, page 113) is well suited to mature pear trees and can be introduced once the tree has become well established. Many varieties of pear spur very freely, leading to congested spur systems within a short space of time, so spur thinning (see Diagram 29, page 188) can be used on a regular basis where this occurs.

The forms of tree used for pears, and the methods of pruning, are so similar to those used for apples that following the pruning instructions in Chapter 10 will give perfectly good results. There are, however, subtle differences between the two, so the methods for pruning a **bush tree** are described here, to illustrate these differences.

The pruning of a mature spur-bearing pear tree is shown in Diagram 37. For tip-bearing pears, follow the methods described in Chapter 10 (page 189).

A branch of a pear tree, showing the blossom arising from fruiting spurs.

Fruiting spurs on a pear.

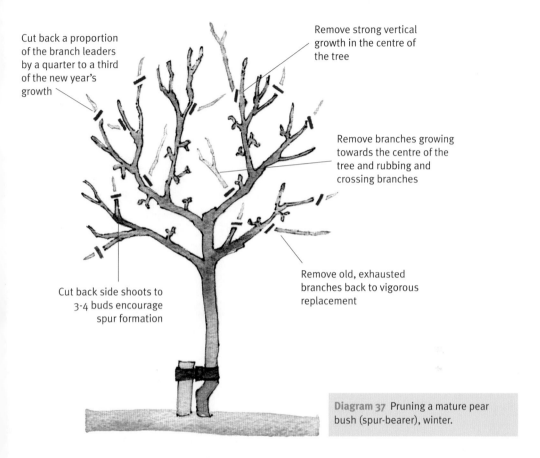

Cut back a proportion of the branch leaders by a quarter to a third of the new year's growth

Remove strong vertical growth in the centre of the tree

Remove branches growing towards the centre of the tree and rubbing and crossing branches

Cut back side shoots to 3-4 buds encourage spur formation

Remove old, exhausted branches back to vigorous replacement

Diagram 37 Pruning a mature pear bush (spur-bearer), winter.

Because of pears' tendency to grow in an upright manner, it can be difficult to keep the centre of a bush open; there is a constant need to cut to outward-facing buds or young shoots. Tying down branches (see pages 96 and 186) will also encourage growth that is upright to assume a more horizontal angle. Pear wood is not as flexible as apple wood, so tying down needs to start before the wood becomes rigid. As with apples, remember that vigorous growth needs to be pruned more lightly than weak growth. When you prune a branch, it will encourage more growth from below the point of pruning, so two or three new shoots will usually emerge from just below the pruning cut.

Growing pear trees in different forms

The bush tree, as just discussed, is the most common form for pear trees, but pears can be grown in a number of different forms, similar to those used for apples (see Chapter 10, pages 186-97). Trees grown on wild pear rootstocks grow into large trees that are suitable only for training as **standards**. The eventual size of tree will depend on the variety grown, but trees on wild pear rootstock can be long-lived and very tall.

The growth habit of the pear lends itself to training as a **dwarf pyramid** – which is somewhere between a bush and a restricted form. It is technically demanding, requiring both winter and summer pruning to keep it artificially small. Designed to allow maximum sunlight and airflow through the tree, it repays the effort required with heavy crops.

Formative pruning of a dwarf pyramid
Because they are kept small by careful pruning, trees trained as dwarf pyramids can be planted closer together than is normal for the rootstock involved: as close as 2m (6'6") apart, providing pruning is carried out regularly so that they do not get out of hand. This is an ideal form for growing pears where space is limited. A permanent 2m (6'6") stake should be inserted at planting time to support

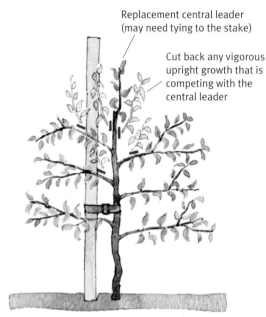

Replacement central leader (may need tying to the stake)

Cut back any vigorous upright growth that is competing with the central leader

First year, summer

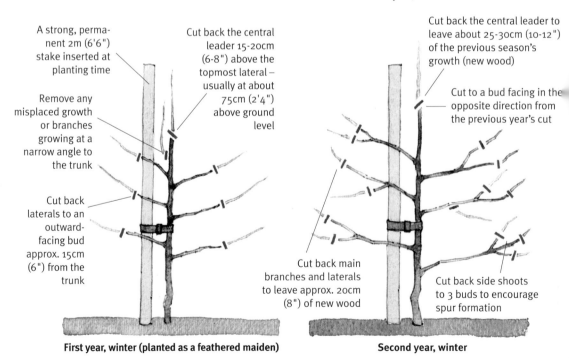

A strong, permanent 2m (6'6") stake inserted at planting time

Remove any misplaced growth or branches growing at a narrow angle to the trunk

Cut back the central leader 15-20cm (6-8") above the topmost lateral – usually at about 75cm (2'4") above ground level

Cut back laterals to an outward-facing bud approx. 15cm (6") from the trunk

Cut back main branches and laterals to leave approx. 20cm (8") of new wood

First year, winter (planted as a feathered maiden)

Cut back the central leader to leave about 25-30cm (10-12") of the previous season's growth (new wood)

Cut to a bud facing in the opposite direction from the previous year's cut

Cut back side shoots to 3 buds to encourage spur formation

Second year, winter

Diagram 38 Formative pruning of a pear dwarf pyramid.

the tree throughout its life. Compact spur-bearing varieties, such as Beth or Concorde, are ideal for training as dwarf pyramids.

Pruning begins once the young tree has formed four to six laterals emerging at a wide angle to the trunk. This will be either after planting a well-developed one-year-old tree, or on a two-year-old tree. The aim of pruning at this stage is to encourage the vigorous upright growth habit to become less vigorous and more horizontal. This is achieved by cutting back the central leader and pruning the laterals hard to outward-facing buds. The process of encouraging strong lower branches

is furthered by removing any vigorous upright growth towards the top of the tree.

Pruning an established dwarf pyramid
Once the tree is established, the majority of the pruning is carried out in summer because this inhibits strong growth. Summer pruning consists of shortening branch leaders and side shoots growing from the main branches. This is carried out in late July in southern England; slightly later further north. Winter pruning consists of spur thinning (see Diagram 29, page 188) and cutting back the central leader, although this can be delayed until spring to discourage regrowth.

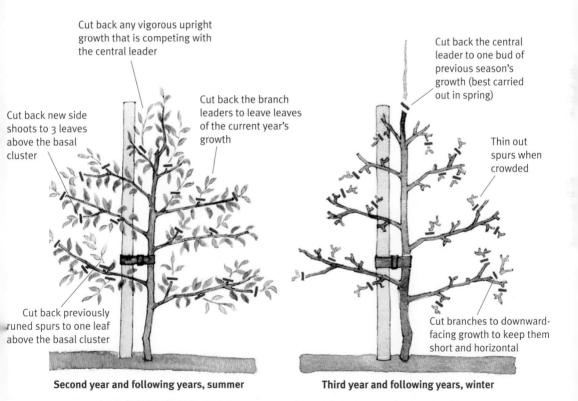

Cut back any vigorous upright growth that is competing with the central leader

Cut back the branch leaders to leave leaves of the current year's growth

Cut back new side shoots to 3 leaves above the basal cluster

Cut back previously pruned spurs to one leaf above the basal cluster

Cut back the central leader to one bud of previous season's growth (best carried out in spring)

Thin out spurs when crowded

Cut branches to downward-facing growth to keep them short and horizontal

Second year and following years, summer

Third year and following years, winter

Diagram 39 Pruning an established pear dwarf pyramid.

Wall-training pear trees

Pears lend themselves well to training on a wall, enjoying the warmth and shelter that it provides. Cultivars that might not ripen sufficiently when grown in the open can be grown successfully against a wall. They are also less prone to developing scab, which can be a debilitating disease for pears. In the north of Britain and in colder spots, training pears against a south- or west-facing wall is the preferred method for growing them successfully.

The methods of training are the same as those for wall-trained apples (see Chapter 10, pages 193-7), with a few subtle differences. Spurs on pear trees can become congested more quickly than on apples, so it is likely that more attention to spur thinning will be needed in winter. Because pear wood hardens quickly, there should be no delay in tying in branches before their flexibility is lost.

Quince C or Pyrodwarf are the most suitable rootstocks for smaller trained trees, such as cordons or espaliers with up to three tiers. Quince A will allow up to six tiers to be trained, particularly on fertile soils. Pears will produce very well on cordons, allowing a number of varieties to be grown in a small space. Pears can also be trained as fans, although this is unusual. Most dessert varieties are suitable for wall training (most cooking varieties are more vigorous), although it is important to check that the varieties chosen are spur-bearers rather than tip-bearers.

Harvesting pears

The harvesting and keeping of pears is more difficult than the growing of pears. This might seem like an exaggeration, but so many pears are spoilt because they are not picked at the correct time and then stored properly until they are perfect to eat. (European pears do not

Pear trees trained into various forms at the Hatton Fruit Garden, East Malling Research, Kent.

Two Conference pears, showing the green colour still evident in the pear on the left, while the pear on the right has taken on an amber shade of yellow. This pear is now very ripe.

ripen quite fully on the tree, but need finishing after picking.) Pick a pear too soon and it will never ripen properly; pick it or eat it too late and it will become 'sleepy', or overripe. This process of spoiling starts in the centre of the pear, so is not detected until biting into it reveals a sickly flesh.

There are two signs that a pear is ready to be picked, the first being a subtle change in the colour. The green colour that a fruit has been showing since it was small slowly turns to a lighter, more yellow shade. This is not a completely reliable indicator, but it is a useful guide. The more significant change is that if you lift the pear and twist slightly, it will come away from the spur. Not all pears will be ready to pick at the same time, so a few repeat visits will be necessary to collect all the fruit.

It is particularly important to pick early fruit at the right time. Some early varieties, such as Williams' Bon Chrétien, Beth and Jargonelle, are particularly prone to spoiling. Once picked, they should be checked regularly in order to catch them at their peak. Later fruit is more tolerant of variations in picking time, but should not be picked too

early or it will fail to ripen properly. Cooking pears and cultivars that will be stored into winter, such as Joséphine de Malines, should be left until the first fruits drop and then all be picked at one time.

Storing and using pears

Although commercial crops kept under optimum conditions can be stored for many months, it is a much more difficult task for the amateur. Pears are best kept in conditions just above freezing. The conditions found in a fridge are excellent for this, so long as the temperature doesn't dip below freezing. Finding room in your fridge for more than a few pears is likely to be problem, but an old fridge in an outbuilding could provide the answer.

Otherwise, wooden trays in a barn or shed are the next best solution; they allow for air circulation and easy inspection of the ripening fruit. Such fruit trays were once widely available but are now hard to find, though they can easily be constructed from old bits of wood or even pallets. Plastic bags should be avoided because they encourage pears to become sleepy.

Look for a slight change in colour, or a softening of the stalk end, to indicate that a pear is nearly ripe. When this stage is reached, a few days in the warmth of the house should bring it to perfection. Once they are in the house, covering the pears with a damp cloth helps to prevent them from drying out too quickly. Regular inspection is needed to catch the fruit at the perfect time for eating. When you get it right, the juice will drip down your chin and the melting texture will fill you with delight.

Because of the ephemeral nature of most pears, it is worth looking at methods of preserving them. With care you can make good use of them when they are all ready at once.

Juicing

Pears can be juiced in exactly the same way as apples, and the juice tastes of pears with a hint of treacle. Depending on the varieties used, pear juice can be slightly thicker than apple juice. If you have a surfeit of apples and not so many pears, as is often the case, you can mix the two together.

The juice can be kept in a fridge for three to four days, or frozen or pasteurised. The methods for making juice are the same as those for apples (see Chapter 10, page 199).

Making perry

Perry is a refined drink, often compared to white wine. Although popular in the past, perry was almost unknown by the middle of the last century, so much so that it became known as pear cider in order to identify it. The area comprising Herefordshire,

Worcestershire and Gloucestershire has traditionally been the centre of perry production in England. Here large trees still stand from perry's heyday in the eighteenth century. There has been a revival in perry production in the last 20 years, both as a traditional drink made by skilled craftsmen and as a commercial drink. Perry is produced from particular varieties of pear that contain high levels of tannin and are more acid than dessert pears.

Drying

Pears can be dried successfully, although, as with apples, precautions should be taken to stop them turning brown when cut. The methods outlined in Chapter 10, page 201, are equally suitable for drying pears.

Bottling and preserves

Pears can be bottled after cooking lightly in a sugar solution. There are numerous variations on this theme, including the use of various spices and bottling pears that have first been pickled. All sorts of pear preparations can be preserved in jars or bottles, including chutney, pear butter, pear honey, jam, jelly and sauce. Various spirits, such as vodka or brandy, combine well with pears.

Other uses

Pears do not freeze particularly well, because they turn to mush. If you do want to freeze pears, it is generally best to cook with them first. A delicious tarte aux poires or pear and cinnamon ice cream can be kept successfully in a freezer. If you still have pears left over, they can be made into a most acceptable wine.

Chapter 12

Plums

"What is more mortifying than to feel that you have missed the plum for want of courage to shake the tree?"

Logan Pearsall Smith

When we think of plums, we usually think of the European plum, of which Victoria is an example, but there are actually many different types of plum. Damsons, bullaces and mirabelles (or Myrobalan plums) are all botanically distinct forms of plum.

The damson is a small, tart plum that can be grown where other plums would struggle.

The origins of the European plum (*Prunus domestica*) are obscure: it is thought to have derived from naturally occurring hybrids in the Caucasus area. Hundreds of cultivars have now been bred, including the greengages, which are a separate group within *P. domestica*. European plums include both cooking and dessert varieties, ranging from the dry acidity of Blaisdon Red through to the toffee-apple sweetness of Kirke's Blue or Jefferson.

Damsons, bullaces and mirabelles all fall into the category *Prunus institia*; they are smaller and tougher trees than European plums and somewhat easier to grow. Damsons are small blue-black fruits with a rich flavour and slightly spicy taste. They are quite sharp and usually used for cooking. Mirabelles, or cherry plums, actually look like large cherries on the tree, in shades of red and yellow. They are generally fairly sweet, perfect for jam making. Bullaces are seen as a wild fruit in Britain. They are small, acid plums that need to be cooked with plenty of sugar.

At the other end of the plum spectrum from the tart bullaces and damsons are the more refined, sweet greengages. Generally, the

THE WESTMORELAND DAMSONS

In the former county of Westmoreland, now part of Cumbria, the Lyth and Winster valleys were home to large orchards of damsons, dating back to the 1700s. The fruits were sent to Lancashire jam factories for making damson jam. In return, charabancs filled with sightseers would visit the valleys in April to admire the wonderful blossom. It is thought that damson skins were used to dye soldiers' uniforms at one time.

Damson Saturday was a local festival in the area, with its heyday between the two World Wars. The area around Kendal was famed for its carts and stalls selling the local damsons. The Second World War saw the demise of the damson trade, as manpower and sugar were in short supply. The Westmoreland Damson Association was formed in 1966 to preserve the damson orchards and encourage the use

The Westmoreland Prune, one of the most widely planted damson varieties in the former county of Westmoreland.

of the fruit. Damson Day is still held each year to promote the remaining orchards and their produce.

more refined the fruit is, the more temperamental it is, so while damsons and bullaces are tough enough to grow in hedges, greengages need a carefully chosen site and plenty of pampering.

The history of plum growing in Britain

The history of plums is more complicated than the history of other fruits, because there is not just one fruit that we can call a plum. The European plum is thought to have derived from crosses between the sloe (*Prunus spinosa*) and the cherry plum (*Prunus cerasifera*). It seems that it spread to Britain from the Mediterranean region, even before the Romans grew it here.

Damsons originated from Damascus in Syria, while bullaces were a native of Britain, their remains having been discovered at Iron Age settlements. Cherry plums, like many fruits, seem to have originated in the Caucasus. Over time, boundaries have become blurred, but these divisions of plums are still meaningful today.

The thousand years after the Romans left Britain saw few advances in plum cultivation; it was largely monasteries that grew plums and perpetuated the few varieties known. Plum growing was reinvigorated by Henry VIII and his fruiterer, Richard Harris, who planted new varieties brought from Europe. In the seventeenth century new types of plums arrived in Britain, such as the German prunes and the reine claudes (later known as greengages), which arrived from France.

By the nineteenth century, deliberate breeding was being carried out in nurseries, the most famous being Rivers of Sawbridge-

worth. Varieties that we still grow today, such as Early Rivers, Czar and several Transparent gages were bred there, while other cultivars were brought in from abroad. Despite all the effort put into breeding new plums, the most famous plum of all, Victoria, was discovered as a chance seedling in 1840.

By the twentieth century, research stations such as Long Ashton and Merton had largely taken over breeding from nurseries. Garden cultivars such as Severn Cross, Thames Cross and Merton Gem were the result of this breeding. Many varieties, such as Opal and Sanctus Hubertus, have been brought to Britain from abroad.

Cultivation of plums

There is a wide range of types of plum, some much more demanding of favourable conditions than others. Greengages fruit and ripen well only in the most favoured locations, while damsons and bullaces will thrive in harsher conditions where other plums would fail.

Plums are susceptible to silver leaf and bacterial canker, both damaging diseases that can seriously damage or even kill trees. It is important to pay attention to correct pruning times and techniques, in order to keep these diseases at bay. Choosing disease-resistant varieties (see Appendix 4.3) will also help to keep your orchard healthy. Some varieties are prone to overcropping, leading to broken branches, which not only disfigure a tree but are an access point for disease.

For details of pest, disease and other problems with plum trees, and how to deal with them, see Chapter 9 (pages 153-5). See Chapter 2 (page 33) for information on rootstocks.

Conditions

Plums prefer a continental climate – that is, a cold, dry winter followed by a warm, dry spring and a hot summer. In Britain, it is only really the south-east of England that can offer such conditions. However, plums will tolerate less favourable climates so long as the soil is to their liking.

The ideal soil is a deep, well-drained, but moisture-retentive loam. Although they detest waterlogging, plums do need a good supply of moisture. For this reason, thin, shallow, or sandy soils will need considerable improvement with organic matter if they are to grow plums successfully. Clay soils are fine as long as the drainage is not compromised.

The addition of manure is helpful because it will aid moisture retention as well as feeding the trees. Plums prefer a slightly acid soil, a pH of 6 to 6.5 being ideal. Lime-induced chlorosis can be a problem on highly alkaline soils. Plums do not enjoy chalky soils, especially where they are thin. Reasonably fertile soils are needed to grow plums: they require good levels of nitrogen to fruit well, but have less need of potash and phosphorus than do some other fruits.

Plums need a sunny, sheltered position to perform well. This is particularly important at blossom time, because they flower early in the season (March to April), when cold, easterly winds can be a problem. Plums are pollinated by bees and other insects that need the encouragement of a sheltered situation at this time of year. Some cooking plums, such as Czar and Pershore, are capable of fruiting well in a slightly shaded position. Damsons and bullaces will also produce decent crops in light shade.

Plum blossom is susceptible to damage by frost. If you are growing plums in an area prone to damaging frosts in late March and April, it is worth choosing late-flowering varieties or those with frost-resistant blossom (see Appendix 4.2). If hard frosts threaten at blossom time, you can protect the blossom with hessian, thick fleece or sheets, keeping the protective material away from the flowers with bamboo canes.

Areas with high rainfall (over 100cm [3'3"] a year) can be problematic for plums, giving rise to higher incidences of bacterial canker and fungal diseases such as brown rot, as well as bringing an increased likelihood of waterlogging.

In essence, plums will do best in a warm, sunny, sheltered location, with deep, fertile soil. However, some are much less fussy than others. Damsons, bullaces and some varieties of plum will grow well in less-than-ideal conditions and areas of high rainfall. In general, early-ripening varieties have less need for the perfect location, whereas late-ripening dessert varieties need as much sun and warmth as possible in order to fully ripen the fruit. Training plums against a wall can improve the warmth, shelter and drainage of a less favourable location.

Feeding and watering

Plums require a good supply of nutrients, particularly nitrogen, although it is also good not to overdo the nitrogen because this will lead to soft, sappy growth that is more prone to attack by pests. Pelleted chicken manure, or blood, fish and bone applied in February will be sufficient, although mulching with manure or compost in the spring will not only add nutrients and organic matter but also help to preserve soil moisture.

Although plum trees appreciate good levels of soil moisture throughout the year, it is unlikely that established trees will need watering in the conditions encountered in the British Isles. Young trees may need watering in dry seasons while establishing. It is worth checking wall-trained trees regularly, because the soil at the base of a wall can dry out quickly.

Pollination

Many plum varieties are self-fertile, meaning that only one tree is needed to obtain a reasonable crop. However, all varieties will produce heavier crops if a suitable pollinator is provided. Some varieties are described as partially self-fertile, meaning that they will set a limited crop on their own, while others are self-incompatible (or self-sterile), meaning that they need another suitable plum tree to ensure pollination. If space is limited, you can get away with one self-fertile tree; otherwise, planting varieties that will pollinate each other will give you heavier crops.

Plum blossom.

Like most fruit, plums are divided into different flowering groups, depending on their time of flowering. In order to pollinate one variety you need to choose a variety from the same group, or an adjacent group. Denniston's Superb (early-flowering), Victoria (mid-season) and Oullin's Gage (late-flowering) are all varieties that are known to be good pollinators.

Fruit thinning

Some varieties will produce very heavy crops in good years. This can lead to broken branches, small fruit and less flavoursome crops. Thinning can be carried out from late to mid-July, after the June Drop (see page 41), ideally leaving one fruit every 5-10cm (2-4") apart, depending upon the size of fruit. Branches bearing large crops can be supported with props, or by maypoling (see pages 95-6), to avoid the branch breaking.

Plum varieties

As with most fruits, disease resistance is an important factor in choosing suitable plums to grow. Get this right in the first place and you will avoid sickly trees later on. It is far better to grow disease-resistant trees in good conditions than to try to control diseases on unhealthy trees.

Victoria, for example, is by far the most popular plum, but this does not make it the best plum to grow. It does have advantages, such as being heavy-cropping, frost-resistant, self-fertile and a good pollinator. Its flavour is pleasant and it is a good plum for jam and cooking, as well as for dessert use. Yet it also has many drawbacks, particularly its susceptibility to bacterial canker and silver leaf. Its heavy cropping is actually its Achilles heel, in that it tends to crop too heavily unless

Kirke's Blue is reputed to be the best-tasting plum, but it crops lightly.

it is thinned and/or propped. Broken branches are a familiar sight on Victoria plum trees, providing a point of entry for disease.

There is, of course, no perfect plum: choosing the best varieties for you to grow is a matter of

compromise between many different factors. For example, Kirke's Blue is a wonderful-tasting plum, but crops only lightly.

Dessert plums

A dessert plum is one that can be eaten straight from the tree. The deliciously sweet greengages are also included here. Although plums do not keep for long, the season can be extended by choosing a range of cultivars that will provide a succession of fruit over a long period.

Recommended varieties

Many plum varieties are listed as dual-purpose, being suitable for both dessert use and cooking. The varieties given here are those known as good-quality dessert plums. Plums will only keep for a short time, so there is no 'season of use' information.

Varieties are listed in order of their picking date.

Recommended dessert plum varieties					
Variety	Characteristics of the fruit	Characteristics of the tree	Flowering group	Picking date	Pest & disease resistance*
HERMAN	Large blue dual-purpose fruit with good flavour.	Upright tree. Reliable cropper. Suitable for northern Britain.	B, self-fertile	Mid–late July	
EARLY LAXTON	A small dual-purpose yellow-and-pink plum with a good sweet flavour.	Weeping tree of low vigour. Good cropper. Frost-resistant flowers. Suitable for northern Britain.	C, self-sterile	Late July–early August	Some suscep-tibility to bacterial canker and fruit split.

(Cont.)

Variety	Characteristics of the fruit	Characteristics of the tree	Flowering group	Picking date	Pest & disease resistance*
OPAL	Small yellow-and-purple plum of good flavour.	Vigorous upright tree. Heavy cropper. Suitable for northern Britain.	C, self-fertile	Early–mid-August	Some resistance to bacterial canker.
EARLY TRANS-PARENT GAGE	Medium-sized, juicy yellow fruit with excellent gage flavour.	Dwarf, bushy tree. One of the most reliable greengages. Suitable to less clement sites.	D, self-fertile	Mid-August	
COUNT ALTHAN'S GAGE	Purple-and-yellow plum with good flavour.	Moderately vigorous, untidy, upright tree. Heavy cropper. Frost-resistant flowers.	D, self-sterile	Mid–late August	Slightly susceptible to bacterial canker.
DENNISTON'S SUPERB	A sweet, juicy yellow plum with an excellent gage-like flavour.	Fairly vigorous, upright tree, later spreading. Heavy and reliable cropper. Can produce good crops in some shade.	B, self-fertile, good pollinator	Mid–late August	Very resistant to bacterial canker.
CAMBRIDGE GAGE	Medium-sized green fruit with excellent gage flavour. Also used for jam.	Hardy, vigorous tree with rounded crown. Moderate cropper. One of the most reliable gages. Happy in chalky soil.	D, partially self-fertile	Mid–late August	

(Cont.)

Variety	Characteristics of the fruit	Characteristics of the tree	Flowering group	Picking date	Pest & disease resistance*
JEFFERSON	Medium-sized yellow fruit with rich, gage-like flavour.	Moderately vigorous, spreading tree. A heavy cropper in good conditions. Frost-resistant flowers.	A, self-sterile	Late August–early September	Some resistance to bacterial canker, silver leaf, brown rot and blossom wilt.
MERTON GEM	Juicy red fruit with good rich flavour. Dual-purpose.	Moderately vigorous, round-headed tree, becoming spreading. Good and reliable cropper.	C, self-fertile	Late August–early September	Resistant to silver leaf.
GOLDEN TRANS-PARENT GAGE	Large golden-yellow fruit with sweet, rich flavour. Suitable for northern Britain.	Low vigour, good for fan training. Heavy cropper.	C, self-fertile	Early–mid-September	
ANNA SPATH	Large purple fruit with good flavour. Dual-purpose.	Vigorous, upright tree. Good cropper.	C, partially self-fertile	Late September	
COE'S GOLDEN DROP	Golden-yellow plum with red speckles. Excellent apricot-like flavour. Plums will keep for a few weeks.	Moderately vigorous, spreading tree requiring good conditions. A light cropper, but worthwhile for its flavour and late season.	B, self-sterile	Late September	

* Where no details are given on pest and disease resistance, this is because information is not readily available for these varieties. This is particularly the case for the less common varieties.

Cooking plums

Although many plums are considered to be dual-purpose, culinary varieties have a distinct tanginess, being low in sugar and high in acidity. Some of the varieties with dry flesh, such as Yellow and Purple Pershore and Blaisdon Red, are particularly good for making jam. As with dessert varieties, it is possible to select varieties that will prolong the season, from Early Rivers, starting in late July, through to Marjorie's Seedling, which will still be cropping in October.

Recommended varieties

These are varieties best known for their culinary qualities. Blue Tit and Reeves, both included here, are dual-purpose plums but are perhaps better known for their culinary value than as dessert plums. There is no 'season of use' information here because plums will keep for only a short time.

Varieties are listed in order of their picking date.

Recommended cooking plum varieties

Variety	Characteristics of the fruit	Characteristics of the tree	Flowering group	Picking date	Pest & disease resistance*
EARLY RIVERS	Small dark-blue fruit with rich, damson-like flavour. Also used for dessert if fully ripe.	Small tree with weeping habit. Reliable and heavy cropper. Will crop in shady conditions.	C, self-sterile	Late July–early August	
BLUE TIT	Medium-sized dark-blue fruit with excellent gage-like flavour. Also used for dessert.	Compact tree, good cropper. Frost-resistant blossom.	E, self-fertile	Mid-August	
PURPLE PERSHORE	Large purple fruit with dry texture and reasonable flavour. Very good for jam.	Vigorous twiggy tree with pendulous habit. Heavy cropper in good years. Will crop in shade. Suitable for northern Britain. Frost-resistant blossom.	D, self-fertile	Mid-August	Resistant to silver leaf.

(Cont.)

Variety	Characteristics of the fruit	Characteristics of the tree	Flowering group	Picking date	Pest & disease resistance*
REEVES	Large, red-purple fruit with a good flavour. Dual-purpose.	A moderately vigorous tree producing heavy crops. Grows well in wetter areas.	E, self-fertile	Mid-August	
BELLE DE LOUVAIN	Large dark-red fruit with dry texture and excellent flavour when cooked.	Very vigorous, upright tree. Reliable and heavy cropper. Sometimes used as a windbreak. Frost-resistant blossom, suitable for northern Britain. Will crop in shade.	C, self-sterile	Mid–late August	
YELLOW PERSHORE (syn. YELLOW EGG)	A medium-large yellow fruit with dry flesh with reasonable flavour. Excellent for jam.	Tree of moderate vigour, upright becoming spreading. Often grown on its own roots (i.e. without a rootstock). Will crop in the shade. Suitable for northern Britain. Frost-resistant blossom.	D, self-fertile	Mid–late August	A healthy tree, resistant to bacterial canker and silver leaf.
BLAISDON RED	Large red plum with sharp, dry flesh. Excellent for jam.	Large, vigorous, upright trees. Very heavy cropper.	D, self-fertile	Late August	Very resistant to bacterial canker and silver leaf.

(Cont.)

Variety	Characteristics of the fruit	Characteristics of the tree	Flowering group	Picking date	Pest & disease resistance*
EDWARDS	Very large purple fruit with juicy flesh of good flavour. Good for jam.	Vigorous, spreading tree. Heavy cropping, reliable. Branches prone to breaking under the weight of fruit	D, self-fertile	Early–mid-September	Susceptible to blossom wilt.
WARWICKSHIRE DROOPER	Medium-sized yellow fruits that hang well on the tree. Sweet and tender yellow flesh.	Vigorous tree with an attractive weeping habit. Heavy and reliable cropper. Suitable for northern Britain and shady conditions.	C, self-fertile	Early–mid-September	
MONARCH	Large dark-blue fruit with firm flesh that has good flavour when cooked.	Vigorous, upright tree with reasonable crops. Tolerates light soils. Will crop in the shade.	B, self-fertile	Mid–late September	Resistant to silver leaf.
MARJORIE'S SEEDLING	Medium-large dark-purple fruit, juicy and sweet for a cooking plum.	Large, vigorous tree. Heavy cropper. Suitable for northern Britain.	E, partially self-fertile	Late September –mid-October	Very resistant to bacterial canker and silver leaf. Resistant to blossom wilt.

* Where no details are given on pest and disease resistance, this is because information is not readily available for these varieties. This is particularly the case for the less common varieties.

Damsons and bullaces

Damsons and bullaces are much tougher than other plums; they will tolerate conditions that other plums would turn their noses up at, growing in any reasonable soils that are not waterlogged. They can therefore be grown all over Britain without difficulty. They suffer much less from diseases than other plums (most are resistant to silver leaf), but are still susceptible to the blossom being damaged by frost.

Recommended varieties

All damsons and bullaces will grow in wet conditions and in northern Britain, and are relatively free of pests and diseases. Most are resistant to silver leaf. Shropshire Prune, Merryweather Damson and Farleigh Damson are known to be well suited to exposed locations.

Specific information on pest and disease resistance in general and, for the less well-known fruits, on suitability for different conditions, is not readily available. Varieties are listed in order of their picking date.

Recommended varieties of damsons and bullaces

Variety	Characteristics of the fruit	Characteristics of the tree	Flowering group	Picking date
MERRYWEATHER DAMSON	Large dark fruit with good flavour.	Vigorous, spreading tree. Good and precocious cropper. Suitable for northern Britain and wet areas.	D, self-fertile	Early September
SHROPSHIRE PRUNE (syn. DAMSON PRUNE)	Large (for a damson) fruit with strong, rich flavour.	Compact, twiggy tree. Regular but light cropper. Suitable for northern Britain and wet regions.	D, self-fertile	Early September

(Cont.)

Variety	Characteristics of the fruit	Characteristics of the tree	Flowering group	Picking date
FARLEIGH DAMSON	A small dark-blue damson with a good flavour.	Dense, compact tree with thorny branches. Heavy cropper if cross-pollinated. Suitable for northern Britain and wet areas.	D, partially self-fertile	Mid-September
LANGLEY BULLACE	Large black fruit, more like a damson than a bullace.	Vigorous tree, upright, but with weeping, twisted branches.	C, self-fertile	Late September–late October
BLACK BULLACE	Small black fruit with an acid flavour. Virtually a wild fruit. Good for jam.	Small bushy tree with thorny branches. Heavy cropper.	C, self-fertile	Nominally September–October, but can be left on the tree until the first frosts.
WHITE BULLACE (syn. GOLDEN BULLACE)	Very small pale-yellow fruit, slightly sweet if left on the tree to ripen.	Moderately vigorous tree. Good cropper.	D, self-fertile	Early October

Mirabelles

Also known as cherry plums, mirabelles are small round plums, mostly yellow or red, that are good for cooking and jam. They can also be eaten fresh when they are fully ripe. In Britain, they do best in the east of England, where they are often seen growing in roadside hedgerows, depositing their colourful fruit on the road in August. They will tolerate a little shade.

Most mirabelles are not included in the normal pollination groupings for plums because they flower earlier in the year. This makes the blossom very susceptible to frost damage. They are all self-fertile or partially self-fertile. Mirabelles are sometimes grown as fruiting windbreaks.

Trees are often sold simply as cherry plums, but there a few improved varieties. As with many damsons and bullaces, little detailed information on specific varieties is available.

Mirabelle (cherry plum) blossom.

Recommended mirabelle varieties

Variety	Characteristics
GYPSY (syn. GYPSY MIRABELLE) 	A later-flowering cultivar with flavoursome large red fruit. The result of recent efforts to breed improved varieties with larger fruits. Partially self-fertile. Pick late August. Best cooked.
MIRABELLE DE NANCY 	A small yellow cherry plum with a good sweet flavour. Somewhat frost-resistant, but still shy-cropping. Partially self-fertile, flowering period late. Pick early–mid-August.
RED MIRABELLE (syn. MYROBALAN RED) 	A small red cherry plum that has been grown in Britain since the seventeenth century. Self-fertile. Pick late July–early August. Best cooked.

THE DITTISHAM PLUM

Dittisham is a small village in South Devon that is famous for its plums. Legend has it that the local fishermen were called to salvage a wreck outside the harbour at the nearby port town of Dartmouth, but all they found on the ship were plums. It is likely that they were actually prunes rather than plums, because plums would not have kept long enough for a sea voyage. The fishermen, used to salvaging more lucrative cargoes, brought the prunes back to the village and planted them.

The Dittisham Ploughman plum.

Although this might seem a fanciful tale, there are still plum trees growing on their own roots (as opposed to being grafted) all around the village. The main variety is the Dittisham Ploughman, whose name is said to originate from the German *pflaumenn* *baum*, meaning plum tree. There are also two local varieties of damson, the Dittisham Black and the Dittisham Damson. The plums are sold locally and also used to produce Dittisham Plum Liqueur.

Pruning plum trees

Plum trees can be trained into a variety of different forms. The **bush** is one of the most common, because it is simple to maintain, requiring little pruning. The **pyramid** is a method of training that keep the trees smaller, but requires more work to keep their restricted shape. (The spindlebush is a similar form, but is mainly used only in commercial orchards.) Although rarely grown these days, large trees on Brompton rootstocks can be trained as **standards** or **half standards**. **Fan training** allows plum trees to benefit from the shelter of a wall, as well as making it easier to protect them against birds or frost. In more northerly areas, wall training allows a wider range of varieties to be grown. **Cordons** are suitable if you would like to grow a number of varieties in a limited space. This can, however, require a lot of work in order to keep them trained properly. Restricted forms are best grown on Pixy rootstock.

Pruning should be carried out with care, avoiding leaving any jagged wounds that can be a point of entry for silver leaf spores. Use a sharp pruning saw, follow good pruning practices (see Chapter 8, pages 104-5), and clean up any problem areas with a sharp pruning knife. It is best not to use loppers on plums unless they are able to make a clean cut. Branches should be pruned as early in their life as possible, so as not to leave large cut surfaces. Careful observation and forethought will allow many cuts to be made instead by 'pinch pruning' – pinching out

TIMING OF PRUNING

The timing of plum tree pruning is largely determined by plums' susceptibility to silver leaf and bacterial canker (see Chapter 9, pages 130 and 139). Silver leaf is a particularly serious problem on plum trees, which can lead to the death of trees and even the grubbing out of whole orchards. Silver leaf spores are released between September and May, so pruning needs to be carried out between June and August. The only exception to this is the formative pruning of young trees, which benefit from pruning when the buds have broken in the spring. Likewise, pruning in summer helps to keep plum trees free from bacterial canker, which can also be contracted through pruning wounds.

growth using the finger and thumb – at an early stage.

A wound paint (see page 140) should be used on any pruning cuts on plums that are large enough to be made with a pruning saw.

It is important to check ties regularly on plum trees, because any wounds formed by rubbing on the stake can allow silver leaf spores to enter the tree.

Plums fruit at the base of one-year-old shoots, as well as along the length of two-year-old and older growth. Fruiting gradually declines on older branches, so the aim of pruning plums is to encourage new growth that will fruit and to remove branches that are exhausted, cutting them back to replacement growth.

Plums are prone to developing suckers, which are best removed during the summer.

Formative pruning of a plum bush

Plum trees can grow vigorously when young. They will need careful training at this stage to prevent the tree from forming an unruly, upright tangle (see photo on page 98).

The bush is an ideal form for easy management and good productivity. However, even using the more dwarfing rootstocks, you will need a ladder to access the top of the tree – for pruning as well as picking.

A one-year-old plum tree is likely to have a number of laterals when planted during the winter. Leave these alone at this stage, unless it is vital to remove them to allow the fitting of the stake to the tree. Once the buds have broken, formative pruning can begin.

A bush tree will have a clear trunk of between 75cm and 125cm (2'6" and 4'2"), so firstly, cut back all laterals below this point by two-thirds; these will then be removed in the following year. Above this, select four or five strong branches, growing with a wide angle to the trunk, to form the main branches of the tree. These branches (or laterals) should be well spaced, so as not to compete with each other later in the tree's life, and they should originate from all sides of the trunk in order to form a well-balanced tree. Any branches growing at a steep angle to the trunk should be removed, because they are weak and likely to break under the weight of a heavy crop when the tree is mature.

If there are not sufficient branches that have formed in the first year, wait until the second year to choose and retain these framework branches. Once sufficient branches have

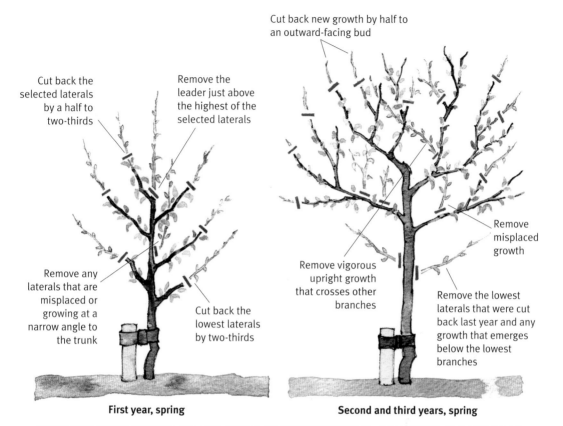

Cut back new growth by half to an outward-facing bud

Cut back the selected laterals by a half to two-thirds

Remove the leader just above the highest of the selected laterals

Remove any laterals that are misplaced or growing at a narrow angle to the trunk

Cut back the lowest laterals by two-thirds

Remove vigorous upright growth that crosses other branches

Remove misplaced growth

Remove the lowest laterals that were cut back last year and any growth that emerges below the lowest branches

First year, spring

Second and third years, spring

Diagram 40 Formative pruning of a plum bush.

developed, remove the leader just above the topmost main branch.

The laterals that are retained should be cut back by half to two-thirds to an outward-facing bud. On horizontal branches, or on varieties with a spreading habit, you will need to cut to an upward-facing bud to prevent the growth from becoming too weeping. Remember that, over time, branches are likely to become more horizontal with age, particularly under the weight of heavy crops.

During years 2 and 3, continue to prune in the spring, shortening the new growth of laterals or sublaterals by half. On weaker branches, half of the new growth can be removed, while stronger growth should be pruned more lightly. Any branches that are crossing, rubbing, misplaced or growing inwards should be removed. Likewise, strong vertical growth should be removed as soon as it is seen. If viewed from above (or below), the main branches should resemble a bicycle wheel in their pattern. During this period in the tree's life, it is important to develop a strong, evenly spaced framework of branches.

This method of pruning continues until the crown of the tree is formed and the tree is fruiting well.

Pruning an established plum bush

The aim of pruning an established plum tree is to maintain its health and to ensure the formation of young wood, on which fruiting takes place. This is largely a natural process that just needs a little encouragement. Any dead, damaged or diseased wood should be removed. Strong vertical growth and misplaced or crossing branches can also be cut out. It is important to ensure that growth does not become too congested, preventing sunshine and light from reaching the ripening fruit. Where this happens, gently thin out crowded areas. It is good practice to keep the middle of the tree clear to allow air to flow and sunlight to penetrate.

Thin out heavy crops in early summer, preferably allowing 6-10cm (2.5-4") between fruits, depending on their size. If a branch has broken due to a heavy crop of fruit, prune it back to a junction with another branch. Do this immediately, whatever the time of year, so as not to allow a wound where silver leaf spores can enter. Where a heavy crop has developed, it is worthwhile propping any branches that look liable to break. Once a branch has been propped, consider whether you can prune to an upward-facing shoot so that the branch doesn't become too low in the following season.

Pruning a plum pyramid

Although they require more regular pruning than bush trees, plum pyramids are ideal for the smaller garden, or where space is at a premium. Grown on Pixy rootstock, they can be kept to 2-2.5m (6'6"-8') tall, depending on the variety.

A pyramid is a tree with the central leader intact and a number of horizontal branches radiating from the trunk. Careful pruning produces a shape like that of a traditional Christmas tree, where the lower branches receive plenty of light because the growth of the higher branches is restricted. The smaller size of the tree makes it more accessible for pruning, harvesting and netting. It can be difficult to train varieties with vigorous upright growth as pyramids, because the aim is to produce horizontal branches.

A strong 2.5m (8') stake is inserted at planting time (see Chapter 6, page 77). Do not try to do this after the tree has been planted, because you are likely to damage the roots. The stake stays in place throughout the life of the tree. Plums trained as pyramids can be planted more densely than would otherwise be possible on the same rootstock. On Pixy rootstock, 2.5-3m (8-10') apart is sufficient, while trees on St Julien A can be planted 3-4m (10-13') apart, depending on the vigour of the variety.

If you are starting with a maiden (one-year-old) tree, remove the central leader in the spring at around 1.5m (5') from the ground (see Diagram 41). Allow the top bud to grow on as the replacement leader, but rub out the

---

MAYPOLING

Maypoling is a method of supporting the branches of a tree using rope that is fastened from the top of a stake to the middle of a branch (see Diagram 14, page 96). It resembles the traditional maypole that children dance around in the springtime. This is particularly suited to pyramid trees, which already have a central stake in place.

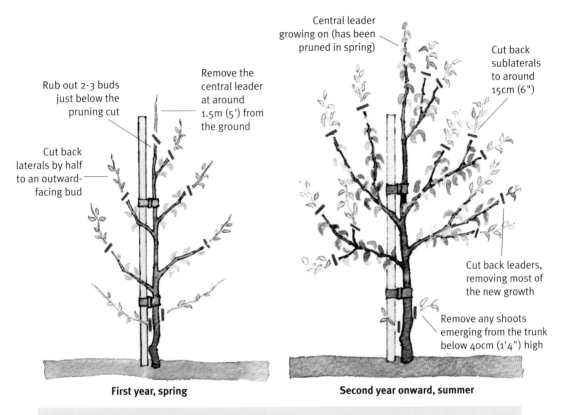

Rub out 2-3 buds
just below the
pruning cut

Remove the
central leader
at around
1.5m (5') from
the ground

Cut back
laterals by half
to an outward-
facing bud

Central leader
growing on (has been
pruned in spring)

Cut back
sublaterals
to around
15cm (6")

Cut back leaders,
removing most of
the new growth

Remove any shoots
emerging from the trunk
below 40cm (1'4") high

First year, spring

Second year onward, summer

Diagram 41 Formative pruning of a plum pyramid.

three buds (or shoots) immediately below the top bud. If allowed to develop, these buds would go on to form branches at a steep angle to the trunk, competing with the leader. Removing the central leader encourages the formation and growth of laterals further down the trunk. Laterals emerging from the trunk can be cut back by about half (the upper and lower ones treated the same), to an outward-facing bud.

In the spring of the second year, again prune back the (replacement) leader, removing two-thirds of last year's growth, and again rub out the three buds (or shoots) below the top one.

The remainder of the pruning takes place during the summer. The laterals that were pruned last year will now have developed sublaterals; prune these back to around 15cm (6") long. Remove any new shoots emerging from the trunk below 40cm (1'4") high. Also, shorten any new laterals that have formed, by removing half of the new growth. The aim is to form a pyramid shape, with the lower branches dominant. The upper branches should not be allowed to shade out the lower branches, otherwise growth will become weaker on the lower ones. This process of shortening sublaterals (side shoots) during the summer helps to produce a small tree.

Once the tree is reaching maturity, the pruning continues in a similar vein, but with all pruning carried out in the summer months, apart from pruning the leader, which is done in the spring (see Diagram 42). The leader is still shortened by around two-thirds each year. A new leader will grow from a bud just below this pruning cut, but this growth will become weak in time. Any vigorous, upright growth is best removed, along with any dead, diseased or damaged growth and misplaced shoots. In time, growth will become congested, needing some thinning to allow air and light to penetrate. Continue to shorten the twiggy growth on the outside of the tree, in order to keep the tree compact.

Pruning standards and half standard plum trees

Plum trees planted on Brompton rootstock (vigorous) can be trained as standards or half standards. The formative pruning is similar to that of a plum bush, except that a taller clear trunk is needed, usually between 1.7 and 1.85m (5'8"-6'2"), and pruning of laterals can be a little less hard. This is a useful form for trees in an orchard with livestock, or for a specimen tree in a large garden.

Pruning a plum fan

This is an excellent method of training plums, with the wall providing warmth and shelter. It means that more temperamental plums, such as gages, can be grown in many locations that would not otherwise prove successful. Fans can also be grown in the open, in warm or sheltered locations, on a system of wires and posts. A plum fan on Pixy rootstock will take up a space about 3m (10') wide by 2m (6'6") high, while a tree grown on St Julien A rootstock will require a space around 3.5m (11'6") by 2.5m (8').

The ideal tree to plant is one with two strong laterals low to the ground and of roughly even vigour. In the spring after planting, the central leader is removed above these two laterals and the two laterals (or arms) cut back by one-third to an outward-facing bud. Tie these laterals to bamboo canes to support them and keep them straight. If one arm is less vigorous than the other, allow this one to grow at a more upright angle, which will increase its vigour. Eventually both arms should be at an angle of 40-45 degrees to the horizontal. Any less vigorous laterals, below the two selected, can be retained until the summer in

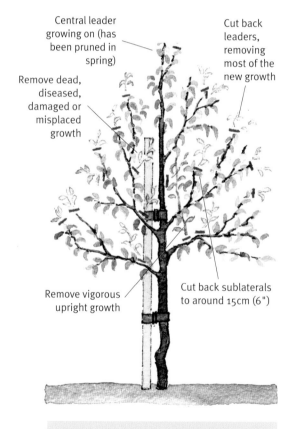

Central leader growing on (has been pruned in spring)

Cut back leaders, removing most of the new growth

Remove dead, diseased, damaged or misplaced growth

Remove vigorous upright growth

Cut back sublaterals to around 15cm (6")

Diagram 42 Pruning an established plum pyramid (summer).

case one of the selected laterals fails to grow successfully.

During the period of active growth in the summer, tie the new growth at the end of each arm to the bamboo cane (see Diagram 43). Because the laterals were cut back in the spring, side shoots (or sublaterals) lower down will be stimulated. Keep the best placed of these to form new ribs that will fill in the space on the wall. Ideally there will be two above and two below the original lateral. These new ribs can also be tied in to bamboo canes. Any growth that is misplaced, or surplus to requirements, can be pinched back (or cut) to one or two leaves at the base of the shoot. All shoots growing directly towards the wall, or away from it, can be removed.

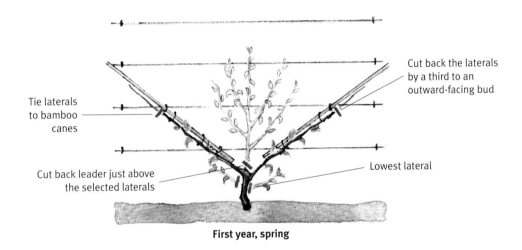

Tie laterals to bamboo canes

Cut back leader just above the selected laterals

Cut back the laterals by a third to an outward-facing bud

Lowest lateral

First year, spring

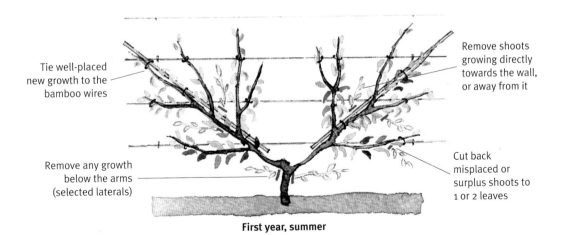

Tie well-placed new growth to the bamboo wires

Remove any growth below the arms (selected laterals)

Remove shoots growing directly towards the wall, or away from it

Cut back misplaced or surplus shoots to 1 or 2 leaves

First year, summer

Diagram 43 Formative pruning of a plum fan.

This process is continued in subsequent years, with the new growth gradually filling in the space in the middle of the tree. Over time, these bamboo canes and main branches will form a fan shape against the wall. In the spring of years 2 and 3, the new ribs can be shortened by removing about one-third of the previous season's growth. Healthy side shoots, in a place where they are needed to fill in gaps in the framework, can be trained into place. Those that are not required can be regularly pinched back over the season to leave just a few leaves at the base. The growth over a season can be quite vigorous, so it is important to keep on top of cutting back new growth, before it becomes congested. It will usually be necessary to prune several times over a season. It is much better to prune young growth regularly, preferably by pinching it out, than to carry out an annual pruning.

Such instructions can seem daunting and complicated, but there is no need to worry too much about getting it exactly right. The important things to remember are training in the new branches and keeping the remaining growth under control.

Once the fan is established, pruning continues to take place over the period from spring through to late summer (see Diagram 44). The branch leaders can be left alone, unless they are growing beyond the space on the wall. In the spring, misplaced and strong vertical growth should be removed, along with exhausted growth and shoots growing away from or towards the wall. The remaining shoots can be thinned to around 10cm (4") apart (see Diagram 45). As the season develops, pinch back the side shoots as described earlier. Cut back any growth that is shading the ripening fruits.

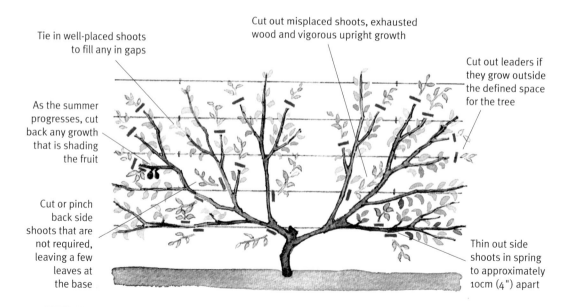

Cut out misplaced shoots, exhausted wood and vigorous upright growth

Tie in well-placed shoots to fill any in gaps

Cut out leaders if they grow outside the defined space for the tree

As the summer progresses, cut back any growth that is shading the fruit

Cut or pinch back side shoots that are not required, leaving a few leaves at the base

Thin out side shoots in spring to approximately 10cm (4") apart

Diagram 44 Pruning an established plum fan (spring to summer).

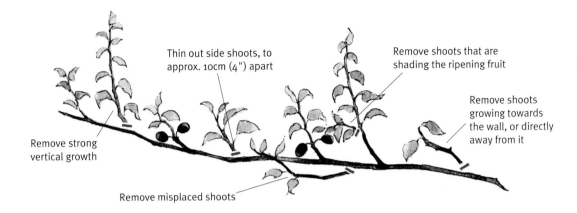

Thin out side shoots, to approx. 10cm (4") apart

Remove shoots that are shading the ripening fruit

Remove shoots growing towards the wall, or directly away from it

Remove strong vertical growth

Remove misplaced shoots

Diagram 45 Pruning one branch of an established plum fan.

Once the fan-trained tree is mature, the centre of the tree is likely to become bare, with the productive growth towards the outside of the tree. This effect can be controlled by selecting replacement shoots to be grown on over a season to replace branches that are becoming exhausted. The following spring, the original branch can be removed and the replacement tied in. It is likely that fruits will need thinning once the tree is cropping well.

Pruning plum cordons

Although it is unusual, plums can be successfully grown as cordons where space is limited. They are best grown on Pixy rootstock and can be planted as close as 1m (3') apart. To form a cordon, first plant a maiden at an angle of 45 degrees. The laterals that emerge from the trunk should be kept to 15-20cm (6-8") long each season. Side shoots that emerge from them should also be regularly shortened to around 5cm (2") long. This involves regular pinching back over the season to keep the tree compact. When a lateral becomes exhausted, it can be replaced by cutting back to a replacement shoot.

Harvesting plums

It is easy to tell when plums are ready to harvest. Ripe plums will be soft and sweet. Picking a plum from the tree and eating it will tell you whether it is ripe or not! Wasps might also give you an early warning that your plums are ripening. They are likely to start eating your plums just before they are ripe – in severe cases, you might need to harvest your plums a little early and leave them on a sunny windowsill to ripen fully. Wet weather can also spoil fruit, by causing the flesh to split. You may need to harvest earlier than planned if hail or heavy rainfall threatens, so it's worth paying attention to the weather forecast.

Not all your plums will ripen at once. You will need to harvest each tree several times to pick all the fruits at their best.

At the same time as harvesting, remember to remove any fruits that are suffering from brown rot (see Chapter 9, page 132). This will help to prevent this troublesome disease from reinfecting the tree the following year.

Storing and using plums

Plums, being a soft fruit, will not keep for any length of time. Once they are at their best, you will need to use them quickly. Of course, you can eat them fresh from the tree – for the finest plums, this is perhaps the best way of enjoying them. It's a special moment when you bite into a home-grown greengage, enjoying its juicy, honeyed, toffee-apple-like taste.

Cooking plums are different: although they also have a wonderful taste, their tartness makes cooking them almost a necessity, but the result is no less a pleasure. Damsons and bullaces are particularly sharp fruits that require plenty of sweetening.

Cooking

There are, of course, many delightful ways to cook plums. I remember the wonder of 'Tinker, tailor, soldier, sailor . . .' to the accompaniment of plum crumble and custard as a child. There are also many equally enjoyable, but more sophisticated, dessert recipes that include plums: Alsatian greengage tart, plum torte and plum cobbler are just a few.

There are also savoury uses for plums, often as accompaniments to poultry or game, where the plums' rich, fruity taste is a perfect contrast to the meat.

Preserves and bottling

Plums are excellent for spicy chutneys and ketchups, while, on the sweeter side, jam and jelly recipes abound. Damson cheese was a traditional use for these fruits in the north of England. Bottling, either in syrup or in alcohol, are other options for preserving plums.

Freezing

There are several ways to freeze plums and damsons, either dry or puréed. There is a tendency for the skins to become tough when frozen; using ascorbic acid or scalding with boiling water will help to avoid this problem. Once the stones have been removed, plums can be frozen, either stewed or puréed.

Drying

Prunes are the dried fruit from particular varieties of plum that have been bred for the purpose, such as La Petite d'Agen from France. School dinners did their best to put a generation of children off prunes, but they are starting to recover their popularity, especially now that their health benefits have been realised.

Dried plums (as opposed to prunes) are now beginning to emerge on to the market. You can dry your own plums at home. If you don't have a dehydrator or drying box, you can dry them cut into slices in a very low oven (the lowest setting possible – around 60°C [140°F]) for 12 to 24 hours. Brushing the plum slices with one part honey and two parts water is said to reduce vitamin loss and discolouration.

Making alcohol

Plums have a long association with alcohol. Even sloes, the bitter relatives of plums, are gathered to make sloe gin. In many eastern and northern parts of Europe, liqueurs are made from plums. Particular varieties of plums are used to make slivovice or slivovitza (the exact name varying from one country to another) – a type of plum brandy. In Britain, plums are more traditionally used to make plum wine.

Chapter 13

Cherries

"Loveliest of trees, the cherry now
Is hung with bloom along the bough
And stands about the woodland ride
Wearing white for Eastertide."

A. E. Housman, *A Shropshire Lad*

Cherries are one of those delicious fruits that make fruit growing so worthwhile. They are not easy – the birds will be desperate to get to them before you, and there are myriad problems waiting to ensnare the cherry grower – but when the trees give up their wonderful ripe fruit, warmed by the summer sun, you are in for a treat.

Black cherries ripening in the sun.

The blossom of a Morello cherry tree.

There are two types of cherry to choose from. The sweet cherry is the one that we all know: with sweet, juicy flesh and a wonderful flavour, it can be eaten straight from the tree. The other type is the sour (or acid) cherry: with a tangy, sweet-and-sour taste, it is normally cooked or bottled. It is very rarely found in the shops, so all the more worth growing, and its flavour is delicately fulfilling in a very moreish way.

Sweet cherries derive from *Prunus avium*, or bird cherry – probably so named because the fruits are so loved by birds that they can strip a tree in a day. Sour cherries derive from *Prunus cerasus,* a wild cherry named after a town on the Black Sea where the trees grow wild. Both sweet and sour cherries carry beautiful blossom that would make them worth growing even if they didn't bear such lovely fruit. In the early twentieth century, day trips were arranged by paddle steamer on the River Tamar, in the south-west of England, to see the magnificent cherry blossom that bordered the river. Many varieties of cherry tree also have attractive autumn colours, which adds to their appeal.

The history of cherry growing in Britain

Like most tree fruits, the sweet cherry originated in Eurasia and was brought to Europe by the ancient Greeks and the Romans. Legend has it that Roman roads in Britain could be identified by the wild cherry trees growing nearby, presumably growing from stones discarded by Roman soldiers.

Morello cherry trees were also brought here by the Romans, probably via southern Spain. After Roman times, cherry cultivation was continued in monasteries, surfacing again in written history when Richard Harris, the royal fruiterer to Henry VIII, was commanded to plant cherry orchards in Kent. Kent became the centre of English commercial cherry growing, because of its closeness to London and its benign climate, ideally suited to cherry cultivation.

The late eighteenth and nineteenth centuries were the heyday of English cherry growing. The breeding of cherries saw huge advances thanks to the efforts of nurserymen Thomas Knight and Thomas Rivers. Varieties that we still grow today, such as Waterloo and Early Rivers, came to prominence at this time. Although Kent continued to be the centre of commercial cherry growing, regional pockets of cultivation developed in Worcestershire, Devon and Suffolk. These early trees were magnificent specimens, growing up to 18m (around 60') tall. In reality, this was completely impractical at harvest time; women were sent up enormous ladders to seek out and cut the elusive cherries.

The development of more dwarfing rootstocks has made the harvesting of cherries a less hazardous pursuit.

The height of these trees was one of the main reasons for their decline, as labour became scarcer and pickers less willing to climb to such dizzy heights. At the same time, transport from European countries became cheaper and more feasible, so imports arrived from countries with climates more suited to growing cherries.

It has only been comparatively recently that dwarfing rootstocks have become available for cherries, enabling cherry trees to be grown in small gardens. These new rootstocks have revolutionised cherry growing, both domestically and commercially, with declining cherry orchards being revived by their introduction.

Cultivation of cherries

Cherries are not the easiest fruit tree to grow: hail, heavy rain and birds can all reduce promising crops to a pitiful handful in a short period of time. However, the rewards are great and it is worth persevering, taking precautions to protect the fruit from damage. Cherries give of their best in warm sunny positions, but where these are not available, sour cherries can be grown, even thriving against a north-facing wall.

For details of pest, disease and other problems with cherry trees, and how to deal with them, see Chapter 9 (pages 155-6). See Chapter 2 (page 34) for information on rootstocks.

Conditions

Cherries prefer a more continental climate than is found in most of Britain. The ideal conditions are a cold winter followed by a warm, dry spring and a hot summer. The east, and particularly the south-east, of England is the area most suited to cherry growing in Britain. Cherries are not suited to growing in areas of high rainfall, partly because of the high incidence of bacterial canker. Summer rainfall can also lead to splitting of the fruit.

The trees are tolerant of a wide range of soil conditions, but prefer a slightly acid, deep, well-drained loam. Badly drained soils can give rise to root-rot diseases such as phytophthora. If you are unsure of whether your soil is badly drained, dig a bucket-sized hole and fill it with water. If any water remains after 24 hours, the site is not well suited to cherry cultivation unless you take steps to improve the drainage (see Chapter 1, page 17). Thin, sandy soils are also best avoided. Cherries will tolerate chalk soils, so long as there is a good depth of reasonably fertile soil. They have shallow roots that can easily be damaged by surface cultivation.

Cherries grow best in a site that is sheltered from strong winds and not prone to damaging frosts. While sweet cherries need full sun to give of their best, acid cherries will grow reasonably well in shade. Cherries lend themselves well to growing against a wall – sweet cherries require a warm, sunny site, whereas acid cherries will even tolerate a north-facing wall.

Acid, or sour, cherries, such as Morellos, are a little different from sweet cherries in their growth habit and requirements. They make a less vigorous tree and prefer a soil that is neutral to slightly alkaline.

Feeding and watering

Feeding requirements are not excessive, particularly in the early years. Little phosphorus is needed, so the requirements of potash and nitrogen can be met by liquid feeds made from comfrey and nettles respectively.

Manure and compost applied as a mulch around the trees are also likely to supply sufficient nutrients. Manure applied in spring, while the soil is still moist, will help to conserve moisture, as well as feeding the tree.

It is worth paying attention to regular watering in summer, because irregular watering can lead to the fruit splitting. This particularly applies to wall-trained trees, which might suffer water deprivation in the rain shadow of a wall.

Pollination

Most sweet cherries are self-incompatible (self-sterile), but there a few recent introductions that are self-fertile, i.e. they can be planted singly and still crop well – although they will produce a heavier crop if grown with a suitable pollinator. The most common of these varieties are Lapins, Stella, Summer Sun, Sunburst and Sweetheart. If you plant any varieties that are not self-fertile, you will need to ensure that you also plant a second variety, so that the two trees will pollinate each other. Most acid cherries are self-fertile.

Cherries suffer from having many varieties that will not pollinate each other, despite flowering at the same time.

Fruit thinning

Cherries can bear a heavy crop, but this doesn't require thinning in order to obtain good-quality fruit. They can suffer from a heavy fruit drop in the early summer.

Cherry varieties

As with most fruits, you need to ensure that your chosen trees will be pollinated successfully as well as meeting your needs for time of harvesting and disease resistance. The fact that many cherry varieties are incompatible with each other means that choosing suitable varieties can be a complicated task. In order to make the selection of varieties simple, the charts in this chapter include suitable pollination partners from within the lists of recommended varieties, rather than giving flowering times. Some trees are listed as universal pollinators – this means that they will pollinate any other cherry flowering at the same time.

Sweet cherries

The large number of traditional European varieties has recently been added to by American and Canadian breeding programmes, which have produced worthwhile cultivars that are also self-fertile. The cherry season is short, with July being the peak, but careful selection of varieties can extend the season at either end. The recommended varieties in the chart below are listed in order of picking date.

Recommended sweet cherry varieties

Variety	Characteristics of the fruit	Characteristics of the tree	Pollination	Picking date	Pest & disease resistance
EARLY RIVERS	An early cherry with large, deep red fruits of excellent flavour.	Vigorous tree with branches that weep with age.	Suitable partners: Merchant, Merton Glory, Noir de Guben.	Mid-June	Resistant to fruit split. Susceptible to bacterial canker.
MERCHANT	An early-to-mid-flowering, medium-sized black cherry. Good flavour.	Spreading tree of medium vigour. Heavy cropper.	Universal pollinator. Suitable partners: Early Rivers, Lapins, Noir de Guben, Merton Glory, Merton Favourite, Stella, Summer Sun.	Late June	Slightly susceptible to fruit split, resistant to bacterial canker.
MERTON GLORY	A large juicy white cherry with a red flush. Excellent flavour.	Vigorous, spreading tree. A regular heavy cropper.	Universal pollinator. Suitable partners: Early Rivers, Merton Favourite, Noir de Guben.	Early July	Susceptible to fruit split. Very resistant to bacterial canker.

(Cont.)

Variety	Characteristics of the fruit	Characteristics of the tree	Pollination	Picking date	Pest & disease resistance
MERTON FAVOURITE	Large juicy dark-red cherries with good flavour.	Tree is initially vigorous, becoming compact. Good cropper.	Suitable partners: Early Rivers, Merchant, Merton Glory, Noir de Guben.	Mid-July	Susceptible to bacterial canker.
LAPINS (syn. CHEROKEE)	Large red cherries with a good, slightly acid flavour.	Vigorous, upright tree. Heavy cropper.	Self-fertile. Universal pollinator. Suitable partners: Bradbourne Black, Stella, Summer Sun, Sunburst, Merchant, Nabella.	Late July	Some resistance to fruit split and bacterial canker.
NOIR DE GUBEN	Large black cherries, quite juicy and with good flavour.	Tree spreading and quite vigorous. Good cropper.	Universal pollinator. Suitable partners: Early Rivers, Merchant, Merton Favourite, Merton Glory.	Late July	Resistant to fruit split, some resistance to bacterial canker.
STELLA	Large dark-red cherries with good flavour.	Tree is vigorous and upright, becoming spreading. Good and reliable cropper. There is also a sport called Stella Compact.	Self-fertile. Universal pollinator. Suitable partners: Bradbourne Black, Lapins, Merchant, Stella Compact, Summer Sun.	Late July	Susceptible to fruit split and brown rot.
SUMMER SUN	Medium-sized dark-red fruits with good flavour.	Spreading and compact tree. Reliable and heavy cropper. Has good frost tolerance, so is suitable for colder locations.	Self-fertile. Universal pollinator. Suitable partners: Lapins, Merchant, Nabella, Stella, Sunburst.	Late July	Some resistance to bacterial canker.

(Cont.)

Variety	Characteristics of the fruit	Characteristics of the tree	Pollination	Picking date	Pest & disease resistance
SUNBURST	Large sweet dark-red cherries with excellent flavour.	Moderate vigour. Good cropper.	Self-fertile. Universal pollinator. Suitable partners: Lapins, Merchant, Nabella, Stella, Summer Sun.	Late July	Prone to fruit split.
BRADBOURNE BLACK	Large black fruit with a rich flavour.	Vigorous, spreading tree with long, drooping branches. Heavy cropper.	Suitable partners: Lapins, Morello, Stella, Sweetheart.	Early August	Some suscept-ibility to fruit split and bacterial canker.
SWEETHEART	Medium-sized red cherries with good flavour.	Vigorous, spreading tree. Heavy cropper.	Self-fertile. Suitable partners: Bradbourne Black, Lapins, Merchant, Nabella, Stella, Summer Sun, Sunburst.	Mid-August	Resistant to fruit split.

Acid cherries

There are fewer varieties of acid cherries available than there are sweet cherries. Most are self-fertile. Morello and Nabella are the most commonly planted varieties, but Wye Morello and Kentish Red are other cultivars that can be found at some nurseries.

Nabella cherries ripening.

Recommended acid cherry varieties

Variety	Characteristics of the fruit	Characteristics of the tree	Pollination	Picking date	Pest & disease resistance
MORELLO	A medium-sized, juicy dark cherry of good quality.	Tree vigorous at first, becoming compact. Good cropper.	Self-fertile. Suitable partners: Bradbourne Black, Nabella.	Mid-late July	Resistant to fruit split and bacterial canker.
NABELLA	Medium-sized, juicy red cherries of good quality.	Upright to spreading tree of moderate vigour.	Self-fertile. Suitable partners: Bradbourne Black, Lapins, Morello, Stella, Summer Sun, Sunburst.	Mid-late July	Resistant to fruit split and bacterial canker.

Other types of cherry

There are also several other types of cherry that are worth planting.

Duke cherries are a cross between acid cherries and sweet cherries, and suitable either for cooking or dessert use. Duke cherries are cultivated as for sweet cherries, although they tend to be more disease-resistant. **May Duke** is the most commonly grown cultivar. It is partially self-fertile, producing better crops if pollinated by another variety, such as Morello or Stella.

Mazzards are traditional West Country cherries that have been selected from wild cherries over many years, becoming distinct varieties. They like well-drained soils, but, unlike other cherries, they enjoy a damp climate. **Dun**, **Large Black**, **Hannaford** and **Bottlers** are all varieties of mazzard. They are sturdy trees that are resistant to bacterial canker.

They do not grow well in the east of England, where the rainfall is low. They all need pollinating by another variety flowering at the same time.

Tamar Valley cherries, such as **Birchenhayes**, **Bullion** and **Fice**, also enjoy a moist climate. They too need pollinating by another cherry variety.

Pruning cherry trees

Cherries require less pruning than apples and pears. Formative pruning is still important, but once the trees are established there is less need to prune to encourage fruit production. Cherries are prone to silver leaf and bacterial canker (see Chapter 9, page 130), devastating diseases of stone fruits; their susceptibility to these diseases can be increased by pruning at the incorrect time of year, or by leaving jagged cuts where spores and bacteria can lodge. Formative pruning is carried out in the spring, but established trees are best pruned between June and August.

Like other stone fruits, cherries should have their larger pruning cuts protected with a wound paint – see Chapter 9, page 140. As with plums (see box on page 238), it is important to prune in the summer, when there are fewer silver leaf spores present, and to ensure that your pruning cuts are left clean.

Cherry tree forms

In the past, the lack of dwarfing rootstocks meant that cherries were large trees, usually (through necessity) grown as **standards** or **half standards**. Now, the availability of the more dwarfing Gisela rootstocks has enabled the training of cherries into **bush** trees, which can be netted fairly easily to stop the birds eating the cherries and to allow easy tree management. **Fan-trained** trees are also appropriate for cherries, using virtually the same methods of training as for plums (see Chapter 12, pages 242-5).

Pruning sweet cherries

Sweet cherries are like plums, in that they fruit on the base of one-year-old wood (the previous season's growth) as well as on older growth. Pruning in the summer checks growth and encourages fruiting. Although the pruning forms and methods described for plums (see pages 237-45) are also applicable to sweet cherries, the following differences apply.

- The growth of cherry trees is a little more sparse than that of plums. Once the tree is established, little pruning is needed on cherries apart from the removal of dead, diseased and damaged growth, together with any rubbing branches.

- The formative pruning of cherries can start earlier in the year than on plums. They can be pruned as soon as the buds burst in spring.

- Cherry branches do not become more horizontal with time and the weight of crops, in the way that plum branches do, so it is doubly important to remove steep-angled branches during formative pruning, lest they split from the tree later on.

- Tying down branches, so that they are horizontal or even below horizontal, can be used as a means to reduce the vigour of trees, where you want to keep them compact. The size of tree can also be kept small by renewing growth on longer branches, cutting them back to replacement growth.

Pruning acid cherries

Acid cherries differ from sweet cherries in that they fruit almost entirely on the previous season's growth. For this reason, it is important to cut back fruited branches regularly, to allow space for and to encourage new growth. When cutting to a bud, in order to direct or stimulate growth, cut back to a triple bud or a single-growth bud, not to a large flower bud. The triple bud is a growth bud surrounded by two flower buds. The flower buds can be rubbed off, to help stimulate the growth bud.

Because of their different growth habits, acid cherry fans are pruned differently from sweet cherry fans, using the same methods as for the peach fan (see Chapter 14, page 266).

The formative pruning for an acid cherry bush is the same as for a plum bush (see page 238). Once the tree is mature, however, the pruning techniques are a little different. Pruning can take place in the spring, when it is

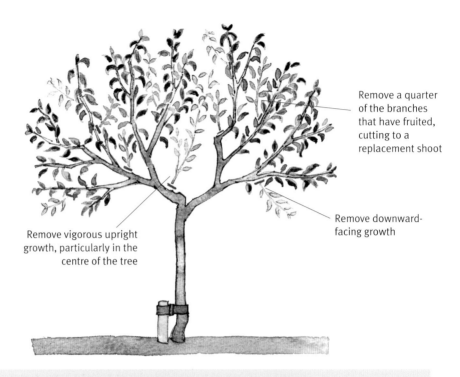

Remove a quarter of the branches that have fruited, cutting to a replacement shoot

Remove downward-facing growth

Remove vigorous upright growth, particularly in the centre of the tree

Diagram 46 Pruning an established acid cherry bush in summer, after fruiting.

easier to see what is happening, or, ideally, it can be delayed until after fruiting. At this point, approximately a quarter of the branches that have fruited are cut back to a replacement shoot lower down the branch (see Diagram 46). Leave any branches growing on the outside of the tree, because this will be fruiting growth for the following year. Any over-vigorous, upright growth, particularly in the centre of the tree, is removed. Any dead, diseased and damaged growth should also be removed, along with growth that is below the horizontal and threatening to become too low.

Harvesting cherries

In the past, when large cherry trees were commonplace, picking was a dangerous affair, carried out on long ladders – a task now made easier by the advent of dwarfing rootstocks. Cherries are ready to harvest when they are ripe and start to taste wonderful. If you are not sure, the blackbirds will let you know by attempting to eat your fruit, even before it is fully ripe.

A Stella cherry tree trained as a fan.

Netting protecting dwarf cherry trees.

Netting is essential at this stage, otherwise birds are likely to strip your trees before any of the cherries are ready to eat. The netting can be a permanent structure, in the manner of a fruit cage. Many fruit cages are sold in kit form; these can be used to build a structure that is taller and thinner than the normal fruit cage. Otherwise, netting can be draped over stout posts a few weeks before harvest, ensuring where possible that no openings are left. The bottom of the netting can be attached to the ground with large staples made of galvanised wire. Birds will go to great lengths to obtain your cherries, so care at this stage is important, not least to ensure that they don't become stuck in the netting.

If you manage to keep the cherries for yourself, the best method of harvesting them is to use scissors. The important part is to ensure that the stalks are with the fruit; if they are pulled from the tree, they can leave scars, where silver leaf spores may enter.

Storing and using cherries

It can be a novel experience having a glut of cherries: we are used to buying them in small quantities at an high price in the shops, so finding a use for an abundance of these delicious fruits can be an enjoyable challenge. Storing cherries in cold water will help them to keep a little longer. Aside from the obvious method of filling up large bowls in the house for short-term consumption, there are various ways of using and preserving cherries.

Cooking

Cherries are usually thought of as a fruit to eat raw, but there are number of different ways of cooking them. Cherry pie, flan or trifle are examples, as are various desserts that include alcohol, for which cherries have a particular affinity. Brandy is a wonderful friend to sour cherries, while cocktail cherries have traditionally been soaked in maraschino or kirsch. The latter is a traditional drink from the Black Forest in Germany, where the abundant Morello cherries are mashed in big wooden tubs and then left to ferment. Cherries soaked in kirsch are a vital ingredient of Black Forest gateau.

Acid cherries are the best for cooking. They have a fantastic sour and fruity taste that is quite different from that of sweet cherries. And you can only really taste them by growing them yourself – you will be very unlikely to discover them in a greengrocer's or supermarket, yet to grow them at home is to discover a rare treat.

Stoning cherries can be a fiddly problem, one that can be solved with a cherry stoner – available from the more select kitchen shops.

Preserving

Cherries can be bottled in alcohol or syrup as a means of preserving them, or made into jam. They can also be dried in a slow oven, or frozen – either dry or in syrup.

Chapter 14

Peaches and nectarines

"Life is better than death, I believe, if only because it is less boring and because it has fresh peaches in it."

Thomas Walker

Peaches and nectarines love warmth. They are at home in Mediterranean countries: if you want to grow them in Britain, you need to find a way of replicating Mediterranean conditions. This could be a warm, sheltered spot, if you are in a very favoured part of southern England, but it is more likely to be a warm wall or even a greenhouse if you are north of the Midlands.

Both peaches and nectarines are difficult to grow in all but the most sheltered of locations, because of their tendency to contract peach leaf curl and to suffer frost damage. However, warming of the climate and the introduction of new cultivars are slowly making peach and nectarine growing a more realistic proposition, at least across southern Britain.

It is worth considering carefully before planting a peach, to make sure that you are not wasting the best site in your garden on a tree that will fruit only every few years, in a good summer. However, the rewards are great, so the decision must be yours. It is very tempting to consider how you will use up a glut of peaches, and English peaches straight from the tree are especially good.

Nectarines are a smooth-skinned mutation of peaches that are grown in the same way. They are a little more tender and are more demanding of warmth than peaches, so are largely confined to unheated greenhouses, apart from in the most favoured locations in southern Britain. At present there a very few parts of the British Isles where they can successfully be grown outside.

Left: Peach blossom.

The history of peach and nectarine growing

Despite their Latin name (*Prunus persica*), meaning 'from Persia', peaches are a native of China. They travelled along the Silk Road towards the Mediterranean, until finding favour in the Roman empire. It was the Romans who called them Persian apples, because they had arrived in Rome via Persia.

Although the Romans spread peach trees throughout southern Europe, it took many centuries for them to reach Britain, probably because of their lack of suitability for the British climate. It was only during the eighteenth century that they became popular in the fruit bowls of the aristocracy, grown in the greenhouses of their walled gardens. Head gardeners would compte to grow the finest peaches for their masters.

Cultivation of peaches and nectarines

Peaches and nectarines are usually thought of as Mediterranean fruits, but they can be grown successfully in the warmest parts of the British Isles, particularly if a sheltered location on a sunny wall can be found. Most varieties suffer to some extent from peach leaf curl, which can be a debilitating disease. The recent introduction of resistant varieties, such as Avalon Pride, has improved the outlook for peach cultivation. Nectarines are even more demanding of a warm, sheltered location.

For details of pest, disease and other problems with peach and nectarine trees, and how to deal with them, see Chapter 9 (pages 157-8). See Chapter 2 (page 34) for information on rootstocks.

Conditions

Aside from their strong preference for a sheltered position, peaches are tolerant of a fairly wide range of soils, so long as they are not waterlogged, particularly during the spring and summer. A deep, well-drained loam with a high humus content is ideal. Sandy soils are tolerated, so long as they are not too dry or shallow. Peaches grown on St Julien A rootstock are more accepting of heavy soils.

Peach blossom is prone to frost damage in the spring, particularly when temperatures fall below 1°C (34°F). Although peaches are thought of as a tender fruit, the trees are actually hardy to around -25°C (-13°F).

High winter and spring rainfall is a problem because it facilitates the spread of peach leaf curl (see Chapter 9, page 157), which can be a debilitating condition in peach and nectarine trees, to the extent that it is best to exclude rainfall during these times in order to prevent the spores from reaching the tree. This is normally achieved by devising some form of removable cover, such as that shown in the photo opposite. This highly effective cover is made from a heavy-duty, reinforced polythene called Monarflex, stapled to a wooden framework; this particular cover is still going strong after nine years. More lightweight versions can also be effective, although they can be difficult to secure in strong winds. The one pictured here is bolted to the wall. Such a cover needs to be in place between December and April.

The other advantage of fitting a cover like this is that it will protect the flowers from frost damage. When the flowers emerge, it is good to open the cover during the day, particularly on warm, sunny days, so that pollinating insects can reach the flowers easily.

A home-made cover that will protect a peach tree from frost and winter rain.

Dwarf varieties of peaches and nectarines, or those grown on Pixy rootstock, are suitable for growing in containers. They have the added advantage that they can be brought into an unheated greenhouse during the late winter and early spring, avoiding the need for fitting a cover.

Feeding and watering

Peaches require careful feeding to give of their best. A good quantity of manure or compost applied in the early spring will provide the basic nutrients, as well as helping to retain soil moisture. From May until harvest, it is helpful to apply a liquid feed of tomato food or comfrey liquid every two weeks. Applying comfrey leaves as a mulch is also effective, though a little slower to have an effect. If you don't have compost or manure available in large quantities, a general-purpose fertiliser, such as pelleted chicken manure, is a good substitute.

Careful attention to watering will also pay dividends: peaches need a good supply of moisture during the growing season. They also detest waterlogged soil, so a balance needs to be struck. Trees grown in the open will only need watering in a dry spell, but trees trained on a wall are likely to need regular watering during the summer months. Pot-grown trees will need watering almost daily in the summer. Remember that a good soaking every so often is much better than frequent applications of small amounts of water.

Pollination

Most varieties of peach and nectarine are self-fertile, meaning that just one tree will give a heavy crop. However, the flowers emerge at a time when few pollinating insects are active, particularly if the weather is poor. Hand-pollination is often necessary in order to produce a good crop. This is a method of spreading the pollen from flower to flower in the same way that a bee might do. The ideal tool for this is a very soft paintbrush, such as one made from wolf or camel hair. Cotton wool is also suitable. All you need to do is dab gently from one flower to another, picking up pollen as you go. (See photo on page 40). Warm, still conditions around the middle of the day are ideal.

Fruit thinning

Thinning peaches as they grow helps to give good-sized fruit in the current season, as well as helping to initiate the development of fruit buds for the following year. It is also best not to let peaches bear too heavy a crop, because the wood is brittle and liable to break. When the peaches are about the size of a marble, they can be thinned to about 10cm (4") apart. The June Drop will naturally occur a little later on; this can be followed by a second thinning to around 20cm (8") apart (15cm [6"] for nectarines). It can be difficult to remove the fruit cleanly, particularly when they are growing in pairs or clusters: using a

A branch of a fan-trained peach before and after thinning the young fruit.

pair of scissors to cut the fruit in half is just as effective. If the trees are allowed to crop too heavily, you will have small peaches and a good chance that the tree will crop only lightly the following year.

Peach and nectarine varieties

There are thousands of peach and nectarine varieties, but only a few that are suitable for growing outdoors in the British Isles. Varieties resistant to peach leaf curl are increasingly available, but none yet are immune to this disease. Some varieties are naturally dwarf, as opposed to being reduced in size by the effect of the rootstock; these are well suited to growing in pots, or in smaller spaces against walls. Varieties that are late-flowering, such as Rochester and Peregrine, are less likely to be damaged by frost.

Recommended peach varieties
There are various types of peach and nectarine varieties suitable for growing in the British

A genetically dwarf peach tree.

Isles, from the traditional British varieties such as Duke of York and Lord Napier through to flat peaches such as Saturn and the recently introduced Avalon Pride – discovered as a chance seedling growing in woods in Washington state, USA. The introduction of this variety has been a breakthrough in peach growing because of its high level of resistance to peach leaf curl.

THE DISCOVERY OF AVALON PRIDE

The discovery of the peach variety Avalon Pride is one of those remarkable stories that light up fruit growing. For many years, the search had been on for a peach that was truly resistant to the debilitating disease peach leaf curl.

While walking in the Issaquah Woods, near her home in Washington state, USA, Margaret Proud had noticed a healthy-looking wild peach tree. Coming from a horticultural background, she realised the potential value of the tree and decided to propagate it, though was almost thwarted by a hungry bear that nearly destroyed the original specimen. Undaunted, she continued with her project, discovering only later that her tree was truly remarkable.

Avalon Pride not only produces delicious peaches but is also highly resistant (though not immune) to peach leaf curl. It is now revolutionising peach growing in the British Isles, where peaches have always struggled to cope with this disease.

Because nearly all peach and nectarine varieties are self-fertile, the flowering date is only relevant in terms of avoiding frost damage – in which respect late-flowering varieties are at an advantage.

The varieties in the chart here are listed in order of picking date.

Recommended peach varieties				
Variety	Characteristics of the fruit	Characteristics of the tree	Picking date	Pest & disease resistance*
DUKE OF YORK	Large crimson-flushed fruits with excellent flavour.	Heavy cropper.	Mid-July	
PEREGRINE	A white-fleshed peach with excellent flavour.	The most reliable cropper in a cool climate. Late-flowering.	Early August	

(Cont.)

Variety	Characteristics of the fruit	Characteristics of the tree	Picking date	Pest & disease resistance*
SATURN	Flat peaches with sweet, firm flesh.	Vigorous tree, heavy cropper.	Early August	Susceptible to peach leaf curl, but included here because it is unusual.
GARDEN LADY	Sweet, yellow-fleshed peaches.	Genetically dwarf tree, good for containers.	Early August	
AVALON PRIDE	A yellow-fleshed peach with good flavour.	Tree of moderate vigour, upright becoming spreading. Good cropper.	Mid-August	Very resistant to peach leaf curl. Seems to be resistant to bacterial canker.
ROCHESTER	Large yellow-fleshed fruit with good flavour.	Vigorous tree, good and reliable cropper. Late-flowering.	Mid-August	Some resistance to peach leaf curl.

* Where no details are given on pest and disease resistance, this is because information is not readily available for these varieties. This is particularly the case for the less common varieties.

Recommended nectarine varieties

Nectarines are more demanding of warm, sheltered locations than peaches, most often being grown in cool greenhouses. For this reason, there is little information available about their disease resistance. The following are the best varieties for growing in the most favoured locations in the British Isles.

Recommended nectarine varieties

Variety	Characteristics of the fruit	Characteristics of the tree	Picking date	Pest & disease resistance*
EARLY RIVERS	Large fruits with melting, soft yellow flesh.	Heavy cropper.	Late July	
LORD NAPIER	Good-quality, melting white-fleshed fruit.	Heavy and reliable cropper.	Early August	
NECTARELLA	Sweet orange flesh with excellent flavour.	A genetically dwarf variety, ideal for pots.	Mid-August	

* Information on pest and disease resistance is not readily available for these varieties.

Pruning peach and nectarine trees

Peaches and nectarines fruit on the previous year's growth, so the main aim of pruning is to remove older wood and encourage new growth that will fruit the following year. As with all stone fruits, pruning takes place during spring and summer, when the trees are growing strongly, allowing pruning cuts to heal quickly. Avoid pruning during the autumn and winter, because of the danger of infection by bacterial canker and silver leaf. Peaches and nectarines are less susceptible to silver leaf than are plums, but the disease can still cause problems. It is essential that all pruning cuts are left clean and that larger cuts are treated with a wound paint in order to avoid infection (see Chapter 9, page 140).

Peaches and nectarines are usually grown as a **fan** or a **bush**. Fan-training against a wall is the most common approach in Britain, because the trees benefit from the warmth and shelter provided by a wall and they are easier to protect from rain and frost. Growing peaches as bushes is probably realistic only for trees grown in containers, which can be

A young peach tree trained as a fan. The growth is becoming too vertical and concentrated in the centre – tying growth down would be beneficial.

brought inside for the winter, or for cultivars that are strongly resistant to peach leaf curl, such as Avalon Pride. Nectarines, being more demanding of warmth and shelter, are best grown against a wall, even in favoured locations in southern England.

Pruning a peach or nectarine fan

Peach and nectarine fans are grown on a support of horizontal wires fixed to a (preferably)

south-facing wall. A fan tree on St Julien A rootstock will need a wall space about 4.5m (14'6") wide and 2.5m (8') high. The first job is to erect a series of horizontal wires, spaced about 30cm (1') apart; the bottom one around 45cm (1'6") from the ground.

Year 1

Plant a feathered tree (one with small branches emerging from the trunk) during the

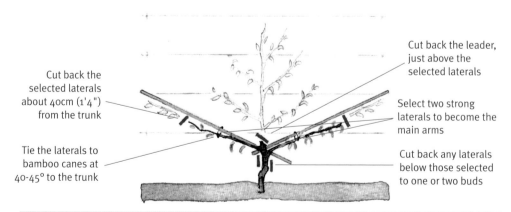

Cut back the leader, just above the selected laterals

Cut back the selected laterals about 40cm (1'4") from the trunk

Select two strong laterals to become the main arms

Tie the laterals to bamboo canes at 40-45° to the trunk

Cut back any laterals below those selected to one or two buds

Diagram 47 Pruning a peach fan, first year, early spring.

winter. Leave it unpruned at this time because of the risk of encouraging disease.

During early spring, select two strong laterals low down on the trunk to become the main arms of the tree (see Diagram 47). Cut back the leader just above these laterals. Tie these two laterals to bamboo canes, then tie the canes to the framework of wires. The arms should be at an angle of 40-45 degrees to the trunk, but if one is less vigorous than the other, keep this one at a more vertical angle for a while. This will induce stronger growth in this arm, which can then be brought back to the 40/45-degree angle later in the year.

Cut back any growth below the selected arms to one or two buds. These will act as reserve laterals in case any problem arises with the selected ones. They can be cut out later in the year, once it is clear that the selected laterals are growing well.

Once the selected arms or laterals reach 40cm (1'4") from the trunk, they can be cut back to an upward-facing shoot. This encourages them to branch out lower down. If these laterals have not reached this length in the first year, wait until the spring of the second year before cutting them back.

Year 2

As more branches grow during the second year, tie the best placed of these to more bamboo canes, to develop the framework of the fan. Ideally you will have two shoots above the original arm and one below it.

Any growth that is not required, or is growing towards the wall or directly away from it, can be cut out. It is good to pinch back unwanted growth early, with fingers and thumb. This not only removes such growth before it causes congestion and shading but also keeps cuts small, making infection less likely.

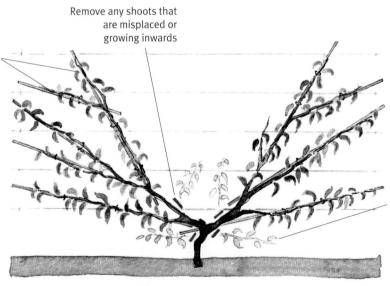

Tie in new leaders and well-placed side shoots to the bamboo canes and wires

Remove any shoots that are misplaced or growing inwards

Once the main arms are established, remove any reserve laterals that were shortened in the first year

Diagram 48 Pruning a peach fan, second year, early summer.

Cut back side shoots to 4 or 5 leaves above the basal cluster where they cross other branches

Cut back the tips of fruiting shoots and other growth that is shading developing fruits

New shoots beginning to fill in the centre of the fan

Cut out misplaced and crossing branches and those growing towards the wall

Thin out side shoots, so that they are 12-15cm (5-6") apart

This young shoot will repla[ce] the main branch when it becomes exhausted

Diagram 49 Pruning a peach fan, third year onwards, spring to summer.

Year 3

Cut back the branches that have been tied in by around one-third, to a bud pointing in the direction of space that can be filled in. As new growth occurs, you are now starting to fill in the shape of the fan, with the centre of the tree the last to be filled in. By now many side shoots will be growing; during the spring, thin these out to 12-15cm (5-6") apart. During the growing season, continue pinching out unwanted growth, as in year 2, and shortening side shoots to around 10-15cm (4-6"). Keep tying in new growth to bamboo canes where it is required to fill in spaces in the framework.

Pruning an established peach or nectarine fan

Continue to remove unwanted growth and thin out side shoots, as described above.

Shoots that are bearing fruit can also be shortened, always leaving a cluster of leaves after the flowers or young fruit. By now, you will notice that peach and nectarine trees grow vigorously: this new growth can lead to shading and congestion if not removed promptly, preferably by pinching out. Make sure that developing fruits do not become shaded. Pruning peach and nectarine fans is not a one-off task; it is a continuous process during the spring and summer.

Branches that have fruited soon become exhausted, so it is necessary to remove them, cutting back to a replacement shoot further back on the branch.

Diagram 50 shows how these replacement shoots are left unpruned in the spring, ready to be tied in as new growth later in the year.

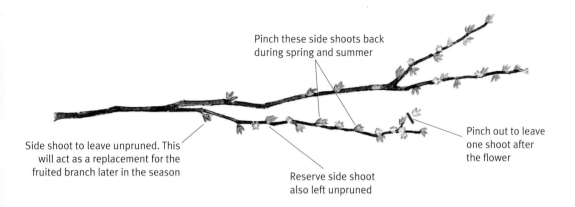

Pinch these side shoots back
during spring and summer

Pinch out to leave
one shoot after
the flower

Side shoot to leave unpruned. This
will act as a replacement for the
fruited branch later in the season

Reserve side shoot
also left unpruned

Diagram 50 A branch of an established peach or nectarine fan in spring.

It is important to keep this process of tying in replacement shoots going, because established fans tend to become bare in the middle, with growth and fruit to the outside of the tree. Training in replacement shoots is the way to prevent this from happening.

After fruiting, cut growth that has just fruited back to a replacement shoot that will fruit the following year. This process of continuing to cut or pinch back side shoots during the summer is important, particularly where the shoots are shading developing fruits.

Pruning a peach bush

Formative pruning is the same as for a plum bush (see Chapter 12, page 238). The exception to this is for genetically dwarf varieties, such as Garden Lady or Dixired. These will naturally form a small bush with minimal pruning. Diseased or misplaced growth can be removed, but otherwise the tree can be left to its own devices when young. Later pruning is the same as for other peach bushes.

Once an open-centred bush has been formed, the aim of pruning is to keep replacing fruited growth with replacement shoots that will

fruit the following year. Firstly, remove any dead, diseased or damaged growth, followed by shoots that are rubbing or crowded. After this, cut back fruited growth and older branches that are becoming bare, to replacement shoots. This is a continual cycle, with about a third of the older branches being replaced each year. Cut out vigorous growth in the centre of the tree, leaving the centre reasonably open. Remove growth that is shading developing fruits, pinching rather than cutting where possible. (See Diagram 51 overleaf.)

Harvesting peaches and nectarines

As the fruits start to ripen, they will become softer and get more of a red flush, depending on the variety. Once you notice this distinct softening, it is time to pick the fruit. It is easy to damage the fruit while picking, because they do not always part easily from the shoot on which they are growing. The best method is to cup your hand around the fruit and pull gently away from the branch. Fruits on one tree will ripen over a week or two, so repeat pickings will be needed.

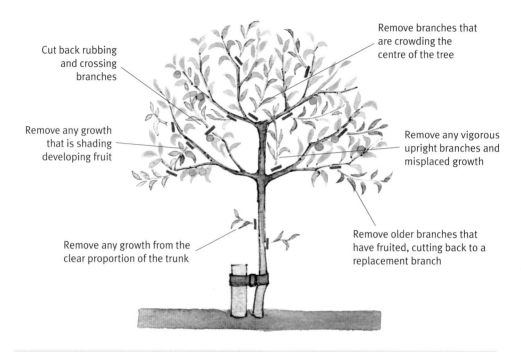

Cut back rubbing and crossing branches

Remove branches that are crowding the centre of the tree

Remove any growth that is shading developing fruit

Remove any vigorous upright branches and misplaced growth

Remove any growth from the clear proportion of the trunk

Remove older branches that have fruited, cutting back to a replacement branch

Diagram 51 Pruning an established peach bush, summer.

Using peaches and nectarines

Fruits picked at this ripe stage won't keep for long, but this is no hardship because they taste so good. Well-ripened home-grown peaches and nectarines are much better and juicier than anything you will find in the shops. I still remember my first English-grown peach. I was shocked that a peach grown in this country could taste so much better than the shop-bought peaches that I had eaten for years.

A mature peach or nectarine fan can produce around 70 or 80 fruits in a good year, so you might have to get used to a glut of the fruit, which can seem rather strange at first. In the event that there are too many for the fruit bowl, there are plenty of ways to cook them. Peach compote, peach flan and peach cobbler are all classic peach (or nectarine) desserts. The fruits also combine well with brandy and coconut, and are excellent baked.

Preserving

Because peaches and nectarines do not keep, you might need to find a way of preserving them for future use. Bottling in syrup or with alcohol, freezing and drying are all ways of preserving them intact. They can also be used for making jams and chutneys, or turned into peach wine.

Chapter 15

Apricots

"No one ever pruned me. If you have been sunned through and through like an apricot on a wall from your earliest days, you are oversensitive to any withdrawal of heat."

Margot Asquith

Usually thought of as a Mediterranean fruit, apricots are a borderline fruit for growing in the British Isles. They need a period of cold in the winter, followed by a warm, dry spring and a hot summer. These are conditions more usually found in Continental Europe, but the climate in south-east England is certainly good enough to grow apricots. Further north, the challenge is finding enough warmth, so a south-facing wall will allow

Apricot blossom.

apricots to be grown in areas that would otherwise be too cold. In the north of England, Wales, Scotland and Ireland, apricots are likely to need the protection of a greenhouse to fruit well. In the west of the British Isles, the higher levels of rainfall can cause problems. The onset of global warming is making apricot growing more viable in Britain; as the climate warms, the areas able to support apricots will move slowly north.

The history of apricot growing

The origin of the apricot is lost in time, with China, India and Armenia all being claimed as the original home of this fruit. China is most often accepted as the apricot's country of origin; they grow wild in parts of China and were certainly cultivated by 2000 BC.

They were brought to the West by traders on the Silk Road. Alexander the Great is credited with introducing them to the Mediterranean area by the fourth century BC. The Greeks referred to them as 'golden eggs of the sun'. Richard Harris, the well-known fruiterer to Henry VIII, brought apricots back from Italy to plant in the orchards of Kent. One variety still grown today is Moorpark, which was introduced by Lord Anson in the seventeenth century.

Cultivation of apricots

Apricots might seem like an exotic fruit, but they can be grown successfully in warm, sheltered areas of the British Isles, or trained against a sunny wall. The recent introduction of improved varieties, suited to cool climates, has made their cultivation more reliable. They make a good alternative to peaches, being less susceptible to peach leaf curl.

For details of pest, disease and other problems with apricot trees, and how to deal with them, see Chapter 9 (pages 158-9). See Chapter 2 (page 34) for information on rootstocks.

Conditions

Apricots prefer a well-drained but moisture-retentive soil. They dislike extremes of drainage, such as heavy, waterlogged soils and light sandy ones. They prefer a neutral-to-alkaline site, with a pH between 6.5 and 8. They can be grown in the open only in the warmer parts of Britain, or in the most sheltered sites elsewhere. Fan-training against a warm wall will give the best results in any location. They can also be grown successfully in containers, at least until they get too big. These can be brought into a greenhouse for shelter during the winter and early spring.

The beautiful blossom of apricots is an attractive feature in the garden and a source of early nectar for bees. However, it arrives early in the year, which makes it vulnerable to frost damage. Planting in frost pockets should definitely be avoided; even in favoured locations, some protection from frost is likely to be needed. This is easiest on fan-trained trees, where sacking or fleece can be draped over the trees in March, preferably held away from the delicate blossom. Remember to lift up the protective covering in the daytime, so that pollinating insects can find the flowers.

Feeding and watering

Apricots prefer a reasonably rich soil, so feeding will be necessary on a regular basis, particularly if the soil is poor. Nitrogen is valuable to apricot trees, but not too much, as this causes the shoot growth to become soft and sappy, making it more susceptible to disease. Good levels of potassium will aid fruit bud development and fruit size. Mulching with manure in the spring, when soil moisture is high, will feed the trees and help to conserve moisture. This addition of humus is particularly important if you are growing apricots on light or sandy soils. It can be helpful to add lime every few years, if there is not sufficient in the soil already. It is best not to add lime and manure at the same time.

Apricots react badly to drought. This is often a problem when an apricot is grown against a wall. Not only does the wall soak up a lot of moisture but it can also create a rain shadow, further reducing the amount of moisture available to the tree. Watering is therefore likely to be needed, particularly in the last few weeks before harvest, when the fruits are swelling.

An apricot tree can provide a plentiful crop where climatic conditions are favourable

Pollination

Apricots are self-fertile, so just one tree can produce a heavy crop, although cropping will be better if two different varieties are planted. However, they flower early in the year, so you cannot rely on insects to pollinate them; hand-pollination will ensure that the flowers are pollinated successfully (see Chapter 15, pages 39-40).

Fruit thinning

If a heavy crop results, it might be necessary to thin the developing fruits. Once the apricots have reached the size of marbles, remove any misshapen fruits and, on a fan-trained tree, those growing towards the wall. After this, thin out the remaining fruits so that there is about 7-10cm (3-4") between them. Thinning the fruits helps to prevent biennial cropping, to which some cultivars are prone.

Apricot varieties

There are hundreds of apricot varieties worldwide, but only a few of them are suitable for growing in cool climates such as in the British Isles. For many years there have been a few traditional varieties grown here, such as Alfred or Moorpark, but recent years have seen new varieties arriving from Canada that are suitable for growing in cooler regions. These new introductions have the suffix 'cot' in the name of the variety – for example, Flavorcot or Tomcot. These trees are likely to be available on St Julien A or Torinel rootstocks. Both will produce apricot trees about 5m (16') tall.

Recommended varieties

Recommended varieties are listed in the chart overleaf, in order of picking date.

Variety	Characteristics of the fruit	Characteristics of the tree	Picking date	Pest & disease resistance*
FARMINGDALE	An American variety with fairly juicy fruits of very good flavour.	Tree of moderate vigour. Crops heavily.	Late July	Resistant to dieback.
TOMCOT	Very large fruit with intense apricot flavour.	Vigorous tree, early flowering. Hardy, suitable for cool areas.	Late July	
NEW LARGE EARLY	Large fruits with good flavour.	Moderate vigour, heavy cropping. Hardy.	Late July–early August	Resistant to dieback.
ALFRED	Small fruit with good flavour.	Tree of medium vigour. Biennial tendency, heavy cropping. Resistant to frost.	Early August	Some resistance to dieback.
HEMSKERK	Large fruit with a sweet, rich flavour.	Vigorous, hardy tree. Good cropper.	Early August	Resistant to dieback.

Recommended apricot varieties

(Cont.)

Variety	Characteristics of the fruit	Characteristics of the tree	Picking date	Pest & disease resistance*
GOLDCOT	Medium-to-large sweet fruit with tough skin.	Late flowering, heavy cropper. Vigorous tree, good for cool climates.	Mid-August	Resistant to brown rot.
FLAVORCOT	A sweet, aromatic fruit with good flavour.	Spreading tree of medium vigour. Good cropper. Frost-tolerant.	Mid–late August	
MOORPARK	Very large fruit with excellent flavour.	Vigorous tree, fairly good cropper.	Late August	Prone to dieback. Resistant to brown rot.

* Where no details are given on pest and disease resistance, this is because information is not readily available for these varieties. This is particularly the case for the less common varieties.

Pruning apricot trees

Apricot trees fruit on one-year-old shoots and on short spurs (two- to three-year-old wood). They are often grown as fan-trained trees in Britain, because of the benefits of the added protection of a wall, but they can also be grown as bushes in the open.

For **bush** trees, formative pruning is the same as for plums (see Chapter 12, page 238), with pruning carried out in the early spring. Once the tree is mature, it is pruned in the same way as an acid cherry (see Chapter 13, page 255).

The formative pruning of a **fan-trained** apricot is the same as that of a fan-trained peach (see Chapter 14, page 266), whereas once it is mature it is pruned in the same way as a fan-trained plum (see Chapter 12, pages 242-5).

Although apricot trees are pruned in the same way as these other trees, it is worth remembering the following points, specific to apricots.

- Little pruning is necessary once a bush tree is mature, unless the growth is becoming crowded, when it will be necessary to thin out some one-year-old shoots. Every few years it is worth replacing one of the laterals, by cutting back to a replacement shoot. This applies to bush and fan-trained trees, and prevents growth from becoming exhausted.
- Mature trees can be pruned in late spring (April to May).
- Apricots can suffer from silver leaf (see Chapter 9, page 139), but are not as susceptible as plums. Large cuts should have wound paint (see page 140) applied as soon as the cut is made.
- Fan-trained apricots need a space on the wall that is about 4m (13') wide and 2m (6'6") high.

Harvesting apricots

Wasps are likely to warn you of the approaching ripeness of your fruit, so it is best to take precautions as soon as they are seen (see Chapter 9, page 128). You can pick the fruit a little early to prevent damage from wasps, but this also prevents the full flavour and ripeness from developing. This premature picking explains why apricots from the shops never have the wonderful, honeyed sweetness of home-grown fruit. If wasps are causing serious problems, you can tie a small paper bag over each fruit, but this is hard work.

It can be easy to damage the fruit if you are picking really ripe apricots. The art is to cup your hand around the fruit, then give a gentle tug, pulling the fruit away with the stalk intact. If it does not part easily from the tree, come back a day or two later.

Using apricots

Ripe apricots will only keep for a week or so, or a little longer in the fridge. Home-grown apricots will disappear readily from the fruit bowl, but they are also wonderful for cooking and preserving.

If you have a glut, treats like apricot crumble, apricot flan or compotes will keep happily in the freezer for a rainy day. Apricots combine well with spirits such as brandy and kirsch, either bottled or in purées. They also make wonderful jam.

They can also be used in savoury cooking – in stuffings, for example. If you need to preserve a large amount of apricots quickly, they can be frozen: either halved or as a purée. Drying is possible, in a cool oven; slice the fruits first.

The kernels of some varieties are quite sweet and reminiscent of almonds.

Chapter 16

Other fruits

"Train up a fig tree in the way it should go, and when you are old sit under the shade of it."

Charles Dickens

This chapter deals with tree fruits that are less commonly grown in the British Isles. This may be because they are not easily usable, as is the case with medlars, for example, or it may be that they grow into large trees not easily accommodated in a garden, as with mulberries. There is also mention of less common tree fruits, such as checkers and elderberries, which are not so easy to use.

Just because these fruits are less common than the apple and pear, however, does not mean that they are not worth growing. Figs are one of the most delicious fruits to be found, and they can be prolific in a good summer. This year, I have harvested nearly 100 figs from a wall-trained tree that has received little attention.

QUINCES

Quinces are rather hard yellow fruits that resemble a knobbly pear. Although they have a grainy texture, they have a delicious aroma when cooked. They are a delightful

Knobbly ripe quinces.

addition to other fruit and make excellent jams and jellies.

The quince is not widely grown because its fruits have a limited value. However it is a fruit that deserves its place in any orchard where space is not too restricted. Even in its Mediterranean homelands, it is rare to see quince orchards. In these warm climates, quinces ripen to become a sweeter fruit than in northern Europe. They are even eaten raw when fully ripe.

The history of quince growing

Like many fruits, quinces originate from the Near East, in particular the Caucasus. As trade between countries spread, the quince was introduced to the eastern Mediterranean. Ancient Greek and Roman writing is littered with references to the quince. By 600 BC quinces were used in Greek wedding ceremonies; the bride would take a bite of quince to ensure her breath was sweet before the first kiss. The golden apple that Paris gave to Aphrodite is thought to have been a quince.

Roman cookbooks tell of stewing quinces with honey and cooking them with leeks.

Although the subsequent spread of quinces through southern Europe was not well documented, we do know that they had reached France by AD 812, when Charlemagne encouraged the French to grow more quinces. Chaucer mentioned quinces, using the old French word *coin*, from which the word 'quince' eventually arose. Quinces were one of the most popular fruits in Britain in medieval times, producing a marmalade similar to the *dulce de membrillo* or *marmelo* that is still popular in Spain and Portugal today. After a brief heyday in the eighteenth century, quince cultivation declined to the marginal level at which it now remains.

Cultivation of quinces

The 'true' quince (*Cydonia oblonga*) is often confused with the oriental or Japanese quince (*Chaenomoles* spp.), sometimes known as 'japonicas'. These are ornamental bushes, often wall-trained, which produce apple-shaped quinces that can be edible.

A Japanese or 'japonica' quince.

Quince blossom.

The quince forms a small tree up to about 5m (16') in height. It is a pretty tree, producing large blush-coloured flowers in the spring. The large yellow fruits also have an ornamental value in the early autumn.

Although usually sold grafted on to Quince A or C rootstocks, quinces can also be grown on their own roots. (See Chapter 2, page 35, for details of rootstocks.) Unlike most fruit trees, quince can be propagated from cuttings and grown from seed.

Quinces are self-fertile, but better crops will usually result if two or more different varieties are planted in close proximity.

For details of pest, disease and other problems with quince trees, and how to deal with them, see Chapter 9 (page 159).

Conditions

Quinces prefer a moist, deep, fertile loamy soil, although they will tolerate a wide range of soil types. They can be grown in more moist conditions than most fruit trees, so if you are planting a mixed orchard, the quince is the tree that can occupy the wettest part of the site. Very alkaline soils can be problematic, leading to lime-induced chlorosis. Light soils may be improved by the addition of manure or compost before planting. Quince trees might need watering during dry spells to perform best.

A sheltered position in full sun is ideal for the quince, particularly for the full ripening of the fruit. In southern Europe, fruits will ripen more thoroughly, to the extent that they are sweet and tender enough to eat raw. So, in the British Isles, every advantage of sun and shelter should be taken to produce the best fruits. For this reason, training quinces against a wall can be beneficial, but other fruits will also be competing for such favoured spots. Quinces can be grown successfully throughout southern Britain, but are likely to need the protection of a wall further north. They flower relatively early, so frost damage can be a problem.

Quince trees will not need much feeding unless the soil is poor. Generally, compost or manure applied as a mulch around the tree will be sufficient, although in poor soils this can be supplemented by a general-purpose fertiliser, such as pelleted chicken manure. A high-potash fertiliser, such as rock potash or comfrey, can help where yields are low.

Quince varieties

Only a limited number of quince varieties are available. Many nurseries will stock only one or two varieties, the most common being Vranja and Meeches Prolific.

Recommended quince varieties

Variety	Characteristics
AGVAMBARI 	Agvambari is a small, regular-shaped fruit that is a reliable cropper in good conditions.
CHAMPION 	Produces large greenish-yellow fruit with a delicate flavour. A vigorous, heavy-cropping tree that fruits at a young age.
KRYMSK 	Produces round golden fruits that soften on ripening. Resistant to quince leaf blight.
LESKOVAC 	Has large quantities of pear-shaped fruit, bearing from an early age. Resistant to quince leaf blight.
MEECH'S PROLIFIC 	One of the most productive varieties in the British climate, unless affected by quince leaf blight, to which it is quite prone. It is a vigorous, heavy-cropping tree that produces sharp fruits with a good flavour.

(Cont.)

Variety	Characteristics
PORTUGAL (syn. LUSITANICA) 	A quince with an irregular habit. It grows in an unruly fashion and produces large, bumpy fruits. The fruit is early to ripen, juicy and mild in flavour. It is reputed to be the best-flavoured quince, excellent for making quince pâté and marmalade. A vigorous tree that crops only lightly, best suited to mild areas.
SERBIAN GOLD 	A newly introduced variety that is said to be productive, healthy and suitable for cooler parts of Britain.
VRANJA 	Produces large, irregular yellow fruits with an excellent flavour and strong fragrance. It is probably the most suitable variety for the British climate, although it can be a light cropper. It crops at an early age and is a good choice for fan training.

Pruning quince trees

Quinces are most commonly trained as **bush** trees, with a clear trunk of around 1-1.2m (3-4'). They can also be trained as a **half standard** or a **fan**. Quince pruning is dominated by the trees' unruly growth habit. Growing quinces as half standards is possible where it is required to lift the canopy, either for access underneath or where animals are grazing an orchard.

Suckers are commonly produced, and should be removed regularly. Apart from this, pruning of quince trees is carried out when the trees are dormant during the winter months. For fan-training, the method is similar to that for plums (see Chapter 12, page 242); the main difference is the unruly growth habit of the quince, which makes it difficult to train it as a tidy tree. A half standard is pruned in the same way as quince bush, but with a longer clear trunk formed during formative pruning.

Quince trees can be grown as fans, though their unruly growth habit makes this difficult.

If you want to grow a half standard, it is advisable to insert a strong bamboo cane next to the tree, in order to train the leader vertically until it reaches the desired height. Remove any unwanted laterals from lower down on the trunk.

The top three to five laterals are retained to form the main branches of the tree, provided that they are growing at a wide angle to the trunk. These laterals are shortened by half to two-thirds at this stage, cutting to an outward- or upward-facing bud. Any growth emerging from the trunk below the selected laterals should be removed. Any competing leaders (see photos on page 109, Chapter 8) can also be removed now.

Formative pruning of a quince bush

Once the tree is planted, it can be grown on until the leader reaches a little taller than the desired height of the clear trunk. At this point, the leader is removed, just above a strong bud or lateral that has already formed.

In year 2 the process continues, with the pruning back of the laterals to outward- or upward-facing buds, removing around one-third of the new season's growth. Any vigorous upright

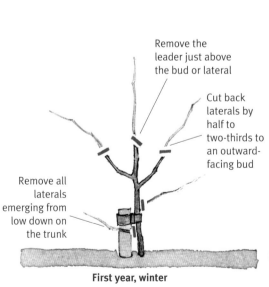

Remove the leader just above the bud or lateral

Cut back laterals by half to two-thirds to an outward-facing bud

Remove all laterals emerging from low down on the trunk

First year, winter

Remove the leader just above the highest of the selected laterals

Remove any wayward growth that is crossing other branches

Cut back laterals by a third of the new growth to an outward- or upward-facing bud

Second year, winter

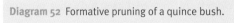

Diagram 52 Formative pruning of a quince bush.

or wayward growth should be removed back to the point where the branch originates. From this stage onwards, it is desirable to keep an open centre to the tree, to allow light and air to penetrate, although in practice the centre of the tree will never be clear of growth because of the wayward nature of the quince. Beware of trying to be too regimented when pruning a quince, or you will end up pruning too hard and over-stimulating the tree.

In year 3, continue this process of shortening the new growth by one-third and removing misplaced and over-vigorous branches.

Pruning an established quince bush

As the tree matures, the main effort of pruning becomes the removal of congested and over-vigorous growth, keeping an open shape to the tree. Fruit will form on one-year-old growth and also on short spurs. Regulated pruning (see Chapter 8, page 113) is a simple way to keep the tree productive, removing tired branches and training in new growth. If spurs become congested, they can be shortened. Remember not to prune too hard because of the risk of over-stimulating the tree. As with all fruit trees, pruning is the art of creating a balance between fruiting and growth.

Harvesting quinces

Quince fruit usually ripen during October, although Meech's Prolific, Champion and Portugal are ready a little earlier. The fruits turn from greenish-yellow to a more golden yellow as they ripen. It is beneficial to leave the fruits on the tree as long as possible, but they should be harvested before the first frosts. It is best to cut the fruits from the tree, because they do not always come away easily, which can cause damage to the small branches.

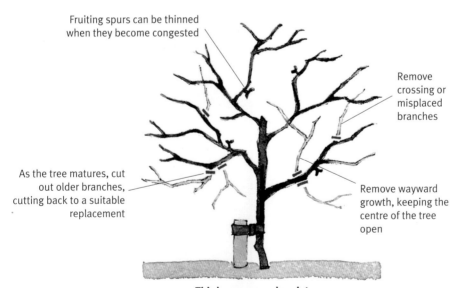

Fruiting spurs can be thinned when they become congested

Remove crossing or misplaced branches

As the tree matures, cut out older branches, cutting back to a suitable replacement

Remove wayward growth, keeping the centre of the tree open

Third year onwards, winter

Diagram 53 Pruning an established quince bush.

Storing and using quinces

Quinces in good condition can be stored for several months, either in wooden fruit trays or cardboard boxes. It is best to store them well away from other fruits, because their powerful aroma can taint other fruit. They are usually not sweet until they have ripened a little further in storage.

The fruit can be used in a variety of ways, but, given their grainy texture, a little inventiveness can be helpful. They are often used to accompany apples in a variety of recipes, enhancing the flavour of apple with their aromatic sweetness. They can also be used on their own in the same ways as apples, such as baked or stewed.

They are well known for their use in various forms of preserve. They contain high levels of pectin, helping preserves to set without the use of large amounts of sugar. Quince marmalade and jelly have both been popular in the past, although less so today. Quince pastes and spreads are popular throughout the Mediterranean, with many regional variations. These can be made in Britain, but remember that quinces from Mediterranean regions are sweeter than those grown here. Quince butter and quince ice cream are other ways of using quinces.

Quinces have occasionally been used in savoury recipes – accompanying game in a casserole, for example. Perhaps their most unusual use is to perfume a room.

Japonica quinces are also edible when cooked, used in a similar way to the true quince. Quince lemonade is sometimes made from blended japonica fruits.

MEDLARS

Although its fruit can be a challenge to use, the medlar is valuable as an ornamental tree, spreading in habit and blessed with white or pink flowers, unusual-looking fruits and clear yellow and red colours in the autumn. Lee Reich described the medlar as a fruit "lost in the Middle Ages",[*] but with inventiveness the medlar can be a worthwhile addition to the fruit garden. The fruits are hard and acidic until they are 'bletted' – a process that involves ripening them until they are semi-rotten and taste like mulled toffee apples.

The medlar is an unusual fruit, tasting rather like a soft toffee apple.

[*]Lee Reich, *Uncommon Fruits for Every Garden.* 2004/2008, Timber Press.

The history of medlar growing in Britain

Medlars are native to northern Iran and the Caucasus region. They spread from there to the Mediterranean, being grown by the Greeks and Romans by the second century AD. Medlars were popular in Britain by the Middle Ages. By the sixteenth and seventeenth centuries they had acquired a rather vulgar reputation, gaining the nickname 'open arse', together with bawdy references in plays and poems of the time. The medlar declined in popularity once more palatable fruits began to be cultivated widely and other fruits were imported from abroad. It is now seen as a curiosity and an acquired taste enjoyed by a few.

Cultivation of medlars

Medlars are attractive trees, whose size will depend on the rootstock on to which they are grafted. Unusually, medlars can be grafted on to a variety of rootstocks from different trees. See Chapter 2 (page 55) for details of rootstocks.

Medlars are self-fertile, so only one tree is needed to produce a worthwhile crop. All varieties flower in late May, when the likelihood of damaging frost has passed.

Medlars are generally healthy trees. For details of the problems that can occur, and how to deal with them, see Chapter 9 (page 160).

Conditions

Medlars enjoy a wide variety of soils, so long as it is well drained. Warmth, sun and shelter are all important for the crop to ripen

Medlar flower.

thoroughly. The flowers and young leaves are susceptible to damage by harsh easterly winds, which are commonplace in the spring. Compost or manure, applied as a mulch in the spring, will provide sufficient nutrients in all but the poorest soils. If need be, a high-potash fertiliser such as comfrey or rock potash can be added to improve the trees' fruiting potential.

Medlar varieties

There is a very limited selection of medlar varieties to choose from, detailed in the chart overleaf. A few other varieties of Dutch and Iranian origin can be found at specialist nurseries.

Recommended medlar varieties	
Variety	Characteristics
DUTCH (syn. LARGE DUTCH)	Has the largest fruits of any variety, although they are usually used for cooking rather than eating fresh. The tree is vigorous and has a spreading habit.
NOTTINGHAM	This variety grows well in Britain, but the fruit is prone to splitting and rotting when ripening. The fruit is small, but has a very good flavour. The tree is more compact and upright in habit than most varieties.
ROYAL	A fairly upright tree. The fruits are medium-sized and have a good flavour.

Pruning medlars

Medlars are spreading trees that are usually grown as bushes on top of a clear trunk of 1-1.4m (3'-4'6"). The length of clear trunk is important in order to prevent the lower branches from dragging on the ground. Medlars should be pruned in the winter, although damaged branches can be tidied up at any time of the year.

Formative pruning of a medlar bush
The methods described here are for a bush tree grown on quince or hawthorn rootstock.

For medlars grown on wild pear rootstock, the most suitable method of training is to grow them as a standard. In this case, follow the methods described for an apple standard (see Chapter 10, page 189). If you are planting a maiden (one-year-old) tree, the only pruning needed in the first year is to cut back the lowest laterals, if they are present, by half.

In the second winter, select the laterals that will be kept to form the main branches of the tree in years to come. Remove the leader just above the topmost lateral. Remove any laterals that were shortened the previous winter.

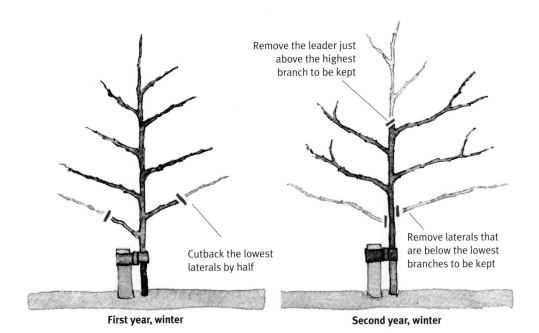

Remove the leader just above the highest branch to be kept

Cutback the lowest laterals by half

Remove laterals that are below the lowest branches to be kept

First year, winter

Second year, winter

Diagram 54 Formative pruning of a medlar bush.

Pruning an established medlar bush

Mature medlars need very little pruning. They form fruit on naturally occurring spurs and side shoots. The main emphasis of pruning is the removal of congested growth and the shortening of long branches, especially where they threaten to reach the ground. Long branches with heavy crops of fruit can benefit from the support of a wooden prop. Medlar trees often produce suckers originating from the base of the tree. It is best to remove these, preferably by pulling, or, if this is not possible, by cutting.

It is important not to prune a medlar too heavily because you will stimulate strong vertical growth. For this reason, it is difficult to renovate a medlar by hard pruning. A soft touch is key when pruning medlars.

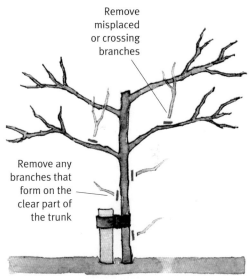

Remove misplaced or crossing branches

Remove any branches that form on the clear part of the trunk

Third year, winter

Diagram 55 Pruning an established medlar bush.

Harvesting and storing medlars

It is best to leave medlars on the tree as long as possible. This usually means picking them in late October or early November, around the time of leaf fall, when they part easily from the tree.

At the time of picking, medlars are inedible due to their astringency; they need to be 'bletted' before they can be eaten. Bletting is the process of allowing the fruit to become soft and semi-rotten during storage. The fruit needs to be kept, calyx down, in a cool, dry, frost-free place for several weeks before it is ready. A wooden tray or cardboard box is an ideal container. The fruits should not be touching, so as to prevent any rot spreading amongst them. The skin becomes wrinkled and darker and the flesh changes from off-white to brown during this process. When the bletting is complete, the fruit tastes like a smoky apple sauce.

Using medlars

The simplest way to consume medlars is to eat the flesh raw; wine and cheese are traditional accompaniments. In some Mediterranean regions, a straw is inserted into the fruit so that the flesh can be sucked out. Medlars can be roasted over a fire or baked in an oven, then served as a dessert, perhaps with cream or wine.

However, most medlars are used for making sweet preserves of some kind. Medlar jelly is perhaps the most well known, but jam is also made. Medlar cheese is a thick, pulpy preserve, with the addition of only sugar and allspice and cinnamon for seasoning. A different type of medlar cheese uses eggs and butter to create a preserve rather like lemon curd. Medlar fudge is another idea, using the thick consistency and sweet, smoky flavour to accentuate the traditional sweet. Although most preserves are used with sweet dishes, medlar jelly can also be served with game.

MULBERRIES

Mulberries are a wonderful fruit, rather like a dark and juicy raspberry with a marked sweet and acid taste that sparkles in your mouth. Sadly, they are rarely appreciated by most people because they do not travel well, so are not to be found in shops. Of course, this is all the more reason to grow your own, although be aware that the mulberry grows to be quite a large tree. It is also a handsome tree, often growing into gnarled and unpredictable forms.

The history of mulberry growing in Britain

Mulberries are native to warm temperate parts of Asia and Europe. They were well known to the Romans and Greeks, who used

The delicious mulberry.

them for medicinal purposes as well as for fruit. King James I is credited with bringing mulberries to Britain in the seventeenth century, planting an avenue of them in London, on the site of what is now Buckingham Palace. He planted them with silk production in mind, but unfortunately he planted the wrong trees: it is the white mulberry that is the only food of the silkworm, but he planted the black mulberry by mistake. The black mulberry is the tree that we know and grow today for its delicious fruit. The mulberry was also used as a medicinal plant in Britain, supposedly expelling tapeworms and roundworms from the intestines. It is still used medicinally today in developing countries, providing protection against tetanus.

Cultivation of mulberries

Mulberries are usually sold as pot-grown trees, ideally planted in early to mid-spring. They have brittle roots that are susceptible to damage. It is preferable to plant a young tree and to take great care not to damage the roots. They grow into large trees up to 15m (49') tall, which start off growing quickly but soon settle down into slow-growing maturity. They can look old and wizened while still comparatively young.

Mulberries are self-fertile, so only one tree is necessary to produce fruit. Mulberries are not usually sold as grafted trees. They can be propagated by cuttings or from seed.

They are susceptible to mulberry canker, which can be a serious problem on young trees if not controlled promptly. For details of this and other problems that can affect mulberry trees, and how to deal with them, see Chapter 9 (pages 160-1).

Conditions

Being a native of warm climates, the mulberry prefers a sheltered site in full sun. It will grow well in southern Britain, but is less successful and less fruitful north of the Midlands. The mulberry is tolerant of a wide range of soil types, but has a preference for well-drained, moisture-retentive soils with a pH of 6-7. It is least happy on thin, sandy soils that drain quickly, and particularly dislikes chalk. The addition of compost or manure will help to improve free-draining or sandy soils.

Because of their preference for moisture-retentive soil, it is worth watering young mulberry trees during dry periods. Adding a mulch of manure or compost in spring helps to retain moisture and feed the tree.

Mulberry varieties

Mulberries are sometimes listed by their Latin name *Morus* in catalogues. *Morus alba* is the white mulberry beloved of silkworms, while *Morus rubra* is the red mulberry, which bears inferior fruit. What you need is the black mulberry, or *Morus nigra*. There are a few named varieties, but in reality there is little difference between them.

King James (also known as Chelsea) is supposed to be descended from the original trees planted by King James I. **Jerusalem** and **Italian** are varieties that are supposedly superior for fruiting and earlier cropping. **Illinois Everbearing** is a vigorous American cultivar that is more suited to cooler climates.

Named varieties will start bearing fruit earlier than the species, usually after three years or so.

Pruning mulberry trees

Mulberries are apt to have a wayward growth habit. Although this is part of the charm of a mulberry, it is best to train the tree carefully when young, in order to create a strong, well-balanced tree. It is good practice to insert a stout bamboo cane 2-2.5m (6'6"-8') tall in order to train the leader vertically – this mitigates the tendency of mulberries to grow lopsided, to the extent that they often fall over when mature. The other structural problem that mulberries are prone to is competing leaders (see photos on page 109). Removing the weaker or less upright of the two leaders helps to avoid a structural weakness that can lead to the tree splitting later in its life.

All pruning of mulberries should take place during early to midwinter because of their pronounced tendency to bleed sap. The only exception to this is the removal of small shoots damaged by mulberry canker.

Formative pruning of a mulberry tree
If you are planting a maiden (one-year-old) tree, the only pruning needed in the first year is to cut back the lowest laterals, if they are present, by half.

In the second or third winters (depending on the height of the tree), select the laterals that will be kept to form the main branches of the tree in years to come. At this stage, you have a choice of removing the leader to form a

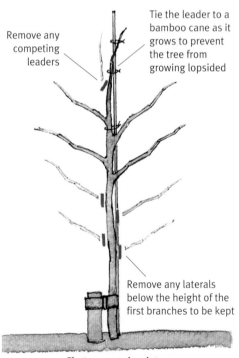

Remove any competing leaders

Tie the leader to a bamboo cane as it grows to prevent the tree from growing lopsided

Remove any laterals below the height of the first branches to be kept

First year, early winter

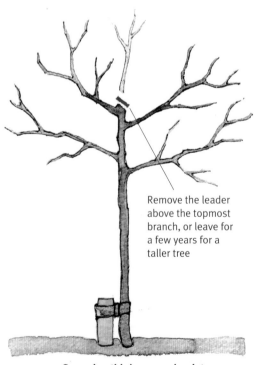

Remove the leader above the topmost branch, or leave for a few years for a taller tree

Second or third year, early winter

Diagram 56 Formative pruning of a mulberry tree.

more spreading tree, or waiting a year or two if you prefer a taller tree. At the desired time, remove the leader just above the topmost lateral. Remove any laterals that were shortened the previous winter. Remove any competing leaders as they form.

Pruning an established mulberry tree
Once a mulberry is established, there is little need for pruning apart from removing damaged or misplaced branches. It is worth paying attention to the balance of the tree. If it starts to lean to one side, it might be worth removing a large branch if this helps the situation. If you are not sure, ask a tree surgeon or fruit tree specialist for advice. Another solution, if the tree is leaning heavily as it ages, is to prop it with stout wooden props.

Harvesting mulberries

Although mulberries can be picked and eaten straight from the tree, the traditional way of harvesting is to place a white sheet under the tree, giving the tree a gentle shake to dislodge any fruit that are ripe. The sheet is then lifted and gathered together gently to collect the fruit. The fruit ripens over a long period in late summer to early autumn.

A word of warning – mulberries stain very easily and stick to shoes, so take care not to plant a tree overhanging the path to your house, or you may end up with carpets spotted with mulberry juice.

Using mulberries

Mulberries will not keep, so either eat them straight away or use them in the various preserves that enjoy their flavour. They can be used in much the same way as raspberries or blackberries in cooking, although they seem to be better when not cooked too long. Mulberry ice cream, summer pudding and fool are examples of good uses. They are great for fruit salad, where their tart sweetness enlivens other fruits.

Mulberry gin is a traditional recipe for the alcoholically inclined. Mulberries can also be frozen, although they will lose some of their wonderful texture.

FIGS

Figs, like many of the less common fruits featured here, are also more at home in their Mediterranean homeland, but are still well worth growing in Britain. They are one of those fruits that is incomparably better when grown at home rather than bought in the shops. Savouring their delicious, juicy stickiness just before the wasps and hornets join in is one of those delights of summer that is barely matched.

The history of fig growing

The fig is thought to be one of the first plants cultivated by humankind. Excavations at Gilgal in the Jordan valley have revealed traces of fig cultivation dated between 9400 and 9200 BC. Figs are thought to originate from the area around Afghanistan and Iran, but they are now naturalised in much of the warm temperate and subtropical world.

Figs were well known during the height of Roman and Greek civilisations. The Greeks claimed that figs were gifted to them by the goddess Demeter. Cato mentions six different figs and Pliny twenty-nine. Archaeological remains have shown that figs were present in Britain in Roman times, although it is uncertain whether they were actually grown here.

Ripening figs. They will turn a purple-brown colour and hang down when ripe.

The first recorded planting of figs in Britain was by Cardinal Pole at Lambeth Palace in 1552. It is thought the variety might have been White Marseille, one still available today. Figs became a fruit that was enjoyed largely by the aristocracy; their cultivation has always been marginal here, so the large walls and greenhouses of stately homes were made best use of.

Cultivation of figs

Fig trees appreciate warm, sunny conditions, but can be grown easily in warm parts of the British Isles, even though their fruits develop and ripen over two seasons because of our cool climate. Even in cooler areas, figs might succeed if they are trained against a sunny wall. Providing a tree is well looked after, you can expect 50 to 100 figs a year, and far superior to any that you are likely to find in the shops.

Figs are grown on their own roots, not grafted on to rootstocks. They are largely untroubled by pests and diseases, apart from those pests that would like to eat the fruit

before you do. See Chapter 9 (page 160) for details.

Conditions

In order to appreciate the art of growing figs, it is worth looking at their native habitat in the heat of the Mediterranean and Middle Eastern climate. They thrive on rocky hillsides, where the drainage is sharp and the heat is reflected by the rocks and warm, bare soil. This is entirely the opposite of the comparatively cold, wet soils and climate of Britain. So, the more we can do to replicate the warm, rocky conditions of the fig's homeland, the better. A sunny and sheltered location is preferable, such as against a south-facing wall of the house. Figs fruit best where growth is restricted by a pot, raised bed or a planting pit (see right and Diagram 57 on page 294).

Fruiting well is not the same as growing well: fig trees will grow well if given a free root run and plenty of nitrogen, but they will not crop well. As with all fruit trees, there is a need to balance vegetative growth with fruit production. With fig trees, there is more of a need to restrict growth in order to encourage fruiting.

Growing figs in a container

Figs are well suited to growing in pots, apart from two potential problems. The first is that figs can become large, heavy trees that can easily blow over. Tying the tree to a stable object such as a vine eye in a wall will overcome this difficulty. The second potential problem is that figs will shed their crop if they become stressed by drought. Although they enjoy warm, dry conditions, figs in pots require a surprising amount of water. They will also need some feeding with a high-potash feed, such as tomato food or comfrey

A fig tree growing in a large container.

than it was before and remove around 20 per cent of the rootball by cutting it back with a sharp knife. Once re-potting becomes difficult, because the tree and pot become too large, the pot can be plunged into the soil in a suitable place. The retention of the pot will still restrict the roots.

Growing figs against a wall

A south-facing wall is an ideal location because figs will enjoy the warmth retained by the wall, the shelter from cold winds and the rain shadow created by the wall. The base of a wall is often an easy place to restrict root growth, either by using paving slabs or a raised border or concrete path. Fig fans can become vigorous plants, so a strong framework of wires will be needed to train them on. Fig fans can be contained in an area about 2.5m (8') high and 4.5m (14'6") wide.

In more northern areas of Britain, some kind of winter protection is preferable. This can be formed of fleece or more natural materials, such as straw or bracken contained by netting or chicken wire.

Creating a planting pit for figs

Sometimes, there will be no obvious place to plant a fig where the roots will be restricted, so the tree will need to be planted in the open; in this case you can restrict the roots by creating a planting pit. Dig a large square hole where the tree is to be planted. Place paving slabs (ideally 60x60cm [2x2']) around the sides of the hole, so that they protrude very slightly above the soil level; this prevents the roots from spreading on the soil surface. Place a thick layer of rubble, bricks, etc. in the bottom of the planting hole to improve the drainage and to hinder the formation of large tap roots (see Diagram 57 overleaf).

liquid, in order to do best. A foliar feed of seaweed will help to strengthen the tree and protect against fungal disease.

Figs can be started off in a 25-30cm (10-12") container, depending on their size when obtained. A soil-based compost such as John Innes No.3 is the ideal growing medium. Crocks or grit in the bottom of the pot will help to keep the drainage sharp. Lifting the pot just off the ground with pot feet or bricks will help to avoid waterlogging in winter. Alternatively, figs will enjoy a spell in the greenhouse over the winter months.

Figs can be potted on every one to two years, gradually increasing the size of pot. When re-potting, plant the fig 2-3cm (1") deeper

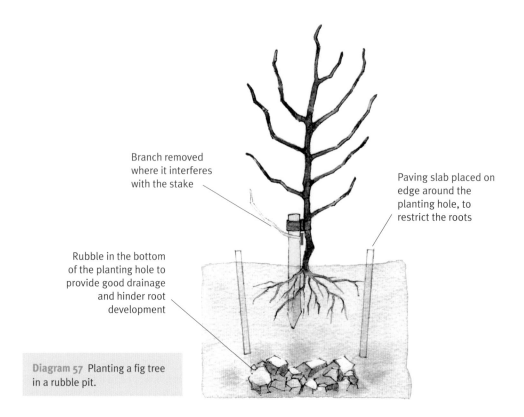

Branch removed
where it interferes
with the stake

Paving slab placed on
edge around the
planting hole, to
restrict the roots

Rubble in the bottom
of the planting hole to
provide good drainage
and hinder root
development

Diagram 57 Planting a fig tree
in a rubble pit.

Some soils that are normally thought of as being difficult will actually suit figs well. Both chalk and heavy clay soils will restrict root development naturally. Although heavy clay soils can inhibit root development, the drainage is likely to be poor, so serious attention will need to be paid to improving this.

Watering might be necessary during drought conditions in the summer. Feeding should veer towards high-potash feeds rather than those high in nitrogen. Farmyard manure or compost applied as a mulch in spring can be supplemented with tomato feed in summer.

The fruiting cycle of figs

It is very easy to become confused by the fruiting cycle of figs, because they carry different generations of fruit on the tree all at the same time. In the British climate, once the ripe fruits have been picked, there will be two types of fruit left on the tree. The larger ones, from about marble size upwards, are fruits produced this season that will not ripen properly. The fruits that will ripen next year are now the size of a pea or even smaller. They can be seen mostly on the final 20-30cm (8-12") of shoots that have grown this year.

The larger fruits are likely to split or fall off during the winter. Removing all the fruits larger than a pea in November allows the tree to put its energy into developing the small fruits ready for next season. In other words, the fruits need to develop over two seasons in our climate. It is the fruits that

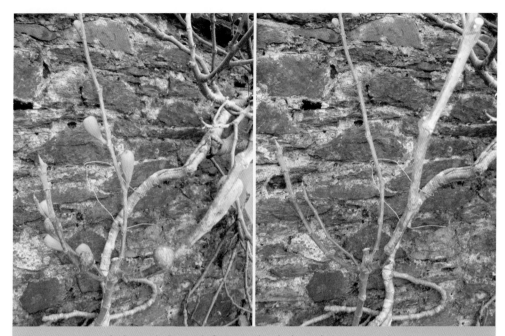

The same section of a fig tree before and after removing the larger fruits in November.

After removing the larger fruits, just the embryonic fruits remain, ready to grow and ripen the following year.

would normally develop and ripen over one season in a warmer climate that are removed in order to help the embryonic fruits develop for the following year.

Fig varieties

There are over 600 varieties of figs in cultivation, but only a small number are suitable for growing in our cool climate. There are many varieties suitable for growing in a large greenhouse (Reads Nursery – see Resources – lists a large selection), but just three varieties that are widely stocked for outdoor cultivation in Britain, listed in the chart overleaf. They are all self-fertile, so only one tree needs to be planted.

Recommended fig varieties	
Variety	Characteristics
BROWN TURKEY	The most reliable variety. It has attractive foliage and bears heavy crops of dark-brown, good-quality sweet figs.
BRUNSWICK	Carries moderate crops of large pear-shaped greenish figs that become tinged with brown in warm summers. They need a hot summer to ripen properly.
WHITE MARSEILLE	Large green rounded fruits with sweet, translucent flesh, which ripen well outdoors in favoured locations.

Pruning fig trees

Fig trees are usually trained as a bush or as a fan, preferably against a south-facing wall, where they will benefit from the warmth and shelter. They are best planted in late winter or early spring, once the harshest of the winter weather has passed. Most pruning of figs is carried out in spring, with April being the normal time in southern Britain, but extending into May in the North. Be aware that the milky sap of figs can be an irritant to the skin.

Formative pruning of a fig bush

Formative pruning of a bush tree is the same as that for an apple bush (see Chapter 10, page 185), except for the time of pruning. Figs benefit from being trained into an open shape, so that maximum amounts of sunlight can reach developing fruits, so ensure that the branch framework does not become too dense.

Pruning an established fig bush

Once the bush is established, spring pruning aims to keep the branch structure clear and open (see Diagram 58). Any crossing branches should be removed and areas of overcrowded growth thinned. Occasionally, older branches can be cut back to a young replacement shoot in order to encourage new growth. Any frost-damaged growth should be removed.

Figs are also pruned in the summer, with the aim of increasing light and helping to reduce

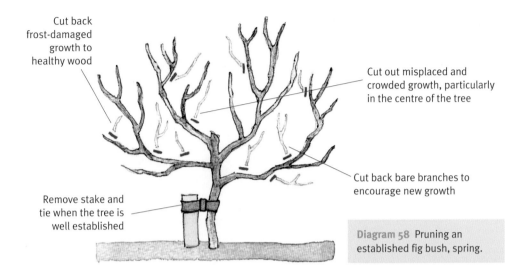

Cut back frost-damaged growth to healthy wood

Cut out misplaced and crowded growth, particularly in the centre of the tree

Remove stake and tie when the tree is well established

Cut back bare branches to encourage new growth

Diagram 58 Pruning an established fig bush, spring.

the crop of unwanted figs that will not ripen. This is done by pinching out all new growth to restrict it to five or six leaves per shoot. Because fig leaves are so large, it can be worth removing individual leaves that are casting a shadow on ripening fruits.

Fig trees that have been neglected can be restored by hard pruning. It is helpful to feed the tree whenever hard pruning is carried

out, because the pruning will encourage the tree to put on lots of new growth.

Formative pruning of a fig fan

Firstly, ensure that the wall is clothed with a structure of strong wires to hold the branches in place. Plant a two-year-old feathered tree at least 20cm (8") away from the wall. Cut back the leader to leave the lowest two laterals (see Diagram 59). These can be tied in

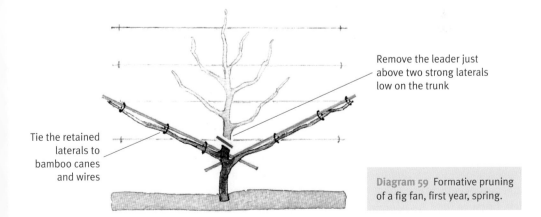

Remove the leader just above two strong laterals low on the trunk

Tie the retained laterals to bamboo canes and wires

Diagram 59 Formative pruning of a fig fan, first year, spring.

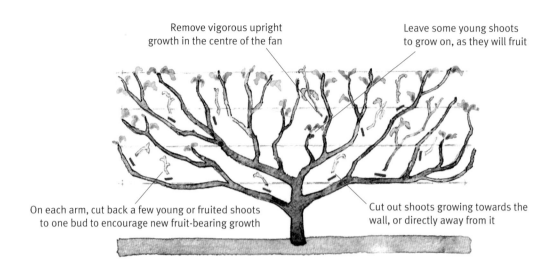

Remove vigorous upright growth in the centre of the fan

Leave some young shoots to grow on, as they will fruit

On each arm, cut back a few young or fruited shoots to one bud to encourage new fruit-bearing growth

Cut out shoots growing towards the wall, or directly away from it

Diagram 60 Pruning an established fig fan, spring.

with bamboo canes at an angle of about 45 degrees to the ground. Shorten these two laterals by about half if weak, or less if growing strongly. If planting a maiden tree, allow it to grow on for a year, until strong laterals are in place. If two strong laterals are not apparent, the leader can be cut back hard in order to stimulate new growth that will produce two suitable branches for the following season.

After this, a fig fan is formed in the same way as a peach fan (see Chapter 14, page 266), except that the branches need to be further apart because of the large size of fig leaves.

Pruning an established fig fan

Once the space on the wall has been filled in, the aim of pruning is to keep an open branch structure and to encourage the growth of young shoots that will bear figs on their tips. Towards the ends of branches, cut back fruited shoots to one bud in order to encourage new growth. Some shoots will need to be left, because they are bearing the embryonic

fruits that will ripen in the coming season (see Diagram 60). Approximately one branch on either side of the fan can be removed each year, or cut back to young growth that will form a replacement. Any frost-damaged wood or vigorous upright growth can also be removed at this time, along with shoots growing towards or away from the wall.

Harvesting figs

As figs ripen, they turn from green towards dark brown or even purple, apart from the so-called green figs or white figs, such as White Marseille: these just turn a little more yellow. They also lose their semi-erect stance and begin to droop.

Once the figs have been picked, there is nothing better than eating them straight from the tree. Even if there are others waiting for them indoors, I consider it the right of the fig harvester to sample a few, to ensure that they are fit for others to eat!

Using figs

If sufficient numbers of them make it into the house, there is a whole range of uses to which figs can be put. To my mind, they are so wonderful that eating them for dessert, perhaps served with a dollop of clotted cream and some walnuts, is pleasure enough. Orange juice is a frequent accompaniment for figs, while blue cheese gives a more savoury flavour. Alcohol, such as brandy or port, is also a suitable companion.

As with most fruits, there is a range of jams, chutneys and other preserves that can be made from figs. Fig ice cream, fig and almond tart and figgy pudding are all delicious desserts. Figs can also be bottled, usually with some form of alcoholic syrup, or dried in a slow oven or drying box. Figs are best kept out of the fridge and freezer.

LESS COMMON FRUITS

All the major types of fruit grown in the British Isles have now been covered in this book; they tend to be popular for a reason, which is that they are either delicious or easy to grow, or in many cases both. There are also a number of other fruit trees that were commonly used in the past, but are now considered marginal. Despite their relative obscurity, these fruits are still worthy of consideration.

Elderberries

The elder (*Sambucus nigra*) is a well-known native tree of the English countryside. It carries flat-topped creamy-white blossoms in May that have turned to deep-purple berries by the end of the summer. Elder is a tree that has strong associations with the superstition and folklore of country people. In centuries gone by it was used as a protection against witches and magic. It has been said that anyone cutting down an elder would be cursed with bad luck.

In addition to its folk significance, the elder has always been a useful plant, both for its wood and for its flowers and berries. The flowers have been used in herbal medicine as well as for making various drinks. Elderflower cordial and elderflower champagne, for example, are available commercially and also commonly made at home.

The berries are used to make a syrup that is said to strengthen the immune system and cure respiratory illnesses. This syrup also makes a delicious cordial or a healthy accompaniment to ice cream. The berries were also used medicinally in the past; the sixteenth-century English herbalist Gerard says that the berries "are good for such as have the dropsie, and such as are too fat, and would faine be leaner". The Romans used the berries to dye their hair black. Elderberry wine and jam are other common uses for the fruit.

Elderberries can be used to make healthy cordials or syrup.

The Devon sorb apple, or otmast. The speckling is a normal feature of this fruit.

While elder is usually thought of as a hedge-row tree in England, it is also grown commercially for use in drinks and medicine. This commercial use has resulted in the development of a number of varieties of elder that have been bred to improve upon the yields of the native tree. There are cultivars from countries in Northern and Eastern Europe, such as Bradet or Samdal, which carry heavy crops of large berries. The American elderberry (*Sambucus canadensis*) bears flowers from July to October. It is not self-fertile, but fruits will follow, so long as pollination takes place. Johns and York are cultivars selected from this tree.

Rowan berries and chequers

There are various berries produced on different types of trees in the *Sorbus* genus. Rowan berries are one example, produced on the rowan or mountain ash tree (*Sorbus aucuparia*). One form of this tree is *Sorbus aucuparia* var. *edulis*, which was introduced in the 1800s, bearing larger berries that are less bitter than the species (*S. aucuparia*). The whitebeam (*Sorbus aria*) and the service tree (*Sorbus domestica*) both carry edible fruits that were eaten by children before more pleasant 'sweets' became available.

Chequers also have their place in British history, as evidenced by the number of pubs called The Chequers. These small fruits of the wild service tree (*Sorbus torminalis*) were used for making an alcoholic drink a little like cider, which probably accounts for the number of pubs bearing their name.

Some of these *Sorbus* fruits are bletted, in the same way that medlars are (see page 288), to sweeten them and improve their texture. Rowan jelly has traditionally been served as an accompaniment to venison and game.

Rowans hybridise easily, producing regional variations. The Devon sorb apple (*Sorbus devoniensis*) is an example; it is a small tree that produces sorb apples or otmasts, which were traditionally used for stuffing turkey and game.

Hawthorn berries

It might surprise you to find hawthorns listed as a cultivated fruit. In Britain we see them adorning hedgerows with blossom in May and red haws in the autumn, but they are rarely thought of as a fruit to be planted in an orchard.

Yet, in many parts of the world hawthorns (*Crataegus* spp.) are perceived as edible. In Mediterranean countries, the azarole (*Crataegus azarolus*) is cultivated for its yellow or red cherry-sized fruits that taste a little like toffee apples. The tansy-leaved hawthorn (*C. tanacetifolia*) also carries fruit like yellow crab apples.

A variety of Chinese hawthorn (*C. pinnatifida*), known as Big Golden Star, bears red

Edible hawthorn berries.

fruit about 2-3cm (1") across that are usually used for cooking. Many of the hawthorn cultivars sold for fruit production come from America. *C. durobrivensis* and *C. ellwangeriana* are examples.

There is even a tree called x *Crataemespilus grandiflora*, which is a cross between a hawthorn and a medlar, producing reddish-brown fruits like a large haw.

BORDERLINE FRUITS

Fruits such as haws and chequers are approaching the borderline of fruits that are worth gathering, let alone those that are worth planting. Yet, if you enjoy experimenting with unusual fruits, or have room for trees that are ornamental as well as productive, you might find a place for such trees in your garden. There are many other trees that are not usually cultivated for their fruits, but which might yield a harvest that is useful or interesting. Examples are juniper berries (*Juniperus* spp.), the fruits of the strawberry tree (*Arbutus unedo*), Cornelian cherries (*Cornus mas*) or juneberries (*Amelanchier* spp.).

Other fruits are in widespread cultivation, but don't quite make it in our temperate climate without the use of a cold greenhouse for winter protection, and thus fall outside the remit of this book. Most of the citrus family falls into this category. Olives will fruit outside, but only just. This might change if global warming gathers pace, but for now olives remain a marginal crop, grown on a pretty tree. I have looked after a loquat tree for the past ten years; it has fruited only once – after two warm summers, one to ripen the wood and one to ripen the fruit. Such a tree, though decorative, is again marginal for fruit production in the present British climate.

Part 4

Traditional orchards

Chapter 17

Restoring a neglected orchard

Despite the best of intentions, many orchards become neglected over the years. It could be that the fruit trees are at the far end of a garden that the ageing house-holder is no longer able to attend to, but more often the neglected site is a farm orchard. Less than a hundred years ago, most farms had an orchard, usually close to the farmhouse, where apple trees pro-vided cider for the numerous farm workers and a variety of other trees gave fruit for use in the farmhouse. Even within living memory, cider made up a part of the wages of farmhands.

These wonderful old farm orchards have often fallen prey to changes in farm manage-ment. The traditional mixed farm has been largely replaced by the specialist farm, as farmers strive to become more efficient in an increasingly competitive world. The numer-ous farmhands of old have been replaced by the single farmer with expensive machinery.

Left: An old farm orchard being restored.

In such a world, the old farm orchard has become largely irrelevant – and the skills and traditions that went with this way of life have been pushed to the edge of extinction.

A typical farm orchard, with a fallen tree.

Throughout Britain, old orchards have been grubbed out to make way for housing development.

With the drive for efficiency, many beautiful orchards were grubbed out after the Second World War. Now, where once whole valleys were covered in orchards, only fragments remain. Devon is thought to have lost 90 per cent of its orchards in the period since 1965.

Government grants were given to grub out orchards – then, a few years later, to plant them again. Despite all this, some farm orchards remain. As farms have been combined, many orchards (and their farmhouses) have come on to the market. Old neglected orchards have passed into the hands of new owners, many of whom are keen to restore them. A renewed interest in orchards has been fuelled by organisations such as Common Ground (see Resources) and local orchard groups throughout the UK.

Some old orchards are remnants of commercial orchards, often with regional interest, such as the damsons of Westmoreland, the plums of Worcestershire, the cherries of Kent, the perry pears of Gloucestershire and the cider orchards of Somerset.

Beginning restoration

The key to restoring an orchard is to take it slowly. Many mistakes are made by rushing what is a delicate process. Start by observing. If possible, watch carefully over a season. Look to see the wonder of what you have already; the intricate play of nature in what is likely to be a wildlife paradise. Watch the comings and goings over the year. See the bare bones of winter transformed into the beauty of blossom time, the richness of summer and the abundance of autumn. Observe the many animals, plants and insects that call your orchard their home.

Before taking any action to restore your orchard, it is worth asking why you are doing it, as the answers will influence how you go about it. What role are you asking your restored orchard to fulfil? Are you wanting to produce as much healthy fruit as possible, or are you interested in the orchard as a wildlife habitat? The answer is probably somewhere between the two, but where you draw the line will determine the methods you use for restoration. It is possible to achieve a healthy, productive orchard that is also a rich and varied wildlife habitat. Restoration will change the nature of the habitat, as shade decreases, but the value to wildlife can be retained.

Orchards and wildlife

In a world where farming is becoming increasingly specialised, the traditional orchard can be a wildlife oasis in the midst of vast swathes of monocultural desert. The value of such orchards was officially recognised in 2007, with the granting of UK BAP (Biodiversity Action Plan) Priority Status. This gives some protection to orchards that may be endangered by development or agricultural improvement.

Traditional orchards are now recognised for their value as wildlife habitats.

Orchards provide a unique and varied habitat, somewhere between open woodland and rough, unimproved grassland. The fruit trees themselves support an array of wildlife, some of it specific to orchards. As long as the mature trees have not been planted too close together, there is likely to be a tussocky sward with its own abundance of species. In many neglected orchards there are areas of scrub that provide valuable shelter, and resources for many creatures.

Fruit trees as wildlife habitats

As fruit trees mature, they begin to develop a wonderful range of features that support particular species. Rot holes, dead wood and hollow trunks provide ideal conditions for invertebrates and specific insects. The noble chafer, for example, is an endangered beetle that lives on decaying fruit tree wood. A vast range of lichens and fungi also thrive in the damp, shady conditions encountered in the middle of large trees.

The thriving insect population is, in turn, a food source for many species of birds, such as mistle thrushes and flycatchers. Little owls will use the holes found in old fruit trees as a nesting site. The dead wood and hollows are enjoyed by woodpeckers, nuthatches and

A mouse nest in a hollow created by pruning.

A tree like this is an excellent habitat for wildlife, including holes and rotting wood.

Mistletoe is a good wildlife habitat as well as a valuable crop.

foxes, hedgehogs, deer and badgers will be attracted by the abundance of fruit available. Mistletoe is a semi-parasitic plant that is found in many old orchards. Aside from its intrinsic interest and value as a crop, it supports its own micro-ecosystem. The mistletoe tortrix moth is one of four insects dependent on mistletoe. The berries are beloved of mistle thrushes.

The orchard sward as wildlife habitat

As long as the orchard trees do not cast too dense a shade, there is likely to be unimproved grassland on the orchard floor. As farming has intensified, this has become a rare and protected habitat, supporting a wide range of native flora and small mammals.

If managed properly, plants such as wild daffodils, ox-eye daisy, green-winged orchid and vetches will grace the orchard floor. These provide nectar for bees and butterflies and

treecreepers. These birds and the ubiquitous tits will do much to keep insect pests under control. A study by Dutch ecologists in 2007[*] found that apple yields increased dramatically where large numbers of great tits were encouraged into orchards. The springtime blossom is a valuable source of nectar for bees and beneficial insects.

Many birds, including winter visitors such as redwings and fieldfares, will delight in sharing your harvest. The now rare hawfinch will feed on cherry stones. Mammals such as

[*]Mols, C. M. M. & Visser, M. E. (2007). 'Great tits (*Parus major*) reduce caterpillar damage in commercial apple orchards'. *PLoS ONE*, 2(2): e202

seeds for birds such as the goldfinch. Rough grassland is home to shrews, voles and mice, providing ideal conditions for owls to hunt. In many a traditional orchard, the rare barn owl can be seen searching for prey at twilight.

Orchard hedgerows and scrub as wildlife habitat

When an orchard has been neglected for some time, areas of scrub will grow up. Brambles provide nectar for insects in the spring and fruit for birds and mammals in the autumn, and the dense cover supplied by brambles, blackthorn and ivy is a useful nesting site for many birds. It can be worthwhile retaining some scrub in parts of your orchard for its biodiversity value.

Hedgerows, likewise, are a wildlife haven, providing food and shelter for a wide rage of species, in addition to their role of sheltering the orchard. Careful management can provide an abundance of fruit and berries that will help sustain birds and animals well into the winter.

Creating a management plan

Once you have begun to understand the rich ecosystem that is your orchard, you will be in a position to create a plan of action. In order to do this, you will need to ask further questions:

- Which fruit are currently growing in your orchard?
- What will you use the fruit for?
- What condition are the existing trees in?
- How will you manage the orchard floor and hedgerows?
- Do you wish to fill in gaps in the orchard by replanting?

By asking such questions, you will begin to build up a picture of the orchard going forward, and the work that you will need to do to achieve this.

Identifying fruit varieties

If an orchard is new to you, it is likely that you will face a collection of trees with little idea of what you can use them for. You can taste them, of course, and you might get an idea whether an apple is sharp, and so used for cooking, or really bitter and astringent, suggesting a cider apple. However, even this may not be the best guide, as many apples become sweeter during storage. A late-keeping apple could taste rather sour at harvest time in October but have become sweet enough by midwinter to be a quality dessert apple.

Pears, likewise, can be used for dessert, cooking and making perry, each with their distinctive taste. It could be that your old fruit tree is the last of its line, valuable not just as a beautiful gnarled tree but as a source of material for gene banks that are now being compiled. If you do have a particularly

Different varieties of apple and pear on display at an Apple Day.

interesting tree, you can propagate it by grafting or budding. Your local fruit tree nursery or orchard group might be able to help you with this (you can find your local orchard group via the website www.orchard network.org.uk).

Some local experts and nurseries, as well as national bodies, offer a fruit identification service. Both the Royal Horticultural Society and Brogdale, custodian of the National Fruit Collection, offer such a service, for a fee. There are specific requirements for sending fruit for identification in the post, so make sure you contact them first. Your local orchard group can also be a source of information on both varieties and experts.

The information that you gain by identifying a variety gives you a much better understanding of its value, use and potential problems. If, for example, you found out that you had a Catillac pear, you would know that you had an old French variety with large crimson-brown fruits, mostly used for cooking, but also acceptable for dessert use in the spring. It is to be picked in October and used from December through to May. You would know that it is flowering group C and that it is a triploid that is very resistant to scab. You would also be able to find out about the nature of the fruit, the habit of the tree and which climate and soil it prefers. If you didn't know about how to use the fruit, you could easily have decided to grub out the tree because its fruit is unpalatable at harvest time.

Grant funding

The recognition of the value of traditional orchards, both as a landscape feature and as wildlife habitat, has led to the availability of grants for planting and maintaining them. Many grants are available for only a short time, dictated by government and European funding policy. The environment department of your local council, or your local orchard group, are likely to have the latest information to hand.

One source of funding that is more constant is the Stewardship grants paid by the Department for Environment, Food and Rural Affairs (DEFRA) to encourage environmentally sensitive farming. Higher Level Stewardship currently provides an annual payment per hectare for traditional orchard management, as well as payments for restorative pruning, tree guards and replacement planting. The Farming and Wildlife Advisory Group (FWAG) provides advice to farmers about conservation and government grants.

Restoring the orchard

If the trees have not been pruned recently, it is likely that they will need restorative pruning (see page 314). If the neglect has continued for a number of years, the first task might be to remove ivy and brambles that have grown up into the trees. A small amount of ivy can be tolerated, but once it starts to grow into the crown of the tree it can seriously affect its wind resistance, making it more likely to blow down in winter storms. Brambles growing into a fruit tree are a prickly nuisance that makes other restoration work difficult. In severe cases, removing ivy and brambles will be sufficient work for the first year's restoration. This process will allow more air and light into the trees. Remember that gradual change is best for the trees as well as for the wildlife inhabiting them.

Once you have removed ivy and brambles, you will be better placed to assess the trees.

An apple tree that has nearly become an ivy tree.

The first task is to decide whether individual trees are worth keeping. If you have observed the orchard over a season, you will have seen the fruiting potential of individual trees. Remember, however, that neglected trees might have reverted to a biennial pattern of cropping, or there may have been adverse weather conditions that affected pollination, so don't write off unproductive specimens too easily. Careful management can increase the quality and quantity of fruit from neglected trees that are bearing small crops. It is more important to look at the general health of the tree.

If you are seeking maximum production from your orchard, you might choose to remove trees that are well past their best, but remember that these are the ones that are likely to offer the most valuable features for wildlife. Even trees that have blown over can live for many years, often starting to grow new upright branches as they adapt to their new position. Because it is not possible to graze or cut right up to the tree trunk, a valuable habitat can arise as nettles or other plants grow up under the branches. So, unless maximising your harvest is the sole aim, nearly all mature trees are useful in one way or another. Even dead trees are important to wildlife. Some species of insect, such as the

Fruit trees will often keep growing after they have fallen over.

noble chafer, live only on rotting fruit tree wood.

The exceptions to this rule are trees that are carrying disease that can spread throughout an orchard. Canker and silver leaf are the worst offenders in this category. Small areas of these diseases can be pruned out, but severely infected trees should be removed. The other disease that will change your plans is honey fungus. Where this is present, remove all dead wood from the orchard floor and take out any dead trees, including the roots, in order to limit the underground spread of the disease. Honey fungus can decimate an orchard, so prompt action is needed. See Chapter 9 for details of these diseases and their control.

Fruit trees can benefit from the management of mistletoe, particularly where large amounts are present. Although only semi-parasitic, mistletoe can have a detrimental effect on its host. Once mistletoe is established, it can be difficult to control.

Mistletoe can harm its host if it is allowed to spread without any control.

Managing the orchard floor

The orchard floor will need some kind of management so that it does not revert to scrub. Once brambles and other scrub have been removed, it will be necessary to keep them under control with a brushcutter or other mechanical means. There are various types of hand-propelled, heavy-duty mowing machines for cutting rough grassland. A ride-on mower can be suitable for more controlled areas of shorter grass, but remember that the more often the grass is cut, the lower the wildlife potential.

Grazing with sheep is the best method of managing the orchard floor, although precautions need to be taken. Firstly, you will need to ensure that the orchard boundary is secure, with either a good hedge or fencing. A water supply and gates will need to be provided, if not already in place. Secondly, the trees might need protecting from grazing animals. Young trees will need the shelter of a tree guard (see Chapter 6, page 84) and even older trees might need more limited protection. Chicken wire wrapped loosely around older trees is usually sufficient. Not all sheep have the same habits – some breeds, particularly mountain sheep, can be much more inquisitive and damaging.

It is best to limit grazing to sheep, but if cattle or horses are admitted to the orchard, protection will need to be more extensive. Larger animals cause soil compaction by poaching the soil around the trees. Also, their extended reach will allow them to reach the lower branches of mature trees. Considerable damage can be caused when they pull branches down or rub against the tree trunk.

Ideally, the orchard floor should be left undisturbed until the third week of July (later in the north of England, Scotland and Northern Ireland). This allows time for some wildflowers to set seed. Another cut (or grazing) can follow later in the year. It is helpful to have the grass short at harvest time, so that windfalls can be collected easily. Where wildflowers are a priority, leaving some of the orchard uncut until September will allow a greater diversity of plants to flourish. Grass cuttings are best removed, in order to avoid a build-up of soil nutrients as the cuttings decay. If space allows, you might choose to leave a few areas of scrub at the edge of the orchard for the benefit of wildlife.

Managing orchard hedgerows

There is an optimum height for hedgerows surrounding an orchard, which will depend upon the size of the trees in the orchard and the degree of exposure to strong winds. If the hedges are too tall they will cast a dense shade on the orchard; too short and the orchard will lack the valuable shelter that a good hedge can provide. Fruit trees are particularly light-sensitive and will lean towards the side where there is most light, causing them eventually to be lopsided and prone to blowing over. Some hedgerows around an orchard will be suitable for laying, but there can be a danger in reducing the height of a hedge too quickly. It is better to remove brambles and ivy from the trees first and then start restorative pruning, before making drastic changes to the hedges. This is because the fruit trees can be prone to blowing over if suddenly exposed to stronger winds than they are used to. It is better to first reduce the wind resistance of the trees, then reduce the hedge.

Where hedges are kept trimmed, it is best to cut them late in the season (January or early February), leaving the berries and seeds undisturbed for as long as possible. Cutting

Grazing with sheep is the traditional method of managing the grass in a large orchard.

Fruit trees will grow towards the light, becoming lopsided if hedges are not kept under control.

distances for each rootstock (see Chapter 2, page 32). Where a number of trees are to be planted, it is helpful to place bamboo canes in the ground to mark their locations. Avoiding the site of trees that have died recently will help to overcome potential problems with replant disease (see Chapter 9, page 137).

Restorative pruning

Once you have observed, assessed and planned the management of your orchard, you can turn your attention to the renovation of individual trees. An initial assessment is, again, the key to carrying out the most appropriate form of pruning. The guidelines for assessing trees given in the box on page 107, Chapter 8, are the same for neglected trees, with the addition of deciding on the severity of pruning, depending on the age of the tree and the degree of neglect.

each side of a hedge in alternate years is another option that ensures a plentiful supply of food for wildlife.

Replanting in an existing orchard

Planting new trees in an existing orchard soon gives an air of renewal and hope where once there was neglect and decay. Through replanting, the life of the orchard is continued indefinitely into the future.

With existing trees, the types of fruit and the varieties are predetermined, but by planting new stock you have the chance to grow trees that will suit your needs – whether this means fruit for dessert, juicing, cooking or cider making. Careful thought when choosing varieties will be repaid at a later date, when you will be rewarded with healthy trees providing heavy crops of the fruit that suit your needs. See Chapter 4 for advice on choosing the right varieties for you.

It is important to choose the planting sites with care, remembering the correct planting

Assessing the neglected tree

Firstly, look at the top of the tree to establish how vigorous it is. You can tell this by seeing if there is strong upright growth or not. Vigorous trees generally need lighter pruning, because of the risk of over-stimulating them by heavy pruning. Trees growing more weakly can be stimulated into growth by pruning, except for really old trees that need to be treated gently to avoid the shock of hard pruning.

If you are uncertain how hard to prune an old tree, start by pruning lightly, then observe it again in a year's time to judge the effect the pruning has had. If there are signs of healthy regrowth where pruning cuts have been made, further pruning can continue. If growth is still weak after a few years, it may be that the tree is in senescence and will not make further growth. Senescent trees can be left alone to end their life peacefully. If there is very strong regrowth, it is possible that the tree has been pruned too hard.

The density of the growth on the tree will also affect the style of pruning adopted. Trees with particularly dense growth can have this growth thinned over a number of years. It is best to think of restorative pruning as a three- to five-year process, depending upon the condition of the tree.

Pruning the neglected tree

No more than 20 per cent of the tree's growth should be removed in the first year, and this amount should then decline each year. For cherries and plums, 15 per cent in the first year is plenty. Keeping a pile of prunings a little way away from the tree will enable you to gauge this percentage easily. It is also good practice from a safety point of view, because it is easy to trip over prunings scattered on the ground while looking up at the tree!

The system of regulated pruning described in Chapter 8 (page 113) is ideal for renovating neglected trees – bearing in mind that apples can produce particularly dense growth when neglected, so are likely to need more pruning than pears, plums and cherries.

SAFETY WHEN PRUNING

When pruning the centre of a large tree, you have a choice of using long-handled tools or a ladder in order to reach the higher branches. The Working at Height Regulations 2005 make it clear that before using a ladder, a safer alternative method should be considered. In the case of pruning large fruit trees, this alternative is the use of long-handled tools. This is a perfectly good alternative in most cases, except that it is more difficult to get a clean cut working from a distance with a pole saw. There may be some areas of really tall trees that cannot be accessed by most pole saws. Good-quality long-handled tools can be expensive, but they are a wise investment if you have a number of large trees to prune.

The Working at Height Regulations are not prescriptive for the private individual, but they are a useful guide. Ladders used in trees can be dangerous. The bottom of a ladder can usually be pushed into the soil, making it unlikely to slip, but it can be difficult to make the top of the ladder secure. Tying the top of the ladder to the tree is one option.

If a ladder is used, one of your hands should always be in contact with it, meaning that a pruning saw or secateurs are the only practicable tools to use, because they can be used with one hand. Your hips should always remain within the stiles of the ladder; don't be tempted to reach sideways to gain access to a branch. Only tackle pruning that you feel comfortable with. If a particular task is daunting for you to tackle, consider engaging a professional.

There are specialist orchard contractors who will prune large trees for you. A good first step is to contact your local orchard group to see if they can recommend someone. Many tree surgeons will prune fruit trees satisfactorily, but there are also some who are not sufficiently experienced in fruit tree work. Don't hesitate to check their qualifications and ask about their experience with fruit trees.

When pruning a large tree, there is an order of working which can prove helpful, especially where growth is dense.

- First, prune what you can reach by using a pruning saw and loppers. This enables you to walk more easily around the base of the tree and also to look up into the tree to observe the pattern of branches higher up. The bottom of the tree usually contains the densest growth, which is most in need of thinning. Sometimes this growth will have started to die back owing to the shade cast by the rest of the tree.

- Next, use long-handled tools to access the centre of the tree. Again, this is an important part of the tree to get right at an early stage, because it is where the major branches originate and because crowded growth in the centre of the tree impedes airflow through the tree. If there is a need to remove any large branches, perhaps because of overcrowding or poor branch structure, it is preferable to do this in the first year. Large branches should have at least 75-90cm (2'6"-3') between them, otherwise their side branches will always have a tendency to be crossing or rubbing.

- Once you have pruned the middle of the tree, you can move on to the higher part of the outside of the tree. This is the area least likely to be congested, because the growth here is the most recent.

When you have finished a season's pruning, the crown of each tree should be thinned, but not look pruned (see photos below – this tree has just been pruned for the first time in many years). An old farmers' saying is that you should be able to throw your hat through the tree when you have finished pruning. After four years maybe, on a neglected tree, but not after one!

A standard apple tree before and after restorative pruning.

When you come back to prune the tree the next year, observe how it has responded to the previous year's pruning. Has the tree made new growth in response to your pruning cuts? The amount of new growth will determine how hard you prune the tree this time, remembering that trees growing vigorously should be pruned more gently in order to avoid over-stimulating them. If a tree produces little new growth after pruning, try feeding it in the spring with a general-purpose fertiliser such as chicken manure pellets.

If you have cut out major limbs in the previous year, you might find 'water shoots' emerging from close to the wounds that have healed. These are upright shoots that grow from larger branches as a result of pruning. They are often in the middle of the tree and not useful for forming new branches. If this is the case, they are best removed during the summer months. If they look as though they could be useful in filling a gap in the branch structure, or replacing an old branch in time, then they can be pruned in the normal way in winter.

Starved neglected trees

Some trees, particularly those on less vigorous rootstocks, respond to neglect by contracting into a torpid state where little new growth is produced. Apple trees in this state will often have overcrowded spur systems producing a lot of small fruit that gradually declines in size and quality. These congested spurs should be thinned out, perhaps leaving three or four fruit buds where there might have been a dozen before (see also Diagram 29, page 188). Gentle pruning each year will result in a gradual renewal of the vigour of the tree. Slowly, new branches will form that will begin to replace the tired old branches.

Often such trees will be suffering from competition from grass growing right up to the trunk. An area of grass should be cleared around the tree, and fertiliser applied. See Chapter 9, page 143, for more details.

Over-pruned trees

The over-pruned tree is one that has suffered a different kind of neglect – that imposed by the over-zealous pruner rather than the non-existent one. If such hard pruning is continued over a few years, cropping will decline heavily and the tree will assume a form not unlike a hedgehog, where excessive upright growth begins to dominate the tree. See Chapter 9, page 142, for how to approach pruning in this situation.

Ongoing management of the orchard

The processes involved in the restoration of the orchard will lead you almost seamlessly into the processes of ongoing management. By three to five years from the commencement of restoration, the trees will be in better health – the pruning having resulted in slightly fewer, but larger and better-quality, fruits. More light and sun will be reaching into the canopy, leading to a reduction in fungal disease. The orchard floor will now be managed, either by grazing or mowing, and scrub will be confined to those areas where it is permitted as a wildlife resource.

Ongoing management is largely a question of keeping these processes going, ensuring that nothing gets out of balance. The traditional orchard does not need to be a high-maintenance operation, but there are particular tasks that will ensure that it flourishes.

- As with any orchard, regular observation is the key to ensuring that nothing gets out of balance. Regular visits to the orchard will show up signs of pests and diseases and broken branches, which can provide a route for disease to enter. Many problems can spread quickly, so prompt action is important.

- Regular pruning should be continued, in order to keep the trees healthy and fruitful. It is far better to prune each tree lightly each year than to neglect some and prune others heavily.

- Any new trees that have been planted will need formative pruning, carried out each year.

- Pay attention to the amount of light reaching the trees. Are surrounding trees or hedges starting to cast too much shade? Lack of light will cause fruit trees to grow in a lopsided fashion and will start to reduce the cropping potential.

- Remember to keep an eye on boundary fences and tree guards. Damage from grazing animals or wildlife can be rapid and severe. A rabbit, for example, can kill a young tree in one night if a rabbit guard becomes detached.

QUICK GUIDE TO RESTORING A NEGLECTED ORCHARD

- A neglected orchard might appear well past its best but it can also be a wildlife paradise. Observe what happens over a full season before making any major decisions.

- Make an effort to identify the varieties of fruit that are growing in your orchard. Local experts, the Royal Horticultural Society (RHS) and Brogdale are the most likely sources of such information.

- Once you have observed, create a management plan for the trees, any surrounding hedgerows and the orchard floor. Consider the balance between wildlife and fruit production.

- Neglected trees, even ones that have fallen over, can be brought back into productivity and health.

- Replanting, where there are gaps, will give a sense of renewal and bring an orchard back to life immediately. Remember to consider replant disease (see Chapter 9).

- Use the regulated pruning system (see Chapter 8) to restore the trees. Remember to view this as a process taking three to five years.

- Consider your safety when tackling large trees. If you feel daunted by pruning at a height, hire a contractor experienced in working with fruit trees.

- Draw up a plan for ongoing management of the orchard. It is best to prune the trees little and often.

Chapter 18

Community orchards

Community orchards are wonderful places. Like all orchards, they are places of beauty and abundance, but – more than that – they bring people together. They are home to such diverse activities as Apple Days, blossom walks, wassailing, apple pressing, wildlife surveys, orchard management courses, moth nights and even apple-based theatre. Community orchards are ideal as outdoor classrooms, so much so that many schools are now planting their own orchards. They are also places of simple rest and contemplation; a refuge from our hectic world.

A community orchard can come in many guises. It could be at the centre of village life, but it could also be a school orchard or part of a nature reserve. It could be a remnant of an old gnarled orchard, or a collection of newly planted endangered local varieties. Community orchards are owned or maintained by all

Lustleigh Community Orchard, complete with children's playground and young trees to fill the gaps where older trees have died.

kinds of groups, from local councils and orchard groups to Wildlife Trusts and The Woodland Trust. They may be diverse in nature, but what they have in common is their community identity. The community pulls together to start a community orchard, enjoys work parties to maintain it and shares the bounty of the harvest. In these times when most of us live isolated lives, sometimes not even speaking to our neighbours, the community orchard can be a focus of local activity.

Although community orchards now seem part of our heritage, it was only in 1992 that they were first promoted by Common Ground, the wonderful charity that champions local distinctiveness and also brought us the idea of Apple Days. Community orchards had no doubt been in existence on an ad hoc basis in various locations, but Lustleigh Orchard in Devon is thought to have been the first unofficial community orchard. Given to the parish in the 1960s, it

is a beautiful old orchard in the heart of the village. It is has been used for the annual May Day festival since 1968, as well as providing a venue for pruning demonstrations and apple pressing events.

When Common Ground proposed the idea of community orchards in 1992, it was the dissemination of an idea whose time had come: the concept spread rapidly throughout the country, to the extent that there are now hundreds of community orchards across Britain.

Starting a community orchard

There are many ways to start a community orchard, but there a few essentials. The main essential is the community. If a group or even an enthusiastic individual has the support of the local community, then a project to start a community orchard is likely to get off the ground. Motivation and commitment can move many a hurdle that is found in the way.

Stoke Gabriel Community Orchard. The path betrays how well the orchard is used by the local community.

The most common method of forming a local group is by friends meeting and talking, outside the school gates or in the village pub. Once a few people are singing from the same hymn sheet, the nucleus of a group can emerge. In a sense, this is the easy stage. What comes later are the 'dreaded' committee and the legalities such as constitutions and leases, but many people have now been there before and help is available.

Enlisting help

Once a few people have come together with the idea of creating a community orchard, and a potential site has been located, it is a good idea to spread the net as widely as possible. The local media will usually be helpful for such a good cause. This can mean the local paper or radio station, or, in a small community, it might be more a matter of posters and networking. By holding an initial meeting you are providing a forum for interested people to share their ideas and to get involved. It is a good idea to collect email addresses at this stage, so that everyone can be kept informed through an email group.

It is important early on to get official bodies on your side. There are so many of these that it is impossible to list them all here, but probably the most important is the local council. In a small community, this usually means approaching local councillors, but on a larger scale – district councils and above – you are likely to find an environmental department. This the legwork stage, where you will need to talk, write letters, send emails and generally persuade officialdom of what a wonderful thing you are doing and how worthy it is of their support. This is all true, so if you present your case well, you are likely to receive the support the project deserves.

There are also many other organisations that are able to help. Depending on your aims, you are likely to have your local orchard group (usually a county-wide or regional group), Wildlife Trust, other conservation groups, and perhaps British Trust for Conservation Volunteers (BTCV) to support you in different ways. There is a list of such organisations in Common Ground's *Community Orchards Handbook* (see Resources). Many parts of the country have volunteer tree wardens who will be keen to help.

Forming a group

Next, you need to form a group and give it a structure. The *Community Orchards Handbook* details several possible forms for such a group. Your local Council for Voluntary Services (CVS) can also be a useful source of advice.

Before long, you will need to consider such legal niceties as a written constitution, risk assessments and insurance. In the appendices to Common Ground's *Community Orchards Handbook* are a number of framework documents to guide people setting up a community orchard through the legal necessities. Everything from the various forms that groups can adopt through to risk assessments is covered. Such documents are also available on other community orchards' websites: Frieze Hill Orchard's website, www.communityorchard.org.uk, is a good example.

Securing the orchard

Once you have a site for the proposed community orchard, you will need to address the legalities of leases and access. It is common for the land for a community orchard to be owned by a local council. If this is the case, and the council is supportive, it will help you find a way through any legal difficulties, with the aim of negotiating a lease on the land. If the landowner is private, negotiations can be more difficult, with solicitors and land agents involved. This can be expensive for an embryonic group, at a time when money is likely to be short. There is a simpler arrangement, known as a Service Level Agreement, with a maximum timescale of three years, which can be a good way to get things moving. Remember, however, that an orchard is a long-term project: fruit trees can last a lifetime, so it is important to consider how arrangements can be extended into the future.

Funding

Before long, you will be spending money, so raising some will be an issue. Grants are likely to be your main source of income at first. Your local council might be able to help you get started, particularly if council land is involved. The availability of grants is constantly changing as new ones come on stream and old ones disappear. Charitable trusts and the National Lottery are two sources of grants that are relatively constant. The *Environment Funding Guide*, published by The Directory of Social Change, is a useful reference tool.

Once the orchard is established, you might be able to institute a small annual membership charge. When a surplus of fruit is available, you can sell it to local juice or cider producers. Making your own juice at Apple Day events can be a good source of income.

Saving an existing orchard

It could be that your intended community orchard is an existing orchard under threat from development or agricultural 'improvement'. The current legal structures surrounding tree preservation provide a number of

avenues that can be pursued to save orchards under threat.

In 2007 traditional orchards were afforded the protection of Biodiversity Action Plan (BAP) status – a measure designed to protect valuable habitats that are under threat. It is implemented by county councils through the creation of local BAPs, which designate the type and means of protection necessary to the locality.

A Tree Protection Order (TPO) is a legal vehicle designed to protect trees that "make a significant impact on their local surroundings". This can include fruit trees and orchards, but the Achilles heel of the legislation is that orchards that are being commercially managed are exempt from protection. They can be felled, providing that such action is in "the interests of the business".

Application for obtaining a TPO is made through the local planning authority. A provisional order can be served if a tree or group of trees is thought to be under immediate threat.

Many outline planning decisions are taken at the time that local plans are drawn up by district councils. These involve widespread public consultation, and this is the time to object to any development that will adversely affect an orchard. However, when planning permission is applied for, there is still time to campaign for the preservation of an orchard. At this point you should attempt to gain the support of local councillors and to use local media to draw attention to the threat. Petitions and letters of objection to the planning authority will help the cause. Many orchards have been saved at this late stage.

Planting a community orchard

Once a site has been secured, you can make a plan for the establishment of the orchard. Carrying out a wildlife survey will help you to find out the value of the wildlife that already exists on the site. The local Wildlife Trust might be interested in helping at this stage. It is important not to carry out any work that will damage threatened species or habitats.

Managing a community orchard

Once a community orchard is up and running, there is still much to do. Drawing up a management plan, detailing the work to be done at different times of the year, will enable work parties to be effective. Apart from pruning, there will be checking guards and stakes, looking out for pests and diseases, weeding around trees, mulching and, of course, harvesting. You might be able to secure the help

QUESTIONS TO ASK BEFORE PLANTING

If you are starting from scratch, try to clarify your aims. Asking the right questions will help you to get clear about how to move forward.

- **Which fruit are you hoping to grow?** Although apples are the most common fruit for community orchards, you could also try pears and plums. And why not a mulberry?

- **What will you use the fruit for?** Will the fruit just be left for the community to enjoy, or are you planning to sell it – to a local cider-maker, for example? If you are thinking of juicing the fruit, are you choosing suitable varieties?

- **Are there local varieties that you can plant?** Your local orchard group can provide valuable advice at this stage. Local nurseries should have an idea of which varieties will grow well in a particular location. (See also Chapter 4.)

- **What size of trees do you want to grow?** Large traditional trees tend to look at home in the landscape and are better for

wildlife, but if space is limited, semi-dwarfing trees might be more appropriate (see Chapter 2). It is worth planning ahead: trees should be ordered by September for planting in the winter. If you will be using stakes, ties, labels, rabbit guards and mulch mats, these will need to be sourced and purchased.

- **How will the orchard floor be managed?** It will need to be cut or grazed at least once a year. Will you be using sheep or cutting the grass? Can you use scythes, or will you need to access machinery for grass cutting? (See Chapter 17.)

- **Do you need to protect your trees?** Tree guards may be needed to protect the trees from grazing animals or deer. Community orchards can be prone to damage from humans as well. One orchard I have worked in, on the edge of a town, was a favourite haunt for dog walkers. The young trees regularly suffered damage from dog owners throwing sticks for their dogs. In some areas, vandalism can be a problem.

of an orchard expert to run a pruning demonstration. Don't forget that newly planted trees also need pruning. Holding a work party on a regular day, such as the first Sunday of the month, helps to get round the need for constant publicity.

When you hold work parties, you will need to ensure that a risk assessment is produced and action taken to avoid accidents. You will need to consider first aid training, the provision of personal protective equipment and means of summoning emergency help. If pruning tall trees, you will need to comply with the Working at Height Regulations 2005 (see Chapter 17, page 315). People using power tools in a public place should attend appropriate training courses.

If the public have access to the orchard, it is your responsibility to ensure that they can do so safely. Any hazards should either be made safe or, if this not possible, signs provided to warn of any danger.

Organising events

There is scope for a wide range of events in a community orchard. Apple Day is 21 October, and many people celebrate it on or around that date. This offers a chance to show people what you are doing and to recruit new volunteers to help in the orchard. The centre of activity on Apple Day is often the making of juice using an apple press. Many local

Pressing apples at an Apple Day event.

Local orchard groups often have a presence at Apple Day events, offering advice and identifying apples.

orchard groups have apple presses for hire. There are various hygiene issues that need to be addressed when serving juice to the public, and, to avoid possible contamination, all grazing animals should be removed from the orchard eight weeks before any windfalls are harvested.

There are many other orchard activities suitable for an Apple Day – fruit identification, longest apple peel competitions, advice from a fruit expert, the sale of apple produce, fruit displays and, of course, games for children. These can include apple bobbing, apple shy and pothering and ponking. Children can make apple dampers, a traditional Australian apple cake, over an open fire. Artists of all kinds can be invited to perform work with an appley theme. The apples and pears can be used for making cider and perry, to be consumed or sold at a later date. In some orchards, it might be more appropriate to have

WASSAILING

Wassailing is a tradition whose roots go back into the mists of time. The Anglo-Saxon 'waes haeil' means to be healthy. For centuries, wassailing apple trees was thought to bring good health to the trees and to ward off evil spirits. It usually takes place between New Year and the Old Twelfth Night, on 17 January. Different traditions abound in various parts of the country, but they are usually based on pouring cider into the tree and placing toast on the fork of the tree. The cider is to nourish the tree's roots and the toast to attract robins, which are seen as the guardians of the trees. Wassail cups are filled with cider and a toast drunk to the trees. There are various wassail songs from around the country, but the most well known comes from Carhampton in Somerset:

Wassailing apple trees in Stoke Gabriel, Devon.

Old apple tree, we wassail thee, and hoping thou wilt bear,
For the Lord doth know where we shall be,
till apples come another year,
To bear well and bloom well, so merry let us be,
Let every man take off his hat and shout to the old apple tree.

CHORUS [shouted]:
Old apple tree, we wassail thee, and hoping thou wilt bear,
Hat-fulls, cap-fulls, three bushel bagfuls
And a little heap under the stairs.
Hip! Hip! Hooray!

At this point shotguns are fired through the branches to ward off the evil spirits!

a plum or cherry theme. The opportunities are endless – the depth of your imagination being the limiting factor.

Other events include wassailing, blossom walks and picnics, and tree dressing. All are an excuse for enjoying the orchard at a different time of year and bringing the public on to the site. Wassailing can be combined with other activities suitable for this time of year, such as bonfires, hog roasts and mummers' plays. Inviting school groups to the orchard is an excellent way of gaining attention for the orchard and using it in a creative way.

QUICK GUIDE TO ESTABLISHING A COMMUNITY ORCHARD

- Gather people together who want to start a community orchard.
- Publicise and hold a meeting to find people of like mind.
- Enlist the help of local councillors and the media.
- Contact some of the many organisations who are able to help you.
- Form a group, paying attention to all the legal requirements.
- Once you have a site, negotiate a lease or Service Level Agreement.
- Find ways of accessing funding and grants.
- If there is a need to save an existing orchard, explore the various legal routes, such as tree protection orders, Biodiversity Action Plan protection and the planning process. Gain support for a campaign if need be.
- Order the trees and accessories for planting in the winter. Consider management of the orchard floor.
- Organise work parties on a regular basis. Remember to take care of health and safety issues.
- Prepare a plan for ongoing management.
- Organise events such as blossom walks, Apple Days and wassailing.

Glossary

Basal cluster The cluster of leaves found at the base of a young shoot.

Biennial cropping The habit of cropping heavily one year and lightly the next.

Chlorosis The yellowing of leaves caused by disease or nutrient deficiency.

Cultivar Another name for variety.

Cultural control The use of cultural practices, such as pruning or creating a wildlife-friendly ecosystem, to control pests and diseases.

Diploid A variety with viable pollen that is able to pollinate other varieties of the same fruit.

Dwarfing A form of rootstock that produces a small tree.

Feathered Having a number of young branches emerging from the trunk (as in a feathered maiden).

Flowering group Another name for pollination group.

Formative pruning Pruning carried out in the early years of a tree's life that forms the branch structure of the tree.

Free-spurring Producing plenty of spurs.

Fruit bud A bud that will produce flowers and (potentially) fruit. These buds are fatter than leaf buds.

Grafting The process of attaching graftwood (or scionwood) to a rootstock to form a new tree.

June Drop The habit of many fruit trees to shed young fruit naturally, usually taking place during June or July.

Lateral A branch growing from a framework (or main) branch, or from the trunk.

Leader The new (or extension) growth at the end of the branch or trunk.

Maiden A one-year-old tree.

Nicking The process of removing a V-shaped piece of wood from just below a bud in order to weaken any growth from that bud.

Notching the process of removing a V-shaped piece of wood from just above a bud in order to encourage growth from that bud.

Pheromone A chemical released (in the case of fruit trees, by insects) to modify the behaviour of others of the same species.

Pollination group A group of varieties that are able to pollinate each other.

Pome fruit A fruit belonging to the *Maloideae* family, such as apples, pears, medlars, quinces, hawthorns and rowans.

Potash-demanding Requiring a higher-than-usual amount of potash to fruit well.

Regulated pruning A method of pruning that aims to open up the tree to the light, renewing exhausted growth and keeping well-spaced branches growing in a radial pattern.

Renewal pruning A system of pruning that involves renewing exhausted branches.

Restricted forms Forms of tree that are trained in a manner that restricts their growth and creates a distinctive shape, such as espaliers, cordons, dwarf pyramids, fans and stepovers.

Rootstock A young tree on to which a variety is grafted to form a new tree.

Scion A cutting that is grafted on to a rootstock to form a new tree.

Self-fertile (or **self-compatible**) Able to set fruit with its own pollen (so doesn't need another variety to act as a pollinator).

Self-sterile (or **self-incompatible**) Unable to set fruit with its own pollen (so requires another variety of the same fruit to act as a pollinator).

Semi-dwarfing A form of rootstock that produces a medium-sized tree.

Shy-cropping Producing only small quantities of fruit.

Sport A naturally occurring variation of a variety that is slightly different from the original variety, often by having more highly coloured fruit.

Spur A side shoot that carries fruit buds.

Spur-bearer A variety that produces most of its fruit on small side shoots or spurs.

Spur pruning The practice of pruning sublaterals to encourage the formation of fruiting spurs.

Spur thinning The removal of excess buds on spurs.

Stone fruit Fruits of the *Prunus* family, such as plums, cherries, apricots, peaches and nectarines.

Sublateral A small branch or side shoot growing from a lateral.

Sucker A shoot emerging from the base of the trunk, usually just below ground level.

Sulphur-shy Harmed by the use of sulphur (sprayed as a fungicide).

Tip-bearer A variety that produces most of its fruit on the tips of the branches.

Trained tree A tree trained into a particular shape against a wall or framework of wires, such as espaliers, cordons, fans and stepovers.

Triploid A variety that has largely sterile pollen, so is unable to pollinate other varieties of the same fruit.

Appendix 1:
Fruit tree calendar
A month-by-month guide

This calendar gives the timing for the many tasks that occur throughout the year in an orchard. It is vital to carry out many of these jobs at the correct time: prune your stone fruits at the wrong time of year, for example, and you are inviting in serious diseases; forget to check for aphids and pear midges, and you could eventually find an infestation instead of a colony. If you can keep on top of your timing in the orchard, you are much more likely to produce plentiful and healthy fruit.

The times given here are for southern England. Further north, these times can be a week or two later.

January
- Plant bare-rooted trees.
- Check and use stored fruit.
- Prune apples, pears, quinces and medlars.
- Begin spraying Bordeaux mixture against peach leaf curl.
- Apply an insecticidal winter wash against overwintering aphid eggs.

February
- Continue planting bare-rooted trees.
- Continue pruning of apples, pears, quinces and medlars.
- Continue spraying Bordeaux mixture against peach leaf curl (before flowering).
- Check and use stored fruit.
- Start feeding fruit trees.

- Hand-pollinate peaches, nectarines and apricots.
- Cover peach, nectarine and apricot blossom to protect against frost.

March
- Finish planting bare-rooted trees.
- Finish pruning apples, pears, quinces and medlars.
- Check and use stored fruit.
- Continue feeding fruit trees.
- Apply mulches of compost or manure when soil is damp.
- Carry out formative pruning of plums, cherries, apricots, peaches and nectarines.
- Cover blossom that is likely to suffer from frost damage.
- Spray apples and pears with sulphur to protect against scab.
- Spray quince with Bordeaux mixture or garlic spray to protect against quince leaf blight.
- Check for aphids and other insect pests. Take prompt action if found.
- Check for blossom wilt and take appropriate action.

April
- Apply mulches of compost or manure when soil is damp.
- Formative pruning of plums, cherries, apricots, peaches, nectarines and figs.
- Pruning of established apricots, peaches, nectarines and figs.

- Check for aphids and other insect pests, including pear midge. Take prompt action if found.
- Check for blossom wilt and take appropriate action.
- Remove covers from peaches and nectarines.
- Spray pyrethrum against apple blossom weevil and apple capsid bug.
- Remove blossom from newly planted trees.

May

- Continue pruning of apricots, figs, peaches and nectarines.
- Check for blossom wilt and take appropriate action.
- Check for the build-up of fungal disease and take appropriate action.
- Apply nicking or notching to pears and apples, if required.
- Spray pyrethrum against apple sawfly.
- Use a tarpaulin to catch fruitlets affected by plum sawfly and pear midge.
- Remove the leaders of apples and pears grown as restricted forms.
- Check for aphids and other insect pests. Take prompt action if found.
- Water if necessary.
- Check for the build-up of fungal disease and take appropriate action.
- Apply liquid feeds, such as seaweed.
- Ensure grass and weeds are controlled around trees.

June

- Prune established plums, cherries, apricots, peaches and nectarines.
- Check for aphids and other insect pests. Take prompt action if found.
- Water if necessary.
- Spray calcium chloride against bitter pit.

- Hang rolled-up corrugated cardboard in trees to attract caterpillars.
- Apply liquid feeds, such as seaweed.
- Protect ripening fruit with netting.
- Use a tarpaulin to catch fruitlets affected by plum sawfly and pear midge.
- Thin fruits where needed (after the June Drop). Prop branches that still have a heavy crop.
- Put pheromone traps in place against codling moth and plum moth.

July

- Continue pruning plums, cherries peaches, nectarines and apricots.
- Protect ripening fruit with netting.
- Spray calcium chloride against bitter pit.
- Thin fruits where needed (after the June Drop). Prop branches that still have a heavy crop.
- Hang rolled-up corrugated cardboard in trees to attract caterpillars.
- Check codling moth and plum moth pheromone traps.

August

- Finish pruning plums, cherries, peaches, apricots and fan-trained plums.
- Protect ripening fruit with netting.
- Check plum moth pheromone traps.
- Spray calcium chloride against bitter pit.
- Remove fruits affected by brown rot.
- Carry out pruning of restricted forms of apples, pears, quinces and medlars.
- Commence monthly spraying of stone fruits with Bordeaux mixture against bacterial canker.
- Take precautions against wasps.

September

- Protect ripening plums with netting.
- Remove fruits affected by brown rot.

- Spray calcium chloride against bitter pit.
- Take precautions against wasps.
- Continue monthly spraying of stone fruits with Bordeaux mixture against bacterial canker.
- Check for the fruiting bodies of honey fungus.
- Place orders for winter delivery of fruit trees.

October

- Remove fruits affected by brown rot.
- Finish monthly spraying of stone fruits with Bordeaux mixture against bacterial canker.
- Check for the fruiting bodies of honey fungus.
- Prepare the soil for winter planting.
- Fit grease bands, or apply fruit tree grease against winter moth.
- Begin putting fruit into winter storage.
- Remove figs larger than the size of a pea.
- Spray peaches and nectarines with Bordeaux mixture against peach leaf curl.
- Spray quince with Bordeaux mixture against quince leaf blight.

November

- Check that stakes and ties are fitted well before winter gales arrive.
- Check that posts and wires supporting restricted trees are in good condition.
- Cut back secondary growth from summer pruning of restricted trees.
- Place container-grown fruit trees in the greenhouse for winter shelter (if required).
- Check stored fruit to avoid storage rots.
- Collect and remove fallen leaves to counteract fungal infections, e.g. scab.
- Prune mulberries.

December

- Check and use stored fruit.
- Prune mulberries.
- Commence winter pruning of apples, pears, quinces and medlars.
- Apply a winter wash against overwintering aphid eggs.
- Commence planting of bare-rooted trees.

Appendix 2: Apple varieties

This appendix lists apple varieties that are suitable for certain locations and conditions, for example, because they are tolerant of frosts or resistant to certain diseases. It also includes a list of apples suitable for juicing. Only well-known varieties or those recommended in this book are listed here. Martin Crawford's excellent reference book *Directory of Apple Cultivars* (see Resources) has more detailed information, should you need it. Another way to access this information is to use a fruit-tree search tool such as that provided by Keepers Nursery (www.keepers-nursery.co.uk).

Here, the following abbreviations denote the type of each apple variety:
D = dessert apple
C = cooking apple
CR = cider apple

Varieties in black are recommended in this book (see the charts in Chapter 10).

Appendix 2.1:
Apple varieties suitable for areas with late frosts

Frosts below 1.5°C (35°F) can damage apple blossom to the extent that crops can be seriously reduced. In areas susceptible to late frosts, it is best to plant varieties from the following list.

FR = varieties with frost-resistant flowers
LF = late-flowering varieties

Variety	Flowering	Type
Adam's Pearmain	FR	D
Annie Elizabeth	FR	C
Blenheim Orange	FR	D/C
Bramley's Seedling	FR	C
Charles Ross	FR	D/C
Chisel Jersey	LF	CR
Court Pendu Plat	LF	D
Crawley Beauty	LF	C
Discovery	FR	D
Dumelow's Seedling	FR	C
Egremont Russet	FR	D
Ellison's Orange	FR	D
Falstaff	FR	D
George Cave	FR	D
Golden Noble	FR	C
Greensleeves	FR	D
Katy	FR	D
Lady Sudeley	FR	D
Laxton's Superb	FR	D
Lord Derby	FR	C
Newton Wonder	FR	C
Peasgood's Nonsuch	FR	D/C
Royal Jubilee	LF	C
Stoke Red	LF	CR
Sunset	FR	D
Suntan	FR	D
Tremlett's Bitter	FR	CR
Warner's King	FR	C
Winston	FR	D
Worcester Pearmain	FR	D

Appendix 2.2:
Apple varieties suitable for northern Britain

This list is comprised mainly of varieties from Appendix 2.1, tolerant of late frosts, together with varieties that are known to succeed in areas with short summers and cold soils.

Annie Elizabeth	C
Ashmead's Kernel	D
Beauty of Bath	D
Blenheim Orange	D/C
Bramley's Seedling	C
Charles Ross	D/C
Court Pendu Plat	D
Cox's Pomona	D/C
Discovery	D
Egremont Russet	D
Ellison's Orange	D
Falstaff	D
Gladstone	D
James Grieve	D/C
Lady Sudeley	D
Lane's Prince Albert	C
Laxton's Superb	D
Lord Derby	C
Newton Wonder	C
Reverend W. Wilks	C
Royal Jubilee	C
Scotch Bridget	C
Stirling Castle	C
Sunset	D
Sykehouse Russet	D
Tower of Glamis	C
Tydeman's Early Worcester	D
Warner's King	C
Winston	D
Yorkshire Greening	C

Appendix 2.3:
Apple varieties suitable for western Britain

In effect, varieties suitable for growing in western Britain means those that are resistant to scab and canker – fungal diseases that thrive in areas of high rainfall, and a serious threat to apple trees. The resistant varieties listed here are not the only ones worth growing in western Britain – others that have resistance to only one of these diseases can still be worthwhile (see Chapter 10 for the characteristics of other varieties). Devonshire Quarrenden is a good example – it is resistant to canker, but slightly susceptible to scab. Local varieties found in these western areas are also often worth growing: they have survived because they are suited to the local conditions.

Annie Elizabeth	C
Ashmead's Kernel	D
Belle de Boskoop	D/C
Brownlees Russet	D/C
Bulmers Foxwhelp	CR
Cornish Aromatic	D
Crawley Beauty	C
Crimson King	CR
Gladstone	D
Golden Noble	D
Grenadier	C
Herefordshire Russet	D
Lane's Prince Albert	C
Lord Derby	C
Newton Wonder	C
Pitmaston Pineapple	D
Rajka	D
Reverend W. Wilks	C
Rosemary Russet	D
St Edmund's Pippin	D
Sanspareil	D
Sunset	D
Topaz	D
Winston	D
Woolbrook Pippin	D

Appendix 2.4:
Apple varieties suitable for areas of low rainfall

In effect, varieties suitable for areas of low rainfall are varieties that are resistant to mildew. These are listed here. Varieties that are highly resistant to mildew are marked with an asterisk.

Annie Elizabeth	C
Ashmead's Kernel	D
Blenheim Orange	D/C
Bramley's Seedling	C
Crawley Beauty	C
Discovery*	D
Egremont Russet	D
Ellison's Orange*	D
Golden Noble	C
Grenadier	C
Howgate Wonder	C
James Grieve	D/C
Lord Derby	C
Orleans Reinette	D
Park Farm Pippin	D
Rajka	D
Red Devil	D
Red Ellison*	D
Reverend W. Wilks	C
Rosemary Russet	D
Sanspareil	D
Spartan*	D
Suntan	D
Tydeman's Early Worcester	D
Winston*	D
Worcester Pearmain*	D
Yarlington Mill	CR

Appendix 2.5:
Apple varieties suitable for chalk or alkaline soils

Although apples will tolerate a wide range of conditions, thin chalk soils or conditions of extreme alkalinity can give rise to lime-induced chlorosis or drought stress. The following varieties are known to tolerate these conditions better than most.

Barnack Beauty	D/C
Charles Ross	D/C
Crawley Beauty	C
Gascoyne's Scarlet	D/C
Miller's Seedling	D

Appendix 2.6:
Apple varieties suitable for juicing

Any variety of apple can be juiced, but some will give better results than others (see Chapter 10, page 199). Some varieties have a high juice content, giving a greater yield, but the flavour of the apple is also important: varieties with a robust flavour make better juice than those with a delicate or insipid flavour. The following varieties are known to make good juice, either blended or as single varieties. Also given here is a description of the juice.

Bramley's Seedling	Full sharp	C
Brown's Apple	Sharp	CR
Charles Ross	Medium sharp	D/C
Cox's Orange Pippin	Medium sharp-sweet	D
Discovery	Medium sharp-sweet	D
Falstaff	Medium sharp	D
Golden Noble	Sharp	C
Greensleeves	Medium sharp	D
Howgate Wonder	Full sharp	C
James Grieve	Medium sharp	D/C
Katy	Medium sharp	D
Lane's Prince Albert	Sharp	C
Lord Lambourne	Medium sharp	D
Northwood	Sweet	D/CR
Roxbury Russet	Medium sharp	D/CR
Royal Jubilee	Sharp	C
Sweet Alford	Sweet	CR
Sweet Coppin	Sweet	D/C

Appendix 3: Pear varieties

This appendix lists pear varieties that are suited to certain locations and conditions, either because they will cope well with frost or because of their resistance to certain diseases. Only well-known varieties or those recommended in this book are listed here. More detailed information can be found in Martin Crawford's *Directory of Pear Cultivars* (see Resources), or by using a search tool devoted to fruit trees, such as that provided by Keepers Nursery (www.keepers-nursery.co.uk).

Here, the following abbreviations denote the type of each pear variety:
D = dessert pear
C = cooking pear
P = perry pear

Varieties in black or bold are recommended in this book (see the charts in Chapter 11).

Appendix 3.1:
Pear varieties suitable for areas with late frosts

Pears suitable for such areas can either be varieties with frost-resistant flowers or those that are late-flowering. Pears flower from mid-April through to early May, so can be vulnerable to frosts, particularly in susceptible locations.

FR = varieties with frost-resistant flowers
LF = late-flowering varieties

Barnet	LF	P
Beurré Hardy	FR	D
Doctor Jules Guyot	FR	D
Doyenné du Comice	FR & LF	D/C
Durondeau	FR	D
Glow Red Williams	FR	D/C
Jargonelle	FR	D
Onward	LF	D
Nouveau Poiteau	LF	D
Red Pear	LF	P
Williams' Bon Chrétien	FR	D/C

Appendix 3.2:
Pear varieties suitable for northern Britain

This list is comprised mainly of varieties from Appendix 3.1, tolerant of late frosts, together with varieties that will cope with a short growing season. Many pear varieties will prosper in areas with a harsher climate only if grown against a warm wall.

Beth	D
Black Worcester	C
Catillac	C
Clapp's Favourite	D/C
Conference	D/C
Durondeau	D
Gorham	D/C
Hessle	D/C
Improved Fertility	D
Jargonelle	D
Louise Bonne of Jersey	D
Onward	D
Williams' Bon Chrétien	D/C
Winter Nellis	D

Appendix 3.3:
Pear varieties suitable for western Britain

In effect, varieties suitable for western Britain means varieties that are resistant to scab and canker – fungal diseases that thrive in areas of high rainfall. Because there is little information available on varieties resistant to canker, some varieties resistant only to scab have been included here. It is also worth considering varieties from the following list if you are intending to grow organically. The diseases that each variety is resistant to are specified. Remember that resistance is not the same as immunity: even resistant cultivars can be prone to these diseases where spore pressure is high.

Arlingham Squash	Resistant to scab	P
Beurré Hardy	Resistant to scab and canker	D
Catillac	Resistant to scab and canker	C
Concorde	Resistant to scab and canker	C
Fondante d'Automne	Resistant to scab and canker	D
Gin	Resistant to scab and canker	P
Glow Red Williams	Resistant to scab	D/C
Gorham	Resistant to scab	D/C
Hendre Huffcap	Resistant to scab	P
Hessle	Resistant to scab and canker	D/C
Jargonelle	Resistant to scab and canker	D
Louise Bonne of Jersey	Resistant to scab and canker	D
Nouveau Poiteau	Resistant to scab and canker	D
Onward	Resistant to scab	D
Winnal's Longdon	Resistant to scab	P
Yellow Huffcap	Resistant to scab	P

Appendix 3.4:
Pear varieties resistant to fireblight

Fireblight is a serious disease of pears. At present, it is mostly confined to southern England, but it is slowly spreading north. The fireblight resistance of many varieties is not known, but Conference (D/C), **Glow Red Williams** (D/C) and Seckle (D/C) are all known to be slightly resistant, while **Gorham** (D/C) is resistant.

The commonly grown cultivars **Beurré Hardy** (D), Doctor Jules Guyot (D/C), Doyenné du Comice (D/C) and Winter Nellis (D) are all susceptible to the disease.

Appendix 4: Plum varieties

This appendix lists those plum varieties that will succeed in more difficult locations, because they can fruit readily in a short growing season, cope with late frost or are resistant to disease. Only well-known varieties or those recommended in this book are listed here. More detailed information can be found in Martin Crawford's *Plums: Production, Culture and Cultivar Directory* (see Resources), or by using a fruit tree search tool such as that provided by Keepers Nursery (www.keepers-nursery.co.uk). Note that although certain gages are listed for difficult locations, they will give of their best in sunny sheltered conditions.

The following abbreviations apply here:
D = dessert plum
C = cooking plum

Varieties in black are recommended in this book (see the charts in Chapter 12).

Appendix 4.1:
Plum varieties suitable for northern Britain

The following are plum varieties that will ripen readily in a short or cool summer.

Belle de Louvain	C
Czar	D/C
Golden Transparent Gage	D
Marjorie's Seedling	DC
Opal	D
Oullin's Gage	D/C
Purple Pershore	D/C
Victoria	D/C
Warwickshire Drooper	D/C
Yellow Pershore	D/C

Appendix 4.2:
Plum varieties suitable for areas with late frosts

The following varieties of plum are more likely to succeed in areas susceptible to late frosts, either because they are late-flowering or have frost-resistant flowers.

FR = varieties with frost-resistant flowers
LF = late-flowering varieties

Belle de Louvain	FR	C
Count Althan's Gage	FR	D/C
Czar	FR	D/C
Italian Prune	LF	C
Jefferson	FR	D
Jubilee	LF	D
Kirke's Blue	FR	D
Late Transparent Gage	LF	DC
Marjorie's Seedling	LF	DC
Old Greengage	FR	D/C
Purple Pershore	FR	D/C
Victoria	FR	D/C
Yellow Pershore	FR	D/C

Appendix 4.3:
Disease-resistant plum varieties

These varieties of plum are resistant to silver leaf (SL) and/or bacterial canker (BC), the most serious diseases to affect plum trees. Growing resistant varieties increases the chances of having healthy trees with success- ful crops, particularly in the wetter regions of Britain. Damsons, bullaces and mirabelles are also largely resistant to silver leaf and bacterial canker. It's worth remembering that resistance is not the same as immunity.

Blaisdon Red	C	Resistant to SL and BC
Jefferson	D	Slightly resistant to SL and BC
Marjorie's Seedling	D/C	Very resistant to SL and BC
Merton Gem	D	Resistant to SL
Opal	D	Slightly resistant to BC
Oullin's Gage	D/C	Slightly resistant to BC
Purple Pershore	D/C	Resistant to BC and SL
Thames Cross	D/C	Resistant to BC
Yellow Pershore	D/C	Resistant to BC and SL

Resources

Books

Many books only mention fruit growing, preserving or foraging in passing, but the ones listed below are a very good start as each is dedicated to the subject.

The Apple Book, Rosanne Sanders. FrancesLincoln Ltd, 2010

The New Book of Apples, Joan Morgan & Alison Richards, Ebury, 2002

Apples of North America, Tom Burford, Timber, 2013

Johnny Appleseed and the American Orchard: A cultural history, John Hopkins, 2012

Cherries: Production and Culture, Martin Crawford. Agroforestry Research Trust, 1997

Cider and Juice Apples: Growing and Processing, R.R. Williams (ed.). University of Bristol Printing Unit, 1996

Community Orchards Handbook, Sue Clifford and Angela King. Green Books, 2011

How to Store Your Garden Produce, Piers Warren. Green Books, 2008

Making Cider, Jo Deal. G. W. Kent, 1993

Getting Started with Growing Fruit, Gerry Edwards, national Vegetable Society, 2015

Ball Blue Book Guide to Preserving, Various, Alltrista Consumer, 1909 to 2015

Peaches and Apricots, Martin Crawford. Agroforestry Research Trust, 2002

The Book of Pears: The Definitive History and Guide to over 500 varieties, Joan Morgan, Ebury Press, 2015

Plums: Production, Culture and Cultivar Directory, Martin Crawford. Agroforestry Research Trust, 1996

Preserved, Nick Sandler and Johnny Acton. Kyle Cathie Ltd, 2009

Principles of Horticulture, C. R. Adams, K. M. Bamford & M. P. Early. Butterworth Heinemann, 2008

The Royal Horticultural Society Pests and Diseases, Pippa Greenwood and Andrew Halstead. Dorling Kindersley, 2018

The Royal Horticultural Society Pruning and Training, Christopher Brickell and David Joyce. Dorling Kindersley, 2017

How to prune Fruiting Plants, Richard Bird, Southwater, 2013

Successful Organic Gardening, Geoff Hamilton. Dorling Kindersley, 2011

Trees for Your Garden, Nick Dunn. The Tree Council, 2010

Food for Free, Richard Mabey, Collins 2002

An Orchard Odyssey, Naomi Slade, Green Books, 2016

Nurseries & Suppliers

Europe

Fruit and Nut, Co. Mayo, Ireland
www.fruitandnut.ie
Supplier of fruit and nut trees. Holds courses and workshops.

Future Forests, Co. Cork, Ireland
www.futureforests.net
Wide range of fruit trees, including native and unusual varieties.

Lubera
www.lubera.co.uk
Swiss breeder and supplier of unusual and interesting soft fruit and, fruit trees.

Weck
www.weck.de
Great German website for steam juicers, water baths and preserving jars.

UK

Agroforestry Research Trust, Devon, UK
www.agroforestry.co. uk
Supplier of fruit and nut trees; courses on Forest Gardening

Otter Farm Shop
www.otterfarm.co.uk
Nursery run by climate-change gardener Mark Diacono. Conventional fruit and nuts plus interesting exotics.

Reads Nursery, Suffolk, UK
www.readsnursery.co.uk
Family nursery offering free expert advice on selection and planting.

Blackmoor Nurseries, Hampshire UK
www.blackmoor.co.uk
A wide selection of popular fruit.

Frank P. Matthews Ltd (Trees for Life), Worcester, UK
www.frankpmatthews.com
A wide selection of varieties, particularly suited to those buying larger quantities.

John Worle Ltd, Hereford, UK
www.johnworle.co. uk
Specialist cider apple and perry pear nursery and advisory service.

J. Tweedie Fruit Trees, Dumfriesshire UK
Many varieties suited to growing in Scotland.

Keepers Nursery, Kent UK
www.keepers-nursery.co.uk
One of the largest selections of fruit varieties in Britain. Includes a very useful search facility that helps with the selection of fruit tree varieties.

Lodge Farm Trees, Gloucestershire UK
www.lodgefarmtrees.co.uk
Specialists in Gloucestershire varieties.

R. V. Roger Ltd, North Yorkshire UK
www.rvroger.co.uk
Useful source of varieties suited to the north of Britain.

Thomhayes Nursery, Devon UK
www.thomhayes-nursery.co. uk
Specialists in West Country varieties.

Walcot Organic Nursery, Worcestershire UK
www.walcotnursery.co.uk
The main supplier of organic fruit trees in Britain.

Chris Bowers & Sons, Norfolk UK
www.chrisbowers.co. uk
A wide selection of fruit trees.

The Farm Forestry Co. Ltd, Shropshire, UK
www.farmforestry.co.uk
Specialist retailers of tree-planting equipment.

Orange Pippin
www.orangepippinshop.com
A wide selection of trees and useful information about growing fruit trees.

Toms Tree Ties, Kent UK
www.jtoms.co.uk
Tree support and protection specialists.

Vigo Ltd, Devon UK
www.vigopresses.co. uk
Suppliers of orchard ladders and equipment for pressing and preserving fruit.

USA

Eastman's Antique Apples, MI, USA
www.eastmansantiqueapples.com
Significant collection of heritage varieties.

Fedco Trees, ME, USA
www.fedcoseeds.com/trees
Supports Great Maine Apple Day in October

Stark Bro's Nurseries and Orchards Company MO, USA
www.starkbros.com
Famous nursery and fruit supplier, home of the original Red Delicious.

Trees of Antiquity CA, USA
www.treesofantiquity.com
Family nursery supplying organic fruit trees and heirloom apple varieties.

Willis Orchard Company, GA, USA
www.willisorchards.com
A good range of trees, with an emphasis on taste

Grandpa's Orchard Coloma, MI, USA
www.grandpasorchard.com
A good selection of fruit on a wide range of rootstocks.

Apple Picking Bags, OR, USA
www.applepickingbags.com
Serious stuff for orchards - bags, pruning kit and more.

Jarden Home Brands, IN, USA
www.freshpreserving.com
Iconic Mason and Kerr jars, water baths, pressure canners plus techniques and recipes on website.

Helpful Organisations and Websites

Europe

European Specialist in Traditional Orchards (ESTO)
www.esto-project.eu
12 partners in 6 European countries with a focus on conservation and the promotion of traditional orchards in Europe.

North America

United States Association of Cider Makers
www.ciderassociation.org
Information for cider and perry makers about production, regulations and growing.

North American Fruit Explorers (NAFEX)
www.nafex.org
Network of fruit enthusiasts in the USA and Canada, devoted to the cultivation and appreciation of superior fruit and nut varieties.

Sole Food Street Farms
www.solefoodfarms.com
Transforms vacant land in Canada into artisan street farms.

Orchard People
www.orchardpeople.com
Toronto-based fruit-tree-care consulting and education organization. Offers workshops.

The Boston Tree Party
www.bostontreeparty.org
Urban agriculture coalition which aims to support civic fruit.

Portland Fruit Tree Project
www.portlandfruit.org
Encourages the community to share in the harvest and care of urban fruit trees, preventing waste, promoting knowledge, and creating sustainable local food sources in this corner of Oregon.

City Fruit
www.cityfruit.org
Seattle-based fruit cultivation to nourish the community and protect the climate.

Jacksonport Cherry Festival, WI, USA
www.jacksonporthistoricalsociety.org/cherry_fest.php
Cheerful cherry-themed event with lots of fresh cherries and cherry products.

UK

The Gardening Website
www.thegardeningwebsite.co.uk
Comprehensive listings of all kinds of gardening information, including nurseries listed by county.

Gloucestershire Orchard Group
www.gloucestershireorchardgroup.org.uk
A local orchard group website, also contains good information about orchards in general.

Old Scrump's Cider House
www.ciderandperry.co.uk
A valuable website that covers cider- and perry-making for the small-scale producer.

Brogdale Collection and Brogdale Garden Centre, Kent UK
www.brogdale.org
www.nationalfruitcollection.org.uk
www.brogdalecollections.co.uk/marketplace/
Leading suppliers of fruit trees and home of the UK National Fruit Collection. Offers fruit identification, advice on growing and information about many varieties of fruit.

People's Trust for Endangered Species (PTES)
www.ptes.org
Wildlife conservation charity providing resources for finding varieties, surveying traditional orchards and managing orchards for wildlife.

Common Ground
www.commonground.org.uk
An environmental charity with projects including Apple Day and the Campaign for Local Distinctiveness.

Farming and Wildlife Advisory Group (FWAG)
www.fwag.org.uk
Independent, dedicated provider of conservation advice to farmers and those planning larger orchards.

Garden Organic
www.gardenorganic.org.uk
UK national organic gardening charity, providing information and support for organic growers.

Natural England
www.naturalengland.org.uk
Government department that provides valuable advice and Technical Information Notes (TINs) about traditional orchards.

Royal Horticultural Society (RHS)
www.rhs.org.uk
The RHS offers a fruit identification service and advice on pests and disease problems.

Index

Photograph credits

All photographs are by the author except for the following:

Pages 2, 51, 54, 57, 126, 162, 273: **iStockphoto**

Page 43: **Amanda Cuthbert**

Pages 46, 53, 123 (right), 136 (left), 146 (left), 152 (top), 159 (left), 170 (Beauty of Bath, Discovery), 171 (Scrumptious) 174 (Rajka), 175 (Orleans Reinette), 182 (Dabinett), 233 (Monarch), 236 (Gypsy, Red Mirabelle), 253 (Sweetheart), 263 (Peregrine), 264 (Saturn, Garden Lady), 265 (Lord Napier, Nectarella), 274 (Tomcot, Alfred), 275 (all), 280 (Champion), 281 (Portugal, Serbian Gold): © **Nick Dunn**

Pages 57, 274 (Farmingdale, Hemskerk), 296 (Brunswick, White Marseille): **Reads Nursery**

Pages 118, 119 (top left): **Tess Nicholls**

Pages 123 (left), 128 (right), 141, 150 (bottom left), 171 (James Grieve), 172 (Worcester Pearmain), 177 (Grenadier, Keswick Codlin), 178 (Stirling Castle), 179 (Newton Wonder), 181 (Frederick Brown's Apple), 207 (Jargonelle, Beth), 208 (Merton Pride, Williams' Bon Chrétien), 215 (Shinsui, Nijisseiki), 228 (Herman, Laxton), 229 (all), 230 (Jefferson, Merton Gem, Golden Transparent Gage), 231 (all), 232 (all), 233 (Edwards, Warwickshire Drooper), 234 (Merryweather Damson), 235 (Langley Bullace, Black Bullace), 236 (Mirabelle de Nancy), 251 (all), 252 (Lapins, Stella), 253 (Sunburst): **The National Fruit Collection, Brogdale**

Pages 124, 125 (top), 127, 128 (left), 129 (right), 146 (right), 148 (top), 150 (bottom right), 152 (bottom), 154 (bottom right), 156: courtesy of **East Malling Research**

Page 142: **A. Harber**

Pages 147, 151 (both), 154 (bottom left): **Sherry Orchard**

Page 148 (bottom): **Dave Hagland**

Pages 174 (Herefordshire Russet), 182 (Harry Masters Jersey): **Orange Pippin**

Pages 180, 181 (Major, Somerset Redstreak), 182 (Kingston Black, Stoke Red, Sweet Coppin), 183 (Yarlington Mill, Crimson King): © **Liz Copas**

Page 198 (left): **Gardena**

Page 199: **Heritage Garden Traders**

Pages 208 (Fondante d'Automne), 209 (Hessle), 213 (Thorn), 252 (Summer Sun), 253 (Bradbourne Black), 264 (Avalon Pride, Rochester), 274 (New Large Early), 280 (Agvambari), 286 (all): **Keepers Nursery**

Page 213 (Judge Amphlett, Hendre Huffcap): **John Worle**

Page 220: courtesy of **East Malling Trust**

Page 235 (White Bullace): **The Friends of Brickfields Country Park**

Page 247: **Devon Wildlife Trust**

Page 249: **David Goodchild**

Page 252 (Merton Favourite, Noir de Guben): **Chris Bowers and Sons**

Pages 263 (Duke of York), 280 (Leskovac): **Blackmoor Nurseries**

Page 265 (Early Rivers): **R. V. Roger Ltd**

Page 280 (Krymsk): **G. V. Bale**

Page 302: **Jacquie Sarsby**

Page 309: © **Jess Whitelock**

Pages 28, 39, 61 (left), 64, 69 (both) 92, 184, 194, 196, 221 (left), 256: photographed with permission of the RHS Garden Rosemoor

Pages 82, 90, 221 (right), 257: photographed with permission of the Hatton Fruit Garden at East Malling Research

Pages 88, 214 (bottom), 223, 224, 235 (Farleigh Damson): photographed with permission of the RHS Garden Wisley

Page 202: photographed with permission of West Dean Gardens

Pages 282, 300: photographed with permission of the Lost Gardens of Heligan